The Crash of
International Finance-Capital
and its Implications for
the Third World

D1569141

Pambazuka Press, an imprint of Fahamu Books
www.pambazukapress.org

 Pambazuka Press is an imprint of Fahamu Books. We are a pan-African publisher of progressive books that aim to stimulate debate, discussion, analysis and engagement on human rights and social justice in Africa and the global South. We publish books and CD-ROMs on Africa, the African Union, capacity building for civil society organisations, China and Africa, conflict, human rights, media, trade, aid & development, and women's rights.

Pambazuka News
www.pambazuka.org

 We also publish the prize-winning weekly electronic newsletter Pambazuka News. With over 1,400 contributors and an estimated 500,000 readers, Pambazuka News is the authoritative pan-African electronic weekly newsletter and platform for social justice in Africa, providing cutting-edge commentary and in-depth analysis on politics and current affairs, development, human rights, refugees, gender issues and culture in Africa.

The Crash of International Finance-Capital and its Implications for the Third World

Dani Wadada Nabudere

Foreword to the second edition
by Yash Tandon

Pambazuka Press
An imprint of Fahamu Books

Fountain Publishers
Kampala - Uganda

Published 2009 by Pambazuka Press, an imprint of Fahamu Books
Cape Town, Dakar, Nairobi and Oxford
www.fahamubooks.org www.pambazukapress.org www.pambazuka.org

Fahamu, 2nd floor, 51 Cornmarket Street,
Oxford OX1 3HA, UK
Fahamu Kenya, PO Box 47158, 00100 GPO,
Nairobi, Kenya
Fahamu Senegal, 9 Cité Sonatel 2, POB 25021,
Dakar-Fann, Dakar, Senegal
Fahamu South Africa, c/o 27A Esher St,
Claremont, 7708, Cape Town, South Africa

Published in Uganda in 2009 by Fountain Publishers Ltd
55 Nkrumah Road, PO Box 488, Kampala, Uganda

British Library Cataloguing in Publication Data

A catalogue record for this book is available from the British Library

ISBN: 978-1-906387-43-3 (2nd edition paperback)
ISBN: 978-1-906387-44-0 (ebook)
ISBN: 0-7974-0911-4 (1st edition)

Manufactured on demand by Lightning Source

Contents

Foreword to the Second Edition

Yash Tandon

Chairman of SEATINI and former Executive Director of
the South Centre

It is hard to believe that this book was first written in 1989 and that
its analysis continues to remain valid to this day. In fact, the original edition was itself an abridged version of the author's larger
and substantial manuscript *The Rise and Fall of Money Capital*, published in 1989 by a not too well-known publisher called Africa in
Transition.

Reading this abridged version again, as I first did in 1989 before its
publication, is like reading history backwards. Professor Nabudere
had predicted the crisis of the global financial system even as, with
the collapse of the Soviet Union, the west was riding triumphant
and neo-liberal globalisation was entering its mature phase.

Between the covers of the book the author explains in both
logical and historical terms the evolution of money and finance-
capital, and their predictable, impending collapse. In language and
arguments that, in the wake of the present crisis, are now all too famil-
iar, the author covers a vast area of issues and subjects, among them:

- Explaining how finance-capital seeks to sustain its profits through
  exploiting peasant labour as largely 'unpaid labour', through the
  exploitation of female and child labour, through ecological waste
  and through speculation
- Documenting how village savings are being mopped up by
  finance-capital, thus putting the much-hyped issue of micro-
  credit in its proper political–economic context

- Showing how the internationalisation of securities was a way of expanding the shrinking national base of western economies
- Explaining the role of the state in the securitisation process, and how this evolved into the 'democratisation' of the stock exchange, the emergence of the 'casino society' and the bubbling of speculative capital. The later (1990s) dot-com bubble and the housing bubble (post-2005) are concrete demonstrations of the professor's succinct earlier analysis.
- Showing how the futures market has 'de-materialised' the commodity market, how poverty has risen to even higher levels, and how the impoverished have become unemployable and now 'fit only for relief'
- Working his way towards analysing why state power is needed to back the 'value' of fictitious capital, and how, among other things, this leads to militarisation. He goes on to analyse the peace implications of speculative capital, and more broadly its implications for democracy and for ecology.
- Showing how the state has been complicit in creating this 'craving for money as a disease', in the now all-too-familiar cant about the 'greed' of corporate managers.

Finally, for those who are now turning to John Maynard Keynes for 'answers' to the present crisis – as somebody once said, 'We are all Keynesians today' – Professor Nabudere has a sobering analysis of Keynesianism. It addresses, he says, only the superficial aspects of a crisis that is more deeply rooted in the capitalist system than is generally understood or appreciated. Writing in 1989, the author offers the incredible foresight that the US deficit-financing difficulty is not a momentary problem to be resolved by measures taken by the US administration; it is deeply embedded within the very fabric of capitalist production.

The author took the October 1987 crisis as the starting point of his journey. That crisis was all but ignored. Ten years later, in 1997, the East Asian economies suffered a serious meltdown, but the west, still basking in its triumphalist illusions, blamed it all on the so-called flawed policies of East Asian countries. Indeed, in the aftermath of the International Monetary Fund's (IMF) moving in to 'save' these economies, the west took advantage of the crisis to

acquire banking and other productive assets in Thailand, Indonesia, the Philippines and Korea on the cheap. Larry Summers, then the intellectual power behind US economic foreign policy and now President Barack Obama's Head of the National Economic Council is reported to have said at the time: 'In some ways the IMF has done more in these past months to liberalise these economies and open their markets to US goods and services than has been achieved in rounds of trade negotiations in the region.' This illustrates Professor Nabudere's argument that the IMF and the other institutions of global economic governance were primarily serving western interests at the cost of Third World people and their economies.

In 2001 as Argentina's economy collapsed on the eve of the Finance for Development conference in Mexico, the world leaders almost completely ignored the crisis, blaming it all on the flawed policies of successive Argentinian regimes. For the west it was always the fault of the leaders in the south for their financial and economic woes. They argued that southern leaders' cronyism, corruption and bad governance were the causes of the collapse of their economies; the global system, they argued, was fundamentally sound.

The shoe is now on the other foot. In the aftermath of the global financial and economic meltdown beginning with the sub-prime rate crisis in the United States in the last quarter of 2008, neo-liberal triumphalism is now eating dust. The leaders of the north are now appealing to those countries in the south that have financial reserves or sovereign funds to put their money into a common winery so that all countries – including those in the north – can drink from it.

Professor Nabudere presents a historical landscape and logical *tour de force* whose arguments may well, again, be ignored by western leaders, but for the leaders of the south to do so would put their peoples and their environment at serious peril.

Author's Introduction to the 2009 Edition

When I wrote *The Rise and Fall of Money Capital* over the period 1985–90 and summarised it as *The Crash of International Finance-Capital and its Implications for the Third World* in 1989, I predicted that the crisis that had built up during the 19 October 1987 Black Monday crash had reached irreversible dimensions. I analysed the fundamental reasons behind that crash and came to the conclusion that what had been seen as the 'immediate' factor behind the crash was in actual fact hidden in the developments of the previous five years of enhanced speculation, developments which had arisen out of the 'de-materialisation' of production and its transformation into the service economy (of which the 'financial services' were the most dynamic 'New Economy'). It is this 'dynamism' of the speculative 'sentiment' that also drove the 'globalisation' process that was getting under way under Thatcherism and Reaganism in the 1990s. This, with the wisdom of hindsight, is what we can now call a 'cannibalistic globalism', a globalism that has devoured million of lives in its expansionism across the globe, especially in the marginalised communities of the world.

We pointed out in 1989 that the loss of 'values' that was brought about by the de-industrialisation of the industrial economies, especially in the 1972–75 recession, was fuelled by the demand of the Thatcherist 'revolution' that there be a new economy rooted in 'new monetary values' and based on 'free markets'. Thatcher famously argued at the time that 'there is no alternative' (TINA) regarding the paradigm shift. Led by Milton Friedman, this new ideology had in fact already been articulated by the Chicago School and its monetarist values. Friedman's main demand was for a 'new monetary rule' which would enable the creation of 'sound money' no longer

based on 'narrow' industrial production but on the 'free market' of the financial system. It is this 'de-materialisation' of the industrial economy, which arose out of the loss of industry's profitability, that elevated the role of technology in the financial management of the 'new values'.

In many ways, Thatcher's 'revolution' was therefore a class war waged in the name of the capitalist class against the working-class and their labour unions. In financial terms, Thatcher even went as far as destroying the basis of the working-class attempt to establish their own cooperative form of economy in the shape of building societies. She attacked this form of property and converted it into a new economy by 'de-mutualising' it. Workers were bought out of their property by being offered significant sums of money for their shares in houses by the new financial classes that were emerging. Many accepted these 'windfalls', unmindful of what might follow under the new regime of new values of fictitious capital. Only a handful of building societies resisted and remained in the hands of their members. Subsequently, Prime Minister Tony Blair's New Labour party adopted a 'relaxed view' of this development and encouraged people to 'create wealth'. As British Chancellor of the Exchequer and later Prime Minister, Gordon Brown managed this 'economic policy' and encouraged banks such as Northern Rock to thrive on this bubble, which finally burst in 2007.

Combined with the de-industrialisation of the British economy, this development became the bedrock upon which global capitalism was re-organised, but also the beginnings of the collapse of that re-organised economy. Northern Rock became the example of a new London, which from 1980 to 2007 had prided itself on having been the financial capital of the world. But when this Northern Rock speculative binge came to an end, the myth of a vibrant London financial market evaporated into thin air just as quickly as it had come. Capital had turned itself into its opposite; it could no longer exploit labour in industrial production to make super-profits. Instead it turned itself into a new economy in which 'money' could be made out of money without substantial industrial production. The New Economy which arose out of the 'financial services' came to increasingly dominate the 'real economy'.

As Marx had correctly observed, for the capitalists the production of goods was an 'unavoidable link' in the chain of

money-making. The capitalists' real motivation in engaging in production was to make money, and therefore, the production of goods was a 'necessary evil' for the sake of making money. In short, the capitalists would if possible rather make money without the intervention of production (of goods). The neo-liberal New Economy came to signal the arrival of a phase of capitalism which, as we are beginning to see, can only implode on the strength of the massive build-up of unquantifiable empty paper wealth which cannot be turned into real money. This 'wealth' has, without the production of real material goods, turned itself into a form of 'toxic wealth' which can only pollute what remains of the 'real' economy, unless the real producers of these material goods find a new means by which they can bury this toxic economy on a new material basis. Unless they succeed in doing this, they cannot save themselves from being consumed by its toxicity.

Considering the 2007–08 'meltdown' in this book's Postscript, we can affirm the economic analysis of the original publication of *The Crash of International Finance-Capital* in 1989. In that earlier analysis, we come to the conclusion that the real underlying cause of capitalist financial crashes and the increasingly shorter and shorter industrial circles that were occurring was capitalists' failure to generate surplus value from living labour, labour which itself alone produces wealth. It is this failure that has resulted from the de-capitalisation of industry, a process which drove financial capitalists to try to substitute old, 'unsound' money and credit instruments based on that form of production with new ones which increasingly put the system into jeopardy before finally bringing it down.

The current global capitalist crisis is therefore the inevitable result of the earlier attempts of the capitalist managers of the system and their owners to try to push the system on for as long as it would take to ensure their survival. The paper money that was being produced became increasingly barren however, unable as it was to generate the material production on which life depends. People do not eat paper nor do they sleep in paper houses. They need food and tangible products like real houses to survive. As soon as the inverted paper pyramid began to eat deeply into the declining material production, the craze to make more money without the production of goods therefore came to a halt, giving rise to

society's demand that people should be left free to engage in new forms of production if they are to survive the crisis that capitalism has created for them. Our conclusion in *The Crash of International Finance-Capital* was that:

> No system [based on capitalist production] can sustain itself in such a situation. It must collapse and with it a new society must emerge, a global community, based on human solidarity and not for profit, a society in which exploitation and class divisions are abolished.

We still hold to that conclusion.

Dani Wadada Nabudere
Mbale, Uganda, 15 May 2009

Part One (1989)

The Crash of International Finance-Capital and its Implications for the Third World

Preface and Acknowledgements

Writing about money and its relationship to production is something that is normally reserved for an obscure chapter because of its alleged 'technical' character. This, as explained in the body of the text, has been due to the separation of money from production in the analysis of capitalism since it was regarded as playing a 'neutral' role as an agent of the circulation of commodities.

This book tries to demonstrate the centrality of money in capitalist production, for if production in pre-capitalist formations is to be referred to as having been production 'for use', then production under capitalism is truly for money. Those who 'use' the products must have money, not momentarily, but all the time in order to be able to buy, and even sell them.

Thus, under the capitalist regime, consumer satisfaction arises out of money transactions of which credit relations are part. Credit enlarges the area of capitalist production and commerce, but it is never a substitute for money as such. As credit it can only circulate commodities, although it may momentarily, hold the value of commodities. It can only act as a producing agent if the credit is in the form of capital. Money is fully *money* if it fulfils all the three historical functions of money: as a measure of value, as a medium of exchange and as a store of value. Only gold (or to some extent silver and, today, platinum) can fulfil all these three functions – and remains so, as Marx observed, even under capitalism as the pivot of the monetary system. It fulfils this role regardless of whether the state recognises it as money, or not.

Money, more importantly, is a *social relation*. It is a social relation because money alone establishes the link between the two main social classes: the worker and the capitalist. The workers' *capacity to work* (labour-power) is money in the form of wages. It is also money in the form of prices (of dead labour), i.e. of machinery and raw

materials. These forms of labour initiate production, the product of which is sold for more money by the capitalist and this is possible only out of the incomes of the workers and the middle strata who earn them in the process of their exploitation.

Thus, as a social relation, money is also a *power relation*. Through money, which is in fact *capital*, the capitalist class as a *whole* establishes its hegemony over the labouring classes in the form of the *bourgeois state*, and it is this state which *guarantees* to the capitalist the social and technical conditions which enable them to exploit labour as a social relation. The state in this form is then a *social-power* of a class which provides *additional* support to the class to subjugate the labourers to capitalist exploitation.

It was with the aim of bringing out these issues through the analysis of *money-capital*, that this project was first attempted. The research started in Nairobi, where I was momentarily in exile in 1980, and continued in Denmark, where it was completed. The main work, entitled *The Rise and Fall of Money Capital*, has been brought out of print in the United Kingdom with the support of the Africa In Transition Trust and for this, thanks must go to Professor Yash Tandon, whose untiring effort to see this project through enabled this publication to come to the readers. Thanks also go to Dunstan Chan of Grassroot Printers, UK, who worked so hard to bring it out in time.

This book is a shortened version of the main work and is being published as a special edition for Africa. Africa In Transition Trust have linked up with the Southern African Political Economy Series (SAPES) to jointly publish it in Zimbabwe. For this, thanks go to Ibbo Mandaza, Yash Tandon and Gilbert Mudenda for enabling this to happen and also SAPES staff working on the publication, especially Sarah Way, Dick Masala and Christina Tunukayi.

Institutional support was rendered to me in the writing of the two books by the International Peoples College, Helsingor, Denmark and in particular the Principal of the College, Erik Holm Hogsbro. Exile life, apart from its inconvenience, also does on the other hand offer one the time to go into research which under normal conditions might not have been possible. The International Peoples College provided me with sustenance and a conducive atmosphere to enable me to complete the research.

The book is now presented to the reader as a contribution to the search for knowledge to enable us to enlighten the path in the process of the struggle to bring about a better world. As such, knowledge is never complete for it develops in the course of such struggle. For this reason, ours is no more than a modest contribution.

Dani Wadada Nabudere
Harare, Zimbabwe, 6 July 1989

Introduction

There can be no doubt in anyone's mind, least of all in the minds of the financial oligarchy that manages and exploits the world's resources, that the international capitalist system is in utter crisis. The crisis of the system has, since the 1929–31 crash and depression, apparently been 'pushed off' from time to time by various adjustment innovations. However, each crisis management innovation has added the ills of the previous solutions to the new ones and complicated possibilities for future innovations. Furthermore, the crisis loops have become shorter and shorter for most of the countries of the world with the result that in a majority of these countries the loops have become merged into one gigantic continuous and ongoing *mega-crisis*.

Many countries of the Third World and weaker capitalist states find themselves caught up in this major crisis, which represents the passing over to them of the ill-effects of the industrial and credit crises emanating from the economics of the major capitalist states. These ill-effects have been added to by the crises of the former socialist countries and people's democracies which, with their own drive to integrate themselves within the capitalist international division of labour, have 'caught the capitalist disease' of cyclical profit crises. These effects have arisen from these countries' restructuring of their economies to respond easily to the rhythms of the world capitalist markets. Such a development is likely to add to the complexities of the world capitalist market.

This then makes the ongoing crisis a world crisis, affecting all the systems of the world encompassing the western capitalist states, the so-called socialist camp and the Third World which is part of these two systems. In this short book, we try to fathom out some of the forces behind these developments and in so doing reveal the real forces behind the crisis, exposing the hidden forces behind the official explanations and theories.

In order to accomplish this task, it becomes necessary to undertake basic theoretical issues connected with the whole question of money-capital, since this is the base of the crisis. After accomplishing this task in Chapter One, we attempt to address substantive questions of the crisis in the remainder of the book.

We first examine the emergence of *finance-capital* on the world scene in the period of generalised colonialisations and imperialist rivalries in Chapter Two. An understanding of the mechanisms in the rise of this form of capital gives us the real basis for understanding the post-war multilateral system which was worked out by the US with the compliance of Britain to sustain the system which was in fact already in crisis. Ridden as it was with cracks caused by the anti-colonial resistance and the movement forward of the socialist system, capitalism had to revamp itself to survive.

We then examine the mechanisms of the post-war Bretton Woods system in depth and try to trace the roots of its later collapse in Chapter Three. The post-war system of economic management, with its Keynesian innovations, is then analysed in Chapter Four. Here we can see that the Keynesian and post-Keynesian prescriptions, with a tinge of neo-classicism that sustained the system to new heights, was itself the culmination of the ongoing forces of crisis which the post-war 'full employment' policy tried to resolve. In turn the failure of post-Keynesianism, while opening the doors for the Chicago School monetarism and 'supply-side' economism, was an opening shot for the further internationalisation of the crisis under the new catch-word 'globalisation'. This drive has, in the last five years, encompassed the world in a wave of 'privatisations' and new financial speculations of finance-capital, which must surely lead to its fall.

In Chapters Five, Six, Seven and Eight we analyse the forces behind the crash of financial markets. We look at the de-industrialisation of the capitalist economies, the growth of the service sector and the undermining of capitalist profit on the one hand, and the negation of wage-labour on the other, as a background to the inevitable collapse of finance-capital and money market crashes. We examine all these matters in great detail in our main book, *The Rise and Fall of Money Capital*, to be published in cooperation with the Africa in Transition Trust.

This special edition for Africa, in a shortened form, brings out the essence of the analysis in the main book. The main book was written in 1983 to mark the first centenary anniversary of Karl Marx's death, but due to publication difficulties, it did not see the light of the day until now. It is clear that Marx's theoretical work was truly a major landmark in humanity's intellectual achievements. His theory of money and credit is at the centre of his analysis of the capitalist mode of production in his four-volume work, *Das Kapital*. The significance he attached to a scientific theory of money and credit explains why he devoted his first major theoretical work, entitled *The Contribution to the Critique of Political Economy* and published in 1859, to a historical study of the theories of money and credit to which he attached his synthesis of the same. This theoretical forerunner was later summarised, with a new precision and dialectical conciseness, in the first three chapters of his *Capital*, Volume 1, published in 1867. It is this analysis of Marx, which was later applied by him in his second volume in the analysis of the turn-overs of capital in the industrial production and circulation circuits, that we try to apply in the understanding of the crisis of today's finance-capital. Without this theoretical understanding, it is in fact impossible to comprehend what is really happening in the world industrial and financial markets. It is hoped that this presentation will provide a basis for further discussion as to the implications of the present crisis of the world economy on Third World countries, and Africa in particular. Are the recent waves of chaotic de-nationalisations in the search for a 'private' solution to the crisis a viable solution? In fact it is clear that privatisation is now itself in crisis with the Black Monday crash of the stock markets on 19 October 1987. This crash is in fact a forerunner of a much deeper malaise of the world capitalist system which must sooner than later lead to its total collapse.

Little attention is sometimes paid to the restructuring which has been taking place in the western economies (and to some extent in the 'socialist' economies) and the link it has to the International Monetary Fund (IMF) and World Bank stabilisation and structural adjustment policies which have been forced on Third World economies. An attempt is made to link up these processes in Chapter Nine, which examines the impact of the crisis of international

finance-capital to the processes of internationalisation and globalisation by these forces. It is shown that the drive to reduce the role of the state in the Third World development (through exchange rate control) and the pressure to strengthen the intermediation of commercial banks in the rural sector of the economy are all connected with the issue of globalising finance-capital in its speculative aspect to encompass Third World peoples. The pressure to turn and convert Third World debt into securities which can be 'marketed' on the stock exchanges is in fact part of this pressure which is highly connected with the drive to 'privatise' the economy and 'divest' the state from economic development activity. By removing the state from the economic sphere, the idea is to establish a *nexus* between the local comprador capitalists with their international 'counterparts' to milk the African countryside and that of the other Third World countries. If this book goes some way to bring to the fore a discussion of these issues in some deep ongoing way, then it will have served its purpose.

1

Marx's Theory of Money and Credit

The international capitalist system is fundamentally undermined by two contradictory forces at work: the over-production of commodities and the money-credit instruments that accompanies it on the one hand, and the economic environment which compels individuals to act as if they are all accumulators of private wealth, on the other. The system at first appeared to have a *rationale* in that, at least as far as Europe was concerned, all individuals had an apparent equal opportunity to work and enrich themselves. Although this was patently untrue, the worker who in fact produced this wealth and had no equal opportunity to accumulate, was nevertheless overwhelmed by the ideological enthusiasm of the period which the new capitalism, counter-poised with feudalism on the opposite side as it was, unleashed. In this way, the system of production based on private appropriation of wealth by a few capitalist individuals out of the labours of the majority constituted by the working-class was accepted as the only natural and reasonable one.

The Dilemma of the Bourgeoisie

But in fact the system was fraught with inner contradictions inherent in this economic arrangement, and this is what explains why the very over-production of commodities and over-expansion of credit should in themselves imply a crisis for the system as a whole which was worsened as the system developed to higher levels. This was because as the capitalist system increased its potentiality to produce ever increasing volumes of commodities, the drive to accumulate wealth in private hands by the few surplus-value appropriators created the necessity that this wealth would be

accumulated in the form of *money*. This was in reality a historical necessity which was imposed on the capitalist system by the material forces of previous society in which money in its latest fully developed form as silver or gold had brought forward a material limit to its unfettered production because of cost. The inheritance of this limitation by capitalism meant that its newly acquired potentiality to increase production, assisted by science and technology to hitherto undreamt levels, would itself be limited by the material conditions of money production and expansion. Although the capitalists tried to overcome this 'metallic' barrier – as David Ricardo came to call it – capitalism has never fully managed to overcome these limitations, precisely because the system of production based on capitalism implied the private appropriation of wealth which was only possible in the form of money. In this way, then, money became a hindrance to the full development of capital, and this is what manifested itself in the recurrent economic crises as the *financial crisis*. The crisis was in reality a *production crisis* because it was connected with over-production of commodities which, at certain points within the production cycle, had led to the 'over-production' of money-credit, for in such events all the capitalists holding money-credit instruments or paper money craved that these instruments, which resembled money, would be turned into *real cash-money!*

The question then which appears to be posed in the understanding of capitalist production and crisis is *what is money?* The bourgeoisie have attempted to answer the question with little success. It is the purpose of this chapter to reveal the reasons for this failure. Nevertheless, the question is a real one and a problem at that for the bourgeoisie. Laughable definitions of money by bourgeois monetary economists such as 'Money is what money does' give one an idea of the quandary in which bourgeois economic theory has found itself with every complication that capitalist crisis has presented to these ideologues of capitalism. According to John Richard Hicks, even that most eminent of bourgeois monetary economists, John Maynard Keynes, ended up with three definitions of money.[1] Thus whilst the bourgeoisie use money in the production process, they still face the dilemma that they cannot explain the process of production based on money-capital.

The reason for this dilemma lies in the fact that the bourgeoisie have always attempted to obscure the function of money within capitalist production because to reveal its true function would expose the true role of money as the basis upon which the labour of the majority in the form of surplus-value is converted into the private wealth of a few. For this reason attempts have been made to present money as a neutral, technical device which serves the circulation of commodities *per se*. The fact that money more fundamentally is a means of expropriating wealth from others and then storing it is only momentarily mentioned in the latter aspect but in a manner that is segmented in order to obscure the total process of production and appropriation. In this way, the organic link between money and capital as a *social relation* between the producers of wealth and its private appropriation is silenced theoretically.

It is for this reason that Joseph Schumpeter points out to us that although debates raged on for years and decades among bourgeois economists as to the true function of money, and hence also on questions of definitions, these discussions and debates 'did not produce very interesting results'.[2] He singles out Georg Friedrich Knapps as having been the exception, although the latter produced a definition of money that obscured its role even more – the so-called state theory of money. But Schumpeter points out nevertheless that the other economists got stuck at the 'neutral' definition of money as 'money is what money does' – a phrase coined by one Francis A. Walker to save them from the embarrassment of having achieved nothing out of the years of talk and writing. The discussion from then onwards was bogged down with drawing distinctions between 'primary money' and 'credit and fiduciary money'. Other bourgeois economists devoted their efforts at examining the four classical functions of money, with one faction within it emphasising the 'separability' of the functions, and another emphasising their combinability.

It was within this theorising that one branch of monetary economists came to try to find the basis for the existence of value in money. Léon Walras and Adam Smith used the concept of 'labour standard value' as the *numeraire* in which labour quantities of labour-power could be expressed as *direct* labour-units created by

labour. On the whole, however, the majority of the new economists increasingly separated the problem of monetary theory from that of the 'theory of value and distribution'. Prices of goods and services were looked at merely as monetary expressions of the quantities of goods and services which did not affect their production. Money was seen as a unit which facilitated exchange in something which was in the nature of barter since money played a non-influential and non-affecting role. In this way economics came to express the 'real analysis' of production and distribution in which abstract 'neutral' money units were used, while monetary analysis was left outside as a different science which was not related to the main issues of production and the existence of real values.

Monetary theory therefore came to look on itself as concerned with the analysis of exchange-value, and this came increasingly to mean examining the origins, meaning and problems of defining the 'purchasing power of money'. It was with this view that many books came to be written examining 'money and prices', as if these were unrelated to the actual problems of production and distribution of goods. With this development, the monetary economists found they had nothing material to their analysis and since money in this role was 'neutral', efforts were made to find neutral index numbers which were created to express the value of money as a basis for calculating prices of goods and services. The Austrian School added to this *de-materialisation* of money by advancing marginal utility concepts to explain how value in money was created, and under this new theory any objective basis to the production of money and its value was denied. Instead a 'subjective theory of money' was advanced in which the value of money was said to lie in the subjective wills of individuals and their desires.

The above tracing of the dilemma of the bourgeoisie can then explain to us why the bourgeois economists came to find it impossible to disentangle the role of money and credit in capitalist production, and yet it was fundamental to the system of production. In fact the 'impossibility' became the necessity for obscuring the reality in order to continue to combat other more scientifically based theories which had already emerged to challenge these obscure theories of the bourgeoisie. It is not surprising then that the bourgeois economists came to see money as only an agent of circulation. Keynes

tried to overcome this weakness by pointing to the storage function of money and tried to build it into the money-capital market operations, but it never sank into the general analysis.

Most quantitative economists stuck to the separation of money into 'primary money' which later came to be called 'narrow money' – meaning currency notes and demand deposits – and 'fiduciary money' or credit which today is called 'broad money', which meant narrow money plus time deposits. This latter classification has been sub-divided so that there is now broad money one and broad money two – MB1 and MB2 – adding further to the confusion as to what categories of 'money' qualify for final payment. The new explosion of financiering that has struck the global financial markets with the deregulation and de-control of money and financial markets had broadened even further the paper claimants to the 'narrow money'. That has undermined the quality of money which has complicated and worsened the 'liquidity' problem of the financial system. In these circumstances, it cannot be surprising for Noboru Takeshita, the Japanese Prime Minister, to have exclaimed recently: 'If I am asked to give you a projection of how far a certain currency can go down, that is a question that only God can answer, especially in the spirit of the floating rate system!'[3] This was said after the 1987 financial markets crash followed by rapid fluctuations of the US dollar and of the other currencies connected with it globewise. It must be clear from this that the bourgeoisie find themselves at a dead-end in their understanding of the system they are supposed to operate as a ruling class. This then is their dilemma.

Money and Credit in Marx's Theory

While the bourgeoisie were struggling in this way to make head and tail of what they were managing, Marx's theory, which was abused and sidetracked, stood the test of time. Even Marxist scholars, who found themselves overwhelmed by this concept of 'neutrality' of money, paid very little specific attention to Marx's theory, except in as much as it concerned capitalist circulation. This is reflected in the writings of Rudolf Hilferding who, despite his major contributions on this matter, still looked at money as an agent. The recent writings of the Trotskyist–Marxist Ernest Mandel also fall into the error of seeing inflation in prices as lying in the over-explosion of credit,

which is the same thing as seeing money as a circulation agent of commodities. The writings of 'neo-Marxists' such as Paul Sweezy and Paul Baran also tended to confuse a proper analysis of money and credit in capitalist production, for in their rejection of the *law of value* in relation to monopoly capitalism, they made it impossible to apply Marx's concepts of value to production.

For Marx, the development of money follows the same path as that of other commodities. Money is a commodity just like all other commodities, except that at a certain stage of its development, it steps aside to act as the sole representative of all other commodities in that it is only through it that all other commodities' values can be expressed.

Marx argues that commodity production does not begin with capitalism. It is, he asserts, *prius* to capitalism. It existed in the earlier modes of production and social formations. It existed under the slave-owning societies as well as under the feudal societies. Indeed, it was on the basis of this commodity production that merchant capital developed and it was under these conditions that the social and economic pre-conditions for capitalist development were created. Nevertheless, commodity production under these conditions was *simple commodity production*. Only under capitalism did it develop into complex expanded forms.

Simple commodity production brought about a certain division of labour among the direct producers under which individual producers specialised in producing and making particular products. It also brought about the existence of *private property* in the means of production in the products of labour. Peasant and craftsman production was based on the personal labour of the commodity producer. But it had something in common with capitalist development in that its foundation was private property in the *means of production*. This petty commodity production is what served as the base and point of departure for commodity production under capitalism and it is under the latter that commodity production became a universal and dominant mode of production.[4]

It is this evolution of commodity production that enabled the labour process to become identified, leading to the emergence of the social division of labour, without which exchanges are impossible. One form of labour became identified with a particular production

and in this way it became a *concrete labour*. The skill of a tailor and that of a shoe-maker became different, but all produced *use-values*. What was important was that both these different forms of labour were human labour and as such they were *abstract labour*. It was only when they were both human labour in this way that exchanges became possible. Different labours and use-values have different measures which are appropriate to their physical characteristics. What expresses this *measure* of the different concrete labours and use-values is the *time* it takes to produce them. Hence *labour-time* became an important element in establishing a relationship which enabled *exchange-value* to be established. Thus it is the two-fold character of a commodity which makes it possible for money-commodity to emerge and develop.

In a society in which private property in the means of production exists, this two-fold character of the labour embodied in a commodity reflects the *contradiction* between the *private labour* of individuals who produce the different use-values, and the *social labour* which can only be carried on in the generalised abstract labour of the commodity producers as a whole. While each producer acts as an individual and regards his production activity as his private affair, he cannot dispose of his surplus or excess product to himself.

This interconnection between the individual producers is established in the market, where every individual meets to compare, measure, evaluate and exchange his particular product for others. The more labour is divided and separated along these lines, the more varied are the products which are manufactured by the different producers and the more extensive becomes the mutual dependence of all the producers one to the other. Consequently the labour of each producer increasingly becomes essentially social in character and in that way it becomes just one particle of the labour of society as a whole. It is within this set of *economic* relationships that the interests of individuals are developed, and it is in the course of this development that *class struggles* emerge and are fought to their conclusion.

Marx points out that he was the first to pin-point and to examine this two-fold nature of the labour process and of the labour contained in commodities, for with this discovery the conception became the 'pivot' upon which a clear comprehension of political economy was

possible.[5] The discovery enabled him to bring into analytical focus the *qualitative* differences in the commodities, because without this their *quantitative* content could not be established.

The common factor in the exchange relation, or in the exchange-value of the commodity is therefore abstract labour. The magnitude of this value is measured by the quantity of the 'value-forming substance', namely the labour contained in the article. The quantity of labour is in turn measured by its duration, and this *labour-time* is itself measured on the particular scale of hours, days and weeks. The labour that forms the substance of value is *equal human labour*. It is the expenditure of identical human labour-power – a *social average unit* of labour-power, which is *socially necessary* to produce *any* use-value under conditions of production normal for a given society, and with an average degree of skill and intensity of labour which prevails in that society. This relation therefore varies with time and space. It is this *relation* which *exclusively* determines the *magnitude* of the value of any article. Commodities which contain equal quantities of labour, or which can be produced in the same time, have therefore the same value.

This time changes as a result of the growth of the productivity of labour. The *productivity* of labour is expressed in the amount of products created in a given unit of labour-time. It grows as a result of the improvement or fuller utilisation of the instruments of production, the development of science, the increase in the worker's skill, the rationalisation of work and other improvements in the production process and other natural conditions. The *higher* the productivity of labour, the *less* the time needed for the production of a unit of the given commodity and the *lower* the value of this commodity. *Intensity* of labour, on the other hand, is determined by the amount of labour expended in a unit of time. A growth in the intensity of labour means an increase in the expenditure of labour in one and the same interval of time. *More* intensive labour embodies a *greater* quantity of products and creates a *greater value* in a given unit of time, as compared with the less intensive labour.

The *skill* of the workers in the production process is either simple or complex. *Simple* labour is the labour of a worker who has no special training or experience. *Complex* labour is the labour of a worker with special training and experience. Complex labour creates value

of a greater magnitude than is created by simple labour in the same unit of time, to which must be added the labour expended in the worker's training. Complex labour is therefore equivalent to *multiplied* simple labour: one hour of complex labour is equal to several hours of simple labour. In the actual process of commodity production based on private property, the reduction of various forms of complex labour to simple labour takes place spontaneously. The magnitude of the value of a commodity is determined by the socially-necessary amount of simple labour-time.

Armed with these findings, Marx then embarked on tracing the evolution of the different functions of money. As we know these functions are: the measure of value, medium of exchange and store of value. It turns out that this analysis is also a historical tracing of money's development, which finally resolves the problem of how it comes about that: 'the thing measured becomes the measuring unit'.[6]

In short, how does one commodity become the universal measurement of all other commodities, that is, how does one commodity become *money*? The singling out of particular commodities at different times leads to one commodity – gold or silver – becoming acceptable universally by different communities as the sole measure of all their commodities' values. This took a very long time and the process of how communities came to accept certain ways of measurement became blurred with the passage of time, as it becomes a habit to accept a certain unit as the basis for measuring. It is this development which expresses the history of price-formation. Gold ultimately becomes the *standard of price*, with a scale of measurements such as 1 ounce of gold = 35 dollars, which is the *price* of gold as a commodity, but also a scale in which the prices of other commodities are expressed. In this same process money evolves as the *medium of exchange* in that gold becomes the only commodity which is acceptable to all commodity producers in the process of *circulation* of their commodities. It is this also which brings about the emergence of *coin*, for gold can be divided in this form and again melted into bars, making it a convenient commodity to act as a medium in coin and yet also as a conserver of wealth as a *gold bar*. This possibility which gold or silver offer to other commodities ensures their evolution into money or gold as a *store of*

value. It also shows that it is only gold acting both as coin, and again as bar, which alone *survives* the process of circulation. Other commodities disappear into private consumption, but gold, although it disappears in private hoards, can and does reappear to act as money.

It is this development of the different functions of money in this dialectical and historical process that ensures the emergence of money as a *means of payment*. It is this which enables the appearance of *money-credit* to develop into the credit system that appears with capitalism. In this function, money enables someone to sell a commodity when another is not yet ready to buy or vice-versa. A seller is able to sell and deliver a commodity to a 'buyer' whose commodity is not yet ready for sale and exchange. In that case, the buyer is able to 'buy' by *means* of the *promise* to deliver when his or her own commodity is ready to deliver or sell. The seller becomes a *creditor* and the purchaser a *debtor*. This transaction enables a *pause* which facilitates the development of *commerce* and *trade*. Here we can already see the emergence of *contract* and *legal relations* in the process of production.

The Rise of Money-Capital

Credit and the credit system have their appearance and initial development under *merchant capital*. Under merchant capital gold is also fully developed as a store of value and as a mark of wealth. Gold is regarded as the 'source of power' and it is this crave for gold that pushed Spain and Portugal to 'conquer the world' in the name of gold. The extermination of aboriginal peoples of what is today Latin America and the enslavement of people to work in the mines of Mexico and Peru marked the drive to achieve this power that gold represented. Thus merchant capital fed on the decay of feudalism, but it also created conditions for the accumulation of wealth that sowed the seeds of capitalist production. Merchant capital established the *merchant estate* and developed credit in the ambit of commerce in which money evolved into a means of payment and gold as *world money*. Capitalism was therefore presented with the material basis for its genesis and full development as *money-capital*. Money could now continue to exist only as *capital*.

Money-capital was therefore a development of money beyond its containment within circulation which merchant capital implied. In this new form, which was a revolutionary leap, capital emerged as the initiator of *production*. The elements of this capital had been created by the pause which merchant capital broadened to include the dispossession of the peasant producers under feudalism through *debt* and bondage. The end product of money as a means of payment was therefore the 'freeing' of the peasant direct producers of their product through the creditor–debtor relation. This act impoverished them and turned them into dispossessed peasantry ready for exploitation by money-capital as workers. The evolution of money-capital is therefore clearly an evolution of social relationships, and capitalism already emerges as a *social relationship* between the capitalist and the worker.

From this moment onwards, *labour* exists in opposition to *capital* in the actual confrontation of production. Labour exists on condition that it shall offer itself as a use-value to capital for exploitation for a wage. This use-value of labour (which takes the form of labour-power) exists in the bodily and mental *capacity* of the labourer, and is consumed when he or she exerts his or her energy to produce. On the opposite side stands capital as an exchange-value, but no longer merely as money. It is *money-capital* in that it exists in the form of commodities such as machinery, raw materials and food products. Capital also continues to exist as money in its role as a general representative of wealth into which commodities are converted after sale. It is the combination of capital and labour-power in the form of commodities which enables capital to expand in production with the amount of *surplus-value* created by the labourer. This is appropriated by capital as *profit* which includes profit of enterprise, rent and interest on money.

The above process of exploitation of labour takes place because the labourer sells his or her labour-power for a wage which is less than the product that he or she is able to produce. With his or her labour-power, he or she is able to pass on to the capitalist two things *free of charge*: first, the surplus value which is over and above his or her wage; and second, the *quality of his or her living labour* which the capitalist uses to *maintain* the value of old products of labour contained in machinery, raw materials and other ancillary materials

which are required in production. The maintenance is achieved in the process of production when the worker is engaged in this process. The labourer *transfers* the values in these old products to the new one in order to form a greater value than before. In this way, the capitalist uses living labour to combine old and new surplus value into a new higher value for himself, which he transforms into money by sale in order to *accumulate* and create greater capitals for further investment.

The formula which this *industrial* activity takes is: money which converted into commodities (machinery, raw materials and labour-power) to produce new commodities which are sold and converted into money, which I have called M-C-M1. These are three stages in the process which constitutes *industrial capital*. Marx states that these three stages of capital must pass into one another in an uninterrupted way in order to maintain the value of capital.

If the process stops short in the first phase, M-C, money-capital assumes the rigid form of a hoard; if it stops in the second phase of production, C-M, the means of production and labour-power will lie idle and remain unemployed, because in this phase capital-money (M) has been transformed into commodities such as machinery, raw materials and labour power, which become idle if the production process is interrupted. Furthermore, if the production and distribution process stops short in its last phase, C-M1, piles of unsold commodities accumulate and clog the flow of circulation. Be this as it may, each stage has a fixed period of its own in which it exists as money, productive and commodity capital.[7]

These interconnected stages of the industrial process ultimately explain why the capitalist system is capable of operating on credit, making it possible for various forms of speculation to exist within the capitalist process of production as part of the crave to make money and accumulate it. This process is possible so long as labour exists continuously, and money-capital existing in these conditions is nothing but a *claim on future labour* of the labourers who alone can keep the system continuously in operation. The bourgeoisie are able to obtain the submission of labour to this process so long as they act as a *social force* in the form of the bourgeois *state*.

What is said above, while presenting a real advantage to the capitalist state, has, nevertheless, in-built constraints to the full

development of capitalism. As already indicated, while it is possible for capitalist production to proceed and produce great amounts of commodities, there is the inherited barrier to its unaffected development in money. Whilst money makes it possible for capital to use the attributes of money as a means of payment to develop new production, nevertheless in its role as a store of value, money presents difficulties for capitalism.

The first problem is posed by the limits of the volume metallic money, as we shall see later. But the more endemic problem arises from the very fact of surplus value creation. This is because with the creation of new values by the labourers, there is no equivalent in the form of metallic money in which to keep the surplus value created. The new value never existed before. This barrier is overcome to a very large extent by the creation of a credit system in which money, acting as a means of payment, is able to come into existence in the form of a *promise*. But the problem nevertheless remains in the final effort by all the capitalists to turn this surplus value so created into *real cash* in periods of crisis which are endemic to the system. This, as we shall continue to observe, presents a real stumbling block to capitalism.

For the most part, and as long as the industrial process proceeds uninterrupted, the credit system fills the gap of the absence of real cash for the preservation of the surplus value created, so that through it the new value is kept at first in credit instruments in the form of banknotes and deposits. In this sense, the credit system becomes reliant and is increasingly based on the future labour of the labourers, which keeps on producing surplus value which gives future 'value' to the new and old credit instruments. It is through this mechanism that new (fictitious) capital is created and invested in productive capital. Thus the existence of *debt* (on which the credit system is based) and its *acknowledgement* become the means of paying for commodities which go into production. In this way credit begins to 'crowd out' real money in the bulk of capitalist production and circulation.

In this development *commercial credit* becomes a means by which the capitalists appear to give credit to one another in the form of *bills of exchange*. The same piece of paper (bill of exchange) can change hands with promises being 'endorsed' in a certain time

progression which, when it begins to wend backwards, ensures that all are paid on time, in many cases by new promises. It is this element which *bank credit* tries to replace and develop even more. The bank was able to concentrate in its hands the savings of lenders so that these could be lent to the borrowing capitalists. While this also enabled capitalist firms to reduce their individually held reserve funds to a minimum while the other portion of their profits served as money-capital for further investment, it at the same time created a new capital within the bank which the banks could use as their own capital to lend out. This bank capital could be in the form of a bill of exchange, a cheque, a credit account or a banknote issued by the bank itself with the authority of the state.

In time the whole banking system came to be based on two branches of activity based on *investment capital* and *borrowed banking capital*. To raise the latter form of capital, the bank relied on savings deposits, note issues (for the deposits) and the drawing of bills. The bank made its capital out of the interest it earned for keeping the deposits while they were not required by the depositor. This became the basis of fictitious capital creation as we shall see in the next chapter. The use of the cheque added further economy to the production of money, since with the issue of a banknote in place of a gold deposit, the metal commodity-money was crowded out of the circulation medium.

The deposit now created the possibility not only of the bank issuing a banknote, but also of it creating a *credit account* which in fact was an imaginary deposit and on the basis of which cheques could be drawn out of the imaginary account. This in turn led to the emergence of new financial institutions, including the *clearinghouse* which enabled the cross cancellation of cheques issued by many banks against one another's cheques to take place. In this role the cheque was acting as a unit of account and no more. This overexpansion of credit also ensured that the new innovative devices *could never* be converted into gold since as capitalism developed new credit instruments were created beyond the gold and silver available in the vaults of banks and central banking authorities.

It can be seen at this stage that in order for the banks to engage in this activity of concentrating money-capital for the sake of lending it *at a profit*, from which the banks are able to build up their own

capital, *interest* as a charge on borrowed bank capital becomes an important aspect of capitalist economic activity. Interest becomes an *offspring* of money-capital while at the same time being a *source* of money-capital. In this respect, it is an inheritance from historical money in which usury was an important element of merchant capital. Now under capitalism, interest arises out of the profit of an industrial enterprise, although it still retains some of the old elements of usury in becoming a parasite on industrial production. This parasitic element on production becomes a major constraint on capitalist development and finally brings it down. Interest turns money-capital into a commodity with its own use-value which the banker now relies on to maintain capitalism. At the height of the crisis as capitalism nears its end with a declining production base, interest assumes a usurious character.

The rate of interest increasingly becomes dependent on the rate of profit of the industrial enterprise. But the rate of interest has a *tendency to fall* quite independently of the fluctuations in the rate of profit due to the activities of the *rentier class*, and the development of the credit system and the attendant ever-growing control of industrialists and merchants over the money savings of all classes of society that is effected through the bankers. The progressive concentration of these savings in amounts which can serve as money-capital, tend to depress the rate of interest. To determine the average rate of interest we must therefore firstly, according to Marx, calculate the average rate of interest during its variations in the major industrial cycles; and secondly find the rate of interest for investments which require long-term loans of capital. This cannot be determined by law of the state despite efforts by the state in this direction.

The rate of interest is similarly related to the rate of profit as the market price is related to its value. In so far as the rate of interest is determined by the rate of profit, this is always the *general rate of profit* and not any specific rate of profit prevailing in some particular industry; and still less any extra profit an individual capitalist may make in a particular sphere of business. The money-capitalists reap their rate of interest from the general rate of profit of *all industry*. In this way, the usurious element of interest begins to make parasitic demands on industrial production, and later helps to undermine it.

The Quantity of Money Debate

The development of the credit system and the existence of gold side by side within the monetary system had already posed a serious problem by the 1840s, at least in England where the capitalist mode of production had by now taken hold. The question then raised was how the quantity of money, which is necessary to meet the circulation needs of capitalism, could be determined. It had become evident that the amount of gold and silver existing in the economy was not sufficient to act as a circulating agent. This problem unleashed a debate between the two schools of thought in England – the so-called Currency School and the Banking School. It also produced a difference of opinion between Marx and one of his followers, Rosa Luxemburg. We cannot deal with the debate in this brief presentation, but the issues raised in these debates are important in the understanding of money and credit in capitalist development. The full treatment of the debate can be found in chapter three of my main book, *The Rise and Fall of Money Capital*.

Marx was of the view that this problem was in fact a false one. Nevertheless, the fact that the bourgeoisie raised it proved how inadequate they were in their understanding of money and the role of credit instruments in capitalist development. By the time Marx wrote his *Contribution to the Critique of Political Economy*, the debate had been settled in favour of the Currency School, which had argued for the need to maintain correct 'proportions' between metallic money and paper money in order to avoid the 'oversupply' of money. Marx had responded by refuting the falsehood behind this solution. He had pointed out that when money acted as a means of payment – which was the latest role in its evolution and development – its volume and quantity was determined not only by the amount of gold or other metals available in the economy, but by the requirements of circulation itself.

This amount would depend on the volume of payments due at a particular date, not of the commodities to be sold, as with simple circulation when gold or silver coin is in use in simple money circulation. Such volume, he added, would be modified by three other factors: the *velocity* and rapidity with which a coin repeated the same operation; the interconnections of the relations of the commodity owners as creditors and debtors in which the same

commodity owner is creditor and debtor at the same time; and, finally, the period of time separating the various dates on which payments were due. If payments were due at the same time and at one place, then with money acting as a means of payments, debts and credits could cancel each other out, thereby reducing the amount of coin or currency required for circulation.[8]

Marx also added that the problem of the quantity of money necessary for capitalist production and circulation was also resolved by the *phases* in which capitalist production and circulation took place within the *industrial cycle*. In the phase of *prosperity*, expansion was brisk and hence circulation also was greater. Wages rose and profits increased as prices also rose with the increase in consumption. In such a case the amount of circulating money only grew within definite limits because of increased velocity of circulation and expansion of creditor–debtor relations. In the period of *slump* on the other hand, the pace of production and circulation slowed down with a decline in prices, profits and wages. Markets began to glut and payments were also delayed. There was an overabundance of commodities which were un-sellable. Credit contractors and every commodity owner demanded *cash* because everyone wanted cash to settle accounts in the absence of credit. Although there was a contraction in the quantity of circulating medium, there was an increase in the demand for *hard cash* – for real money. This is what contributed to the *monetary* and *financial crisis*.

In this way, Marx exposed the whole basis of credit and showed that this acted so long as production was uninterrupted. With the onset of crisis every one demanded cash: 'But now the cry everywhere is: money alone is a commodity', as each capitalist 'pants after fresh water'.[9] It now becomes clear that capitalist production stands for the sake of making and accumulating it as a social power in the form of money, which ultimately means gold.

Ricardo's argument of proportionality was therefore proved to be false. Ricardo, following Smith, advocated the replacement of coin by paper money in the form of banknotes and cheques. Although Ricardo acknowledged that the value of commodities was determined by the labour-time, he nevertheless drew this value directly from particular labour magnitudes, which gave a false picture of prices. This caused him to draw the wrong conclusion that

since exchange-value was derived *directly* from concrete labour, and therefore, money being no more than a medium of exchange, money was no more than a 'voucher' for effecting exchanges. This understanding ignored money's role as storage of value. His concept led to the adoption in 1844 of the Bank Act in England under which 'proportions' between gold and currency were fixed once and for all, while at the same time banknotes and cheques were permitted to expand with the needs of circulation, although they were assumed to do so in proportion to the gold reserves as expressed in the *reserve ratio*.

In fact this sharp division was not necessary because gold's function as store of value and its value had nothing to do with the proportionality in which gold was held in official stocks and the issue of banknotes. Because of this wrong conclusion, Ricardo had believed that the value of gold and silver rose or fell with the increase or decrease in the quantity of currency which had to do with exports and imports of goods. This theoretical formulation of the issue by Ricardo was in real fact a demand by financiers to buttress their gains when commodity prices were too high. The demand was to increase the discount rate in such a case and to reduce it when prices were too low. The demand that the rates of interest be raised because of the over-extension of credit or the over-supply of money was a demand that the value of money be increased. This in fact had nothing do to with gold's role as a store of value. This misconception led to a lot of bank panics and bank failures in the 1846–90 period, as we shall see in the next chapter.

Notes

1. Hicks, J.R. *Critical Essays in Monetary Theory*, Clarendon Press, Oxford, 1967.
2. Schumpeter, J.A. *History of Economic Analysis*, Oxford University Press, New York, 1954, p.108.
3. *The Herald*, Harare, Zimbabwe, 23 December 1987, p.13.
4. Marx, K. *Capital*, vol. 1, Progress Publishers, Moscow, 1977.
5. *Ibid.*, p.49.
6. *Ibid.*, p.39 (Marx here quotes Montanari).
7. Marx, K. *Capital*, vol. 2, p.50.
8. Marx, K. *Contribution to the Critique of Political Economy*, pp.144–6.
9. Marx, K. *Capital*, vol. 1, p.138.

2

The Emergence of Finance-Capital

The development of money-capital which we have outlined in the previous chapter set the ground for the emergence of finance-capital. Looking at this phenomenon purely from monetary-credit side, the device of the banknote to replace gold in circulation had already established a solid basis for the development of banking, which became the centre for developing fictitious capital as a means of restructuring capitalism into a monopoly phase. The fiction that banknotes were as good as gold did not start with the 'almighty' dollar. It began with the British imperial 'almighty' pound. It was in reality part of the techniques for broadening money-credit to meet the demands of capitalist production, circulation and *speculation* which was a necessary aspect of capitalism. If we are to understand the bank crises of 1846–90, the financial crash of 1929–31 and the Black Monday financial crash of 19 October 1987, we have to understand the basis of this fiction.

The Bank Act of 1844 had created the myth that the banknotes which were 'backed' by gold in the vaults of the Bank of England's banking department were as good as gold. The myth was maintained by a new technique called the *reserve ratio*, which required the Bank of England to maintain a certain reserve of gold as back-up to banknote issue. In fact the ever-increasing demand for credit, and the crises connected therewith, blew this illusion to the skies with the Overend–Gurney crisis of 1866. From this date onwards it was a situation of uneasy compromise between the illusion and the reality. By this time it had become clear that the amount of banknotes could have no relation whatever to gold.

The reality was also expressed in the practice of over-stepping the reserve ratio by a system of 'window-dressing' by which the banks were made to appear to have the necessary reserves to meet depositors' demand for 'liquidity', when in fact they did not. Under

this juggling of statistics, the impression was given in the balances of the bank at the end of weekly accounting periods that the banks possessed the stipulated reserves, when none in fact existed. Behind this cover the banks had in fact extended much more credit based on *deposits* held by other banks on 'make up' days. The fact that they did not make up their balances on the same day, of course, made it possible for them to engage in this practice.

By the same token, the banknote, as a major instrument of credit having the advantage it apparently had of 'gold backing', was reinforced by the *deposit* which now increasingly came to play a much larger role in the credit-creation of banks. The deposit thus became another foundation for the credit system on the bases of the capitalist claim to the future labour of the labourers and this, in turn, formed the basis for the emergence of a new breed of capitalist agents in the persons of brokers and promoters as conduits in the financial market. Later it became the new basis of linkage with state debt in the 1920s.

But the development of this new form of capital created by banks was not understood by the bourgeois economists as well, and this came to lead to another illusion about the actual functioning of the money-capital market and the credit system that was part of it. According to Joseph Schumpeter, almost all the economists believed that credit was extended by capitalist to capitalist and the bank did not have any function other than passing on this credit between capitalists. This was held to be true under the so-called commercial theory of banking, which made the commercial bill and the financing of current commodity trade the centrepiece of the analysis of bank credit.

This misconception is again traceable to the Currency School. The view persisted until very recent times that the 'public lent each other money', thus obscuring the role of banks and the financiering activities which were connected with stock and share issuance on the stock exchange. Bankers were seen as no more than middle-men and agents of the 'public' who did the actual lending on behalf of this amorphous 'public'. The financial oligarchy was obscured from the view of the 'public'. Their speculative activities to create fictitious capital as *bank capital* for investment beyond the deposits made by the public, as well as the social power which was wielded

behind this shield of ideology, were tremendous. This also obscured the distinction which existed between circulating credit and *capital credit*.

Whilst the earlier confusion about the definition of money had helped to obscure the fundamental role of money by referring to it as a mere instrument of circulation, ignoring the real function of money under capitalism, the new confusion added to the clouds of bourgeois obscurantism. It hid the fact that whereas circulating credit carried out money's function as a medium of exchange, capital credit on the other hand was able to *transfer* money-capital *in this form* from one capitalist to another for the *purposes of transforming it into productive capital*.

The Evolution of Finance-Capital

It can now be seen that the new credit devices of the banknote, the deposit and the cheque enabled the creation of new forms of capital which Marx refers to as 'fictitious capital'. Part of the gold-stock was used to achieve this objective by giving temporary relief to the fear that the banknote was not 'money'. But soon, as we shall see, the deception was over-ridden by reality. The banker was now charged with the responsibility by the bourgeoisie as a collective social power to open credit lines beyond the available 'cash', i.e. gold and banknotes, and lend it out as investment capital on the condition that the borrowing capitalist shall turn it into *productive capital*. To do this, the borrowing capitalist had to ensure that the capital credit would reproduce itself with a surplus value over and above the credit extended in the form of interest. In doing so, the new capital credit must expeditiously turn itself into commodities (including the commodity labour-power); realise itself in new commodity values with the assistance of labour; exchange itself through sale and purchase (and in this process help *transfer* capital to other capitalists); and to realise revenue out of which interest is to be paid to the bankers. In this process, the deposit of one capitalist is utilised by another to increase production. The same capital is money to one capitalist and a *claim* to another – a mere *title* to ownership.

But it should not be forgotten that it is this process which in the same activity led to the concentration of production into greater units of monopolies. The interjection of money – capital in the

circuit of industrial production – increasingly led to a situation whereby the various mechanisms of credit-creation got embedded in the very fabric of production itself. This further led to a situation in which the interests of the money-capitalists – represented by the bankers – and the industrial capitalists, gradually integrated into a coherent interest of the upper stratum of the bourgeoisie – the *financial oligarchy* as the controllers of *finance-capital* which was the *merger* of industrial capital and money-capital. This is because although bankers appeared to control the process of credit-creation and fictitious capital formation, they in fact acted as representatives of the entire capitalist class, which in this way became a *social capital* based on industrial production. This control was achieved through the process of production and credit extension. As we noted earlier, the capital which was centralised through the banks upon which the credit structure was built was allocated according to the profitability of enterprises. In competition each capitalist tried to realise a profit above the average, but since not all of them could make such a profit without others losing in the competition, there arose a tendency for rates of profit to equalise.[1] This equalisation took place on the stock exchange on the basis of capitalist competition. But in time this same competition gave way to monopolistic competition as smaller unprofitable capitals became swallowed by bigger and more profitable capitals. In this process of concentration, the banks added their own process of centralisation of money-capital which we have seen above, but which took the form of *joint-stock banks*.

The formation of joint-stock banks was very much assisted by the first line of speculators called the *bill-brokers*. They were the ones who assisted the process of centralisation of credit in the hands of the banks by transforming 'credit material' into capital through the money-capital market which emerged in this period. The banks passed on that part of the deposits of which the bankers had no immediate use to the bill-brokers. The latter gave the bank as security his bills of exchange which he had discounted with the merchants and manufacturers to whom he had given it at a profit to himself. The bill-broker thus enabled the bank to take over the business of commercial credit and link it to a new process of bank capital creation. This also represented the first phase of fictitious capital formation and the new stock exchange speculations.

Some of the deposits used by the banks came from the bank's reserve cash and thus further 'decentralised' banknote issues, since it at times meant that the banks had no reserves to back up their banking activities as required by the Bank Act. Furthermore, the bill-broker, to whom these reserve-less deposits were passed by the banks, had no reserve of any kind! This helped the banks to keep their funds 'liquid' all the time, making it possible for them to make greater profits from their clients' deposits which they increasingly turned into new bank capital. The banks themselves began to overstep the old limits of credit-creation without doing serious injury to the system because the capitalist production continued with minimum levels of speculation in credit instruments. Since they knew by experience when payments were made, they were able to use the 'idle' periods to 'make an extra quid' by lending deposits on short notice or 'at call'. The bill of exchange was particularly useful to bring about this transformation, for it could 'automatically turn itself into cash on the due date'![2]

This process of 'financiering' which the banks themselves were engaging in nevertheless helped to bring about a greater economy in the use of money as medium of circulation. It eliminated further the use of actual money in these transactions, and thus also increased the velocity of the new 'currency' which multiplied with each passing day. But the process also created a 'paradox' for the system. While the new 'credit materials' had the apparent 'procreative power', with the capacity and facility to validly transfer capital with 'stability of value' in sufficient quantities to meet all the needs of expanded production and trade, it became clear that only part of it was capable of 'conversion' with 'maximum celerity and certainty into a form such as gold'. It was recognised that only that part was capable of easiest assimilation 'even when the (new) organism was disturbed and diseased'.[3] As the credit instruments grew in volume, this 'maximum celerity and certainty' became diminished, even for that part of paper which was capable of 'conversion' giving rise to recurrent financial crises on the markets. Thus it became necessary to perfect the 'organism' so that the process could go on in a self-sustaining manner even in times of stress. As one observer of the period noted:

> With the credit material we require a credit mechanism [which
> is] highly coordinated and correlated, freed from the shackles of
> medievalism and prejudice, and capable of cooperating with the
> currency in fostering, by means of distributed and redistributed
> credit facilities under adequately centralised control, a maxi-
> mum of legitimate financial, commercial and industrial activity,
> proceeding evenly and not spasmodically.[4]

The above passage underlines the difficulties which faced David
Ricardo and his solution as we saw. His viewpoint that 'correct
proportions' between gold and credit material must be maintained
in order to stop the possibility of creating an 'over-supply' of money
is shown by the experience to be unwarranted. This was considered by him to be necessary in order to maintain the 'value' of these
instruments at the level of the 'intrinsic value' of gold. But the process became complex with time so that it became a system requiring
an 'exceeding delicacy of adjustment'.[5] The whole purpose of banking and the stock exchange operations were increasingly to try to
maintain these 'proportions' in order to maintain the value of the
credit materials being created 'to the uttermost limits of contemporary possibility'.[6] As we shall see, this task became increasingly
a difficult one. In any case the maintenance of the 'value' of this
depended not on the 'proportions' but on the assured claim by the
bourgeoisie of future labour.

The Stock Exchange

Here we are concerned with the issue of how the institution of the
stock exchange emerged within these developments to advance fictitious capital formation and the new element of speculation that
arose with it. We have already indicated that the Exchange became
one of the institutions for equalising the profits of capitalists and
for assisting in the maintenance of the value of paper money. In
this respect, the stock exchange became truly the 'citadel of capital'
as well as the 'temple of values', the 'mart where a man's courage,
ingenuity and labour were marketed'.[7] It is here that capital was
able to get an additional source in the form of new devices such as
stocks and shares, which were 'floated' in order to mobilise new
capital. It is also here that capital which was raised in this way was
standardised and evaluated both quantitatively and qualitatively.

The Exchange also enabled the emergence of joint-stock companies because it is here that they could float their prospectuses for the raising of capital. By offering its shares for public subscription, the company 'democratised' the operations of the enterprise for all subscribers who were now said to have a stake in it, and through the vote at general meetings, they could exercise control over the management of capital so subscribed. By 1860 the Exchange, through the company, had 'abolished the capitalist private industry on the basis of the capitalist system'.[8] It consolidated social capital and strengthened the capitalists' control over 'social labour'. The industrial capitalist was transformed from an individual functioning capitalist of the family enterprise into a manager of collective capital, and with this development, according to Marx, 'capital itself becomes purely a basis for the superstructure of credit'. Capital becomes no more than a 'book-keeping concept' for the aim of exploiting labour.[9]

In the Exchange every share was as good as another, if it earned the same profit as the other. Hence every investor in the shares of a company was entitled to an equal portion of the profit realised in every enterprise in which he or she had shares according to his or her holding. The more profitable an enterprise, the more shareholders it attracted, and vice-versa. This was the economic 'democracy' of capitalism behind which liberal democracy as a dictatorship of the bourgeoisie thrived.

This is the environment that led to the establishment of the *finance company* and *investment trust*. The aims of these two new institutions were to aggregate large sums of money out of small investments in order to 'distribute risk' and earn profits on them in the process of investing them. In fact, the finance company had its continental variant, the investment trust, which was a response to the crisis which finance-capital brought about with the first major money-capital crisis of 1866, the so-called Overend–Gurney crisis in London. Overend–Gurney was a bill-broker which later formed a financial joint-stock company. By the 1860s the company had turned itself into a 'commercial banker's bank'. It engaged in the first activity of 'financiering' by extending credit with the back up of banks to companies engaging in corn, shipping, iron and railways, 'leaving no reserves'. It became an institution 'next to the Bank of England'

as the 'mainstay of British credit'.[10] It over-extended itself, and as the borrowing companies failed to meet their obligations with the industrial crisis of 1865, Overend failed to meet their own obligations to the banks leading to a major financial crisis. It resulted in panic and a run on the banks in fear that the banks did not have enough money to pay depositors. The crisis was resolved by the Bank of England merely releasing more banknotes to the banks. But the experience was not lost on the system, which responded by tightening the concentration process in the form of finance companies and investment trusts which got underway soon after.

According to J. K. Galbraith, a typical British trust held securities in 500 to 1,000 operating companies. As a result, the man with a few pounds, or even a few hundred in the trust, was able to spread his risk far more widely than he could have done on his own investment. In this way, the management of the trust could be expected to have a far better knowledge of companies and their prospects in Singapore, Madras, Cape Town and Argentina – the places where British funds were invested. The smaller risk and better information justified this form of mobilisation and utilisation of invested capital, and the trust soon became an established part of the British scene, as a new form of monopoly.[11]

By the 1890s the activities of these trusts had merged with those of big banks, creating a new speculative boom. In the American experience, trusts were created as part of what Galbraith called 'speculative architecture', for 'cashing in' on prevailing speculative sentiment with which these formations were connected:

> The investment trust did not promote enterprise or enlarge old ones. It merely arranged that people could own stock in old companies through the medium of new ones.[12]

It was in fact this speculative activity that helped bring about the 1929 financial crisis connected with the economic depressions of the period. It is the same technique that Friedrich Engels described in relation to the England of 1866, but the new American trust added new elements into the situation, enabling the 'doubling' and 'trebling' of fictitious capital beyond its production basis. In the words of Galbraith:

> The virtue of the investment trust was that it brought about an almost 'complete divorce' of the volume of corporate securities outstanding from the volume of corporate assets in existence. The former could be twice, thrice, or 'any multiple' of the latter. The volume of underwriting business and of securities available for trading on the exchanges all expanded accordingly. So did the securities to own, for the investment trusts sold more securities than they bought. The difference went into the call market, real estate or the pockets of the promoters.[13]

The 'fiduciary innovation' and improvement of the earlier English experience described by Engels above was built up in the US more particularly after 1921, where the stock exchange was perfected for this speculation. By 1927, 160 of these trusts existed. Another 140 were formed that year. During 1928, 186 were organised and in the early months of 1929 they were being promoted at the rate of approximately 'one each business day'. A total of 286 trusts made their appearance during the course of the year.[14] In 1927 they sold to the public about $400 million worth of securities; in 1929 $3 billion worth, a third of all the new capital issues in that year. By autumn 1929 the total assets of the investment trusts were estimated to exceed $8 billion, increasing *eleven-fold* since the beginning of 1927. Thus, if we go by Galbraith himself and accept the fact that the total volume of *corporate assets* had by 1929 increased eleven-fold since the beginning of 1927, and if corporate securities were twice, thrice, or any multiple of the assets, then it must be seen that the fictitious capital which was built upon the $8 billion of assets must have been several times, if not a hundred times, this amount.

But then the only 'corporate assets' the investment trust owned were common and it preferred the stocks, debentures, mortgages and bonds it had sold and the cash it owned. In many cases, the trust did not have an office or furniture. These were owned by the sponsoring and promoting company. Yet it was precisely these 'assets' which were much less than the securities held by the investment trusts upon which they had borrowed several times. The 'property' was in fact paper and the manipulative ability of the promoters. The 'value' of the assets of the trust could still be increased several times if the trust 'joined' a pool or formed a syndicate.

The above fictitious capital super-structure was lifted degrees higher by a new technique called *leverage*. By the summer of 1929, Galbraith says, one no longer spoke of investment as such. One spoke of high-leverage trusts, low-leverage trusts, or trusts without leverage. This new fiduciary innovation was achieved by issuing bonds, preferred stock, as well as common stock to purchase. When the common stock so purchased rose in value, 'a tendency which was always assumed', the value of the bonds and preferred stock of the trust would be largely unaffected. These had a fixed value derived from a specified return.[15] Most of the gain from rising portfolio value was concentrated on the common stock of the investment trust, which meant that these would rise more percentage-wise than if they were held as preferred shares stock.

Galbraith gives the following illustration: An investment trust has capital of $150 million. A third of it was realised from the sale of bonds, a third from preferred stock and the rest from sale of common stock. If the capital was invested it would have appreciated by 50% in six months at the time. The assets would then be $225 million. The bonds and preferred stock would still be worth only $100 million as before; their earnings would not have increased. The remaining $125 million, therefore, would be attributed to the common stock of the trust, the increase in assets being in the order of 150% (from $50 million to $125 million), which was the result of an increase of only 50% in the value of the assets of the trust as a whole.

This miraculous increase would be 'leveraged' furthermore if this common stock in this trust was held by still another trust with a similar leverage. In that case the common stock of that trust would get an increase of between 700% and 800% from the original 50% advance, and so on, right up to the 'ultimate man behind all the trusts'.

This ultimate man behind this vast super-structure of fictitious capital with a diminishing material value base would hold the structure together by an institutional innovation of the *leverage company*, through which the concentration of management and control would be exercised, which was also a 'striking feature of the period'.[16] The holding company would invest in and exercise control over the operating company (which could be a trust or

another holding company). Since most investment trusts were promoted by other companies, a holding company could set up several investment 'operating' trusts under its control through the holding company, and in that way increase the leverage just described. This structure was built up still further into a gigantic monopoly if it was joined up to the *corporate chain system* which established new outlets. It was this over-blown credit structure of fictitious capital that led to the 1929 financial crash.

The Gold Standard and International Exchanges

Whilst it is clear that the above credit structure was quite adequate to ensure capitalist development through its competitive phase and the initial stages of monopoly capitalism, for Britain in particular, this super-structure of credit on which finance-capital was erecting itself was very much interconnected with the emergent world economy. The lie that gave sanctity to the belief that Britain, on the basis of 'free trade', had established international links was that it did so with the 'gold standard'. In fact the gold standard was part of this super-structure of credit and without the colonial and semi-colonial linkage of Britain, such a vast credit system could never have been sustained on the belief that Britain could pay back in gold what it owed in paper.

In fact it was this banking that monetary and financial institutions built around London that enabled gigantic countries like India and the African continent to be webbed into this exploitative system. As London broadened its linkages, it increasingly became 'cheaper' to use London as a commercial and financial centre to transact other international exchanges. Bills drawn on London had an international reputation because of the fact that they could be accepted world-wide. This also added to their profitability and popularity. It did not matter very much in these circumstances whether Britain's imports exceeded her exports or not. If, for instance, Country A had trade with Country B alone, such an imbalance mattered very much. But if A had trade links with B and C, and if C did not have any trade with B, it followed that B's trade with C could only be transacted with the currency of A, which could help them balance their own imbalances. In this kind of arrangement, it mattered very little whether A had gold or not so long as its currency and credit instruments were acceptable to both B and C.

This is in fact how the so-called gold standard operated to the advantage of Britain. It was able to apply the operations of the 'inland bills' and 'accommodation bills' which evolved within the internal sphere of her commerce to the external and international operations. At the same time these external operations were brought to bear on the internal operations as they both got inter-married to the economic activities of the London banks, stock exchange and finance companies combining them into a coherent system of imperialist economy.

The system of the gold standard which evolved under the terms of Peel's Act of 1819 did not consolidate until the 1860s. Under the terms of the Act, the Bank of England was obliged to exchange its notes for gold bullion at a price of £3.17.10 per ounce. When in 1866 it was established that the Bank would operate as a 'lender of last resort' in Britain, the basis was laid to establish London as the financial centre of the world. The Bank of England became the world's central bank because of the fact that most other countries had their trade financed in London. Already this new role of the Bank of England turned it into a bank 'of the last resort' of many countries, as well as making it a banker in their international exchanges. The operation of the gold standard was ostensibly based on two rules: that gold is the recognised standard value of money and was therefore convertible at fixed price; and secondly that a country on the gold standard was obliged to permit the free export and import of gold. In fact these rules were observed only formally. Britain had neither the gold reserves nor the capacity to mobilise enough to convert all the paper devices it created into gold. It used the rules to draw in the gold of other countries.

The main credit device with which this stability in gold reserve levels was achieved *in the absence* of a large gold reserve was the wide use to which the *sterling bill* was put for financing commercial and financial operations throughout the world. According to P. Einzig:

> This alone went a very long way towards maintaining [the] stability of sterling. Only on very rare occasions such as the Baring Crisis (in 1890) did it become necessary to supplement the Bank rate device by financial support from abroad.[17]

Thus by use of a small stock of gold plus its international imperialist connections, Britain was able, with the use of international commercial bills of exchange, finance bills, sterling bills and the discount rate to build a vast international means of payment system to mediate its operations of finance-capital, with the British currency being looked upon as the store of value for most of the world.

In fact, before the appearance of the sterling bill one of the major steps had come with the introduction of the *finance bill*. This technique arose in the period of the 1857 crisis. With this new device, the bill of exchange 'lost its objective basis'.[18] It became purely subjective when it took on the 'purely "finance" form'.[19] It further assisted the bridging of the separation between purchase and sale of seasonal crops across oceans 'which would otherwise have had to be settled by sending bullion forwards and backwards'.[20] It now occurred that although 'a bill should "pay itself" by means of the sale of the commodities which originally brought it into existence... there was no absolute necessity for adherence to this rule'.[21] If the creation of a bill was convenient to its creators, there was no need to undertake it when there was an actual transaction behind it. The purely fictitious finance bill then had no actual commodities behind it. Furthermore, it could be applied to transactions with other countries, other than British colonies. Its creation depended on two finance houses in different countries and involved an arrangement in which one would draw and the other would accept the bill on sight.

An American banker could, for instance, create bills on London, at a time when bills were scarce there, not against goods, but against collateral in anticipation of the goods. Governments also resorted to this 'specie' of 'kite flying' to raise credit in foreign money markets in anticipation of resources to be created by an intended loan issue.[22] This 'bank credit', so long as it was kept within legitimate limits of actual transactions, did relieve the need to await actual resources before productive activities could proceed in many countries.

For instance, for seasonal crops like corn, the revenue derived from foreign countries would come in at the end of the harvest, when cargoes of corn began to be despatched and the bills of exchange were drawn against the shipments. In the meantime, the corn growing country would have been importing commodities

from the manufacturing country all the year round, and the corn growing country would have been requiring bills on foreign countries in order to pay for these imports long before the corn bills of exchange could be drawn and become available for this purpose. In the absence of bills to pay for the manufactured commodities immediately, gold had to be shipped, and arrangements had to be made to receive back gold when their own bills on the corn cargo were paid.

To avoid this risk and expense, and to economise on the use of gold, the device of the finance bill was used, whereby bankers in Country X could draw on the banks in Country Y to finance bills at the time when no actual commercial bills representing bona fide transactions could be bought. By the use of those finance bills, a fictitious capital was created with which to pay for the imported commodities, pending the shipment of the corn. The acceptors of the corn bills had in fact received blank bills since it was not known how much the corn crop would be. The finance bill was therefore used to pay for blank bills held by the acceptors.

The same device was used by exporting houses in both countries receiving permission from those to whom they sold or consigned their shipments to draw bills in anticipation of the goods being actually dispatched. By this means they indirectly obtained loan capital in advance at a premium, instead of waiting for the time when the bulk of the exports were despatched, and when consequently, from the number of those who had to draw bills, they would have to accept a lower price.[23]

It can be seen here how the earlier and speculative practices were being harnessed to develop the credit system under more refined methods. Credit instruments developed in the internal circulation were being brought in constant use in the international arena as gold became more expensive and risky to utilise in the increasing volume of international trade. The finance bill, it can be seen, was akin to the inland bill or 'accommodation bill' in the domestic transactions. What had been condemned earlier in the 1840s was being defended in the 1860s. In fact, on the basis of this finance bill, a new form of bill, a hybrid between the commercial bill of exchange and finance bill was devised, which went further to sophisticate the system.

The *hybrid bill* was drawn against a blank credit on the same lines as the finance bill proper, but it was secured by the merchant giving the acceptance house a general lien on all his shipments, or all his shipments to particular markets, with a promise to pay back the proceeds arising to a separate account earmarked for the purpose of repaying the loan to the accepting house. Once this bill was repaid, it was provided for that the merchant could re-open the credit on the same basis and in this way a *'revolving credit'* was created for the merchant which put him in funds throughout the year. This was an improvement and a much better arrangement for British commerce overall, and became the basis for developing the sterling bill which helped reduce the reliance on gold.

The State Debt: Taxation and Credit-Creation

We must now take note of the fact that the state debt and public credit was the *credo* for the emergence of capital. In the formative stages of capital, state debt was used to endow barren metallic money 'with the power of breeding', thus helping it in the process to become real capital 'without the necessity of its exposing itself to the troubles and risks inseparable from its employment in industry.'[24]

According to Marx, the birth of great banks was associated with public credit. They were 'decorated with national titles' from humble associations of private speculators, who placed themselves by the side of the governments. They received privileges from the state and became lenders to the state in the process. The Bank of England began its operations by lending its money to the state at 8%. In return it was empowered by the state to coin money out of the same capital by lending it again to the public in the form of banknotes. This was bank credit based on state debt. It was then allowed to use the same notes to discount bills of exchange, make advances on commodities and buy the precious metals. This same credit, made by the bank itself, became the basis on which the Bank of England made its loans to the state and paid, on behalf of the state, the interest on the public debt. Gradually the Bank became inevitably the receptacle of the metallic hoard of the country, and the centre of gravity of all commercial credit.

The state-creditors who buy state securities actually give nothing away, for the sum lent to the state is transformed into public bonds, which are easily negotiable and these go on functioning in the hands of the borrowers as much hard cash would. The national debt has for this reason given rise to joint-stock companies, to dealings in negotiable effects of all kinds as we have seen, and to stock exchange gambling and the modern bankocracy of financiers, rentiers, brokers and stock-jobbers – an 'aristocracy of finance'. As Marx had earlier remarked in the *Eighteenth Brumaire*:

> By the 'aristocracy of finance' must be understood not merely the large bond negotiators and speculators in government securities, of whom it may be readily understood that their interests and the interest of government coincide. The whole banking industry is most intimately interwoven with the public credit. Part of their business capital must be invested in interest-bearing government securities that are promptly convertible into money. Their deposits, i.e. the capital placed at their disposal and distributed by them among merchants and industrialists, flow partly out of the dividends on government securities. The whole money market, together with the priests of this market, is part and parcel of the 'aristocracy of finance' and in every epoch the stability of the government is synonymous to them with Moses and the prophets.[25]

Since the national debt finds its support in public revenue, which must cover yearly payments for interest, the modern system of taxation was the necessary complement of the system of national loans. The loans enable the government to meet extraordinary expenses without the tax-payers feeling it immediately, but they necessitate, as a consequence, increased taxes. At the same time the raising of taxation caused by the accumulation of debts contracted one after another compels the government always to have recourse to new loans for new extraordinary expenses. Marx adds:

> Modern fiscality whose pivot is formed by taxes on the most necessary means of subsistence (thereby increasing their price), thus contains within itself the germ of automatic progression. Overtaxation is not an incident, but rather a principle.[26]

Thus the 'public fund' from which a class of state-creditors draw their annuities is nothing but imaginary capital, which represents that portion of the annual revenue which is set aside to pay the debt. It represents an equivalent amount of capital which has *been spent*, and it is this which serves as the *denominator* for the loan. But it is not this which is represented by the public fund, for the capital no longer exists. New wealth must be created by the work of industry (labour-power) and a portion of this wealth must annually be set aside in advance for those who have loaned that wealth which has been spent. It is this portion which is taken by means of taxes from those who produce it, and is given to the creditors of the state in the form of interest and repayment of the nominal value.

The emergence of techniques of finance-capital is closely connected with the development of the activities of the state and the evolution of the national debt. In England, before the reforms of 1688, most government borrowing had been on a *temporary* basis. The debts were incurred by the monarch, acting as head of the feudal state, who pledged state revenue from certain duties as security for their repayment plus interest. With the reforms of 1688, Parliament could impose taxes, and with this it became possible for the state to borrow on a more permanent basis, and it was with these developments that the idea of a national debt became reality. The importance of this development, however, is its connection with the establishment of banking and credit systems, and in particular the creation of the Bank of England and credit for England.

To be sure, the demand for the creation of a bank was connected with the importation in England of sophisticated ideas of finance of the Venetians and Lombards which came with a new Dutch King, William of Orange. The new King wanted money to wage a war against France and needed £40 million for the purpose. The idea for the creation of a national bank to provide the loan came from William Patterson. The idea gained ground and proposals for the establishment of the Bank of England were approved and by 1694 the Bank was in a position to raise a subscription of £1.2 million. This sum was to be lent to the King immediately at a rate of interest of 8%. The King, for his part, agreed to give the Bank a royal charter granting it, among other privileges, a right to issue notes payable on demand up to the amount of the loan. A 'perpetual fund' of

interest of £100,000 was to be secured by the duties on wines, spirits and ship tonnages, and £4,000 of this was to be set aside to pay administrative expenses.

The management of the national debt, finally, was deeply connected with the evolution of public credit and finance. It was part of the evolution of finance-capital. In 'managing' the national debt, the Bank had the responsibility of paying interest from the *'consolidated fund'* into which national revenue was paid. There was also the duty to pay the expenses of the debt, as well as the duty to reduce it. For this reason the debt was divided into two portions for proper management, namely the floating and permanent. The *floating* debt was concerned with the issue, circulation and redemption of exchequer bills, and the *permanent* debt was concerned with the maintenance of the amounts outstanding.

In this latter function, the Bank paid interest to the 'fund holders' to maintain the value of the debt. When it turned out that the consolidated fund was not adequate to meet these expenses and the interest, it became a practice to meet the difference from the issue of a financial device of the special exchequer bills known as *deficiency bills*. In 1866, in line with the developments of the period in which finance-capital began to consolidate itself with the Overend–Gurney crisis, an analogous but simpler plan was adopted and *deficiency advances* were substituted for the bills. Such advances had, however, to be refunded in the following quarter.

It is this structure that made it possible for Britain and other capitalist states to raise funds for waging the two world wars and in the process increasingly strengthened the hand of the bourgeois state in the monopoly capitalist economy. With the collapse of the so-called gold standard in 1931, the state increasingly found it necessary to intervene in the money-capital markets to give stability to the market through 'open market operations' with an increasing resort to the *gold exchange standard*. In the same period the activities of the US Federal Reserve Board broadened to include the management of the gold which was fast slipping through the fingers of the European imperialist powers. The Treasury was, in this way, 'put into the Bank of England'.

The Value of Money

But all these developments had serious implications for the maintaining of the value of these credit and state credit instruments to approximate to the value of money. This was, of course, an impossibility, for most of the credit power was not backed by actual production as speculation became part of this activity, as we have seen. How could such approximation be achieved and how could it be maintained? David Ricardo's 'proportionality' had not stood the test of time. To overcome this difficulty, a number of bourgeois economists tried to address this problem afresh and one of these economists was Irving Fisher. According to him, capital was 'simply' *future income* which was discounted or *capitalised*. Based on the expectation of the availability of future labour and its instruments, it was possible to argue theoretically, as Fisher did, that the value of *any property* or property right was the value of its value as a *source of income* which is 'found' by discounting the expected income. Wealth became the ownership of 'material object' in partnership rights, shares of stock, bonds, mortgages and state bills. But in order to discount these material objects, the *rate of interest*, became the 'bridge and link' between capital and income, so that interest was seen as the price of money. Through this gimmick, it became possible to de-link capital from its historical roots, and to see its value as lying in the future instead of the past:

> Income is derived from capital good. But the value of the income is not derived from the value of the capital goods. On the contrary, the value of the capital is derived from the value of the income... Our valuations are always anticipations.[27]

Thus we start with capital goods, through the *flow* of incomes and services, through money income values, to capital value: 'Not until we know how much income an item of capital will probably bring us can we set any valuation on that capital at all'.[28] In this scheme of things therefore, capitalist production can go on on the basis of a credit system very much backed by the fictitious capital of the state and the private aristocracy of finance, based on some idea of the value of future benefits that will accrue, as well as some idea of the rate of interest by which these future values may be translated into present values by discounting.

Although we know that interest derives from profit and is obtained through the competition of capital in which an average rate of profit is realised by all capital, in fact this is not possible unless the production and social conditions are guaranteed by the state. By acting as a *guarantor* of interest payments, the state, historically, also ensures that the various credit devices that capital must create to transmit and transfer capital values have value. The value of a paper note or device, denominated in the standard of value which the state guarantees will be the discounted value of the future payment to which it entitles the holder, who is assumed, regardless of who he is, to a property right.

It is this which imbues capital with a *social* power and force. In this sense, capital value becomes 'income capitalised and nothing else'.[29] Only as a social force can the average rate of profit, and eventually, the average rate of interest, be realised, and this is the basis of the political rule of the bourgeoisie, the basis of the dictatorship of the bourgeoisie, without which private appropriation of wealth is impossible. In the money-capital market this social force expresses itself as a guarantor of future earnings on money incomes, in which all social wealth is expressed because, according to Fisher, 'it is only money which is traded as between present and future'.[30] Charles Rist refers to the same thing when he says that money as a store of value is the link between the present and the future.[31] Here the credit system with state assistance imitates money's function as a store of value to preserve current wealth through the rate of interest on all money-credit devices.[32]

Despite these flashes, bourgeois monetary theory remained segmented, with different schools of thought contending with one another. On the one hand we had the old quantity theory of money re-emerging, from time to time, fastened to the basic propositions of Ricardo. New theories emerged around the so-called purchasing power theory of money, around which efforts were made to make the value of money be tied to certain consumer goods indexes. Then emerged Georg Friedrich Knapps's theory of money by which the value of money was made to depend on the state establishing the standard of money, which had nothing to do with value but the medium through which it was expressed through prices. Also Marxist efforts in the person of Rudolf Hilferding to join the

discussion at this time failed to bring out the true content of Marx's theory, since it too got stuck at the level (theoretically at least) of money being seen as a means of purchase. He argued that money was no longer a real measure of value but what he called 'socially necessary value in circulation'.[33] He did this because he conceived money purely at the level of circulation. His references to gold as a final value under capitalism are imprecise.

The real breakthrough for the bourgeoisie seemed to have come with John Maynard Keynes's writings before his *General Theory*.[34] In his *Treatise* on money, we have a glimpse of his efforts to resolve the problem of money as a store of value.[35] His main contribution lay in drawing attention to the crisis of the capitalist economy, which he saw as lying with the inability to maintain a stable standard of money in the face of inflations and deflations. He saw the labour cost unit as being the only stable one since the wage of all prices was the 'stickiest downwards', meaning that the money wage of the worker tended to be stable relative to prices. His proposals for 'ironing out' the industrial cycle, which brought about the instability of the standard of money, involved the state intervening to manage what he called 'the credit cycle'. In *General Theory*, he developed his theories a little more and refined his tools for managing the macro-economic variables of the economy to increase employment through a higher generation of income. As we approached the Second World War, there seemed to be no bourgeois theory of money except his.

Notes

1. Hilferding R. *Finance Capital*, Routledge & K. Paul, London, 1981, p.183.
2. Walter, H.C. *Foreign Exchange and Foreign Debts*, Methuen, London, p.118.
3. Powel, E.T. *The Evolution of the Money Market 1385–1915*, Frank Cass, London, 1966, pp.261–2.
4. *Ibid.*, p.262.
5. *Ibid.*, p.265.
6. *Ibid.*
7. Armstrong, F.E. *The Book of the Stock Exchange*, quoted in Jenkins, A. *The Stock Exchange Story*, Heinemann, London, 1973, p.4.
8. Marx, K. *Capital*, vol. 3, p.439.
9. *Ibid.*
10. Jenks, L.H. *Migration of British Capital to 1875*, Nelson, London, 1971, p.247 and pp.260–1.
11. Galbraith, J.K. *The Great Crash 1929*, Penguin, 1980, p.72.

12. *Ibid.*

13. *Ibid., op. cit.*, pp.72–3.

14. *Ibid.*, p.82.

15. *Ibid.*, p.83. Galbraith gives the example of Harrison Williams, who in this way controlled a billion dollars.

16. *Ibid.*, p.84.

17. Einzig, P. *The History of Foreign Exchange*, London, 1970, pp.227–8.

18. *Ibid., op. cit.*, pp.171–4.

19. Powel, E.T. *op. cit.*, p.379.

20. Einzig, P. *op. cit.*, p.175 and p.179.

21. Powel, E.T. *op. cit.*, p.379.

22. *Ibid.*, p.380.

23. Goschen, G. *The Theory of the Foreign Exchanges*, London, 1932, p.26.

24. Marx, K. *Capital*, vol. 3, p.755.

25. Marx, K. *Eighteenth Brumaire of Louis Bonaparte in Revolutions of 1848*, Penguin, London.

26. Marx, K. *Capital*, vol. 3, p.756.

27. Fisher, I. *The Theory of Interest*, Kelly, New York, 1930, p.12.

28. *Ibid.*, p.15.

29. *Ibid.*, p.19.

30. *Ibid.*, p.13.

31. Rist, C. *History of Monetary and Credit Theory from John Law to the Present Day*, New York, 1940, p.58.

32. *Ibid.*

33. Hilferding, R. pp.46–7.

34. Keynes, J.M. *The General Theory of Employment, Interest and Money*, Macmillan, London, 1936.

35. Keynes, J.M. *Treatise on Money*, vols. 1 and 2, Macmillan, 1953.

3

The International Monetary System

The Second World War brought to an end an era of dominance by the European powers over the economies of the whole world. US imperialism saw to that. Having used their rivalries to strengthen their economy, they worked tirelessly to impose a new world order based on a system of multilateral imperialism in which the US dollar was to play a leading role. In various agreements signed with these powers, the US was able to articulate its demands including the need to abandon the currency blocks which Europe had established in the inter-war years to compete against one another in the trade and currency wars that were characteristic of the period. Britain, in particular, was required to dismantle its sterling block as *quid pro quo* for a loan of $3.5 billion which it required to pay off its war debts. The effect was to make it possible for the US to introduce its own dollar in the international exchanges for its own imperialist activities, since it would make it easier for the US to spread its own debts around the world.

A New Dollar Monetary Order

This 'settlement' between the old and the new superpowers merely carried forward the antagonisms of the previous period and heightened the crisis for money-capital, now increasingly operating on the basis of international finance-capital. The US preparations for a new monetary order, worked out as the European powers consumed themselves in a war, were directed at removing the problems that had arisen for US finance-capital. In a paper entitled 'Suggested Plan for a United Nations Stabilisation Fund and a Bank of Reconstruction of the United and Associated States', it was stated that the US aimed at preventing the disruption of

foreign exchanges and the collapse of monetary and credit systems. It also wanted to assure the restoration of foreign trade and to supply the huge volume of capital that would be needed throughout the world for reconstruction, relief and economic recovery. This would be achieved by 'stabilising' the monetary and financial system as a first step. It would also necessitate the creation of a *new international currency* that would be a basis for providing the capital. Furthermore it aimed at creating an international bank that would invest the capital 'virtually throughout the world'.[1]

It was not surprising that the issue of monetary stabilisation, which involved the creation of a 'stabilisation fund', took the foremost and urgent position for US policy. It was the only means of creating the super-structure for the emergence and hegemony of US finance-capital. The US Assistant Secretary of State for the Treasury, Harry Dexter White, was put in charge of this task. Gardner has observed of this emphasis:

> White's great emphasis on the problem of monetary stabilisation was not a personal foible; it reflected the general Treasury attitude born in the experience of the post-war period... Accordingly the Treasury planners considered the elimination of such (post-war) practices one of the primary tasks of post-war reconstruction.[2]

It is important to put this issue in a dialectical perspective in order to avoid the error of many writers of this period. In the preparatory stages of working out the new international monetary system, many writers examined the positions offered by White for the US and John Maynard Keynes for Britain in terms of the abstract ideas each one of them put forward or the personal positions of the individuals involved. In fact each of these individuals represented the two forces at work and the struggles inherent in the imperialist struggles. Most important, however, was the US interest to produce an international monetary system that would protect private wealth on world scale under US hegemony, which European inter-imperialist rivalry had threatened.

The Keynes Plan

The Keynes Plan, based on a position of a debtor imperialist country, envisaged the setting up of an international clearing union, which would make large overdrafts available to its members, facilities which were to be related to their pre-war share of world trade. This, of course, favoured Britain and at worst placed the US on equal terms with Britain. According to the Keynes Plan this overdraft should have amounted to $26 billion. There was no limit set on the value of individual credit balances. Surpluses and deficits in the balance of payments of member countries were to be reflected in credits and debts on the books of the union, expressed in *'bancor'*, an international unit of account. With these vast reserves of liquidity, members would have been able to eliminate all exchange restrictions on current accounts, maintain stability in their exchange rates, and pursue policies of domestic expansion without fear of adverse consequences on their foreign balances. This view of the matter catered for Britain's concern with domestic economic expansion on the lines of Keynes's theories referred to in the last chapter. The concern was to avoid the re-emergence of unemployment, and the large overdraft facilities were intended to cater for imbalances in Britain's payments.

The 'bancor' was to be defined in gold, and members were to accept the bancors as the equivalent of gold for the purpose of settling international balances, through transfers on the books of the union. Each member would also continue to hold and use all his or her own separate gold and currency reserves as he or she chose. Keynes tried in this way to implant a system of an internal money-credit regime and a closed banking system and superimpose it on a world money regime. Describing the concept in his 'Christian English' to the Governor of the Bank of England, Sir Montagu Norman, Keynes simplified the issues as follows:

> The essence of the scheme is very simple indeed. It is the extension to the international field of the essential principles of banking by which, when one chap wants to leave his resources idle, those resources are not therefore withdrawn from circulation but are made available to another chap who is prepared to use them – and to make this possible without the farmer losing his

liquidity and his right to employ his own resources as soon as he chooses to do so. [I]t is only by extending these same principles to the international field that we can cure the manifest evils of the international economy as it existed between the two wars, after London had lost the position which had allowed her before 1914 to do much the same thing off her own bat.[3]

Keynes then hoped to forget the entire history of why London lost her position in order to superimpose an ideal international credit system. The Plan also pre-supposed the existence of stable exchange rates, but which could vary according to need. In this way the deficit country would lose control of its exchange rates, since it was provided that if the deficit exceeded one half of her quota, the clearing union might require a stated reduction in the value of the country's currency if that seemed to be the proper remedy.

But the fact is the Keynes Plan did not eliminate gold from the system and for good reason, although his other proposals contradicted the role of gold, as would money under a capitalist regime. Apart from its function as a unit of account, Keynes also saw its other functions as a medium of exchange relevant to his system. For countries that owned gold and wished to use it as such, gold was to be a form of international liquidity. It could be turned into the clearing union for *bancor* balances, but national central banks were also allowed to retain separate gold reserves as we have seen, and transfer it among themselves for official settlements at the official par. This plan would have protected gold producers as well as those investing in gold shares, not to speak of the gold hoarders who are a necessary component to the system. Despite the fact that Keynes provided for some form of future gold de-monetisation, gold remained the central pivotal point in the international arrangement that emerged, but only formally.

The White Plan

The White Plan, as the US Plan came to be called, started from the position of a strong imperialist creditor country. It was more down to earth than the more idealist Keynes Plan, which could never have been accepted by the US under the existing conditions. It was no wonder that the US took the issue of the blocked balance by Britain as the starting point to any financial and monetary

stabilisation programme in the post-war period. The US sought to solve this problem through a financial stabilisation fund. The fund was to buy up these blocked balances from the creditor nations, mainly colonies and dominions, and re-sell part of them over a period of years both to the creditors and to the countries whose obligations they represented. The fund, the creditors, and the debtors would each have borne part of the burden. But this would have taken the initiative from the hands of the British, and the issue got mixed up with other problems of the period.

As already indicated, the White Plan was intended to put the international monetary and financial house in working order under its hegemony. It provided for no overdrafts. It called for the establishment of 'an international stabilisation fund' with resources and powers adequate to the task of helping to achieve monetary stability, and to facilitate the restoration of international trade. Unlike the Keynes Plan which required no initial contributions from members, the White Plan required members to contribute a specified amount or quota to the fund, the total of the quotas being at least $5 billion, determined according to the agreed formula. This formula took into account factors such as a country's gold holdings and foreign exchange, the fluctuations to which the country's balance of payments were liable, and the country's national income. Voting power in the management of the fund was to be weighted *pro rata* with the size of the quota. This, in effect, meant US dominance of the fund's activities.

There was to be no automatic access to the drawing rights from the fund. On the contrary, these were to be made conditional. In every case of a withdrawal, the fund would have the right to place restrictions on supplying currencies to a deficit country. A country that reduced its deficit could buy back the fund's surplus holdings in her currency for gold or other approved currencies. On the issue of adjustment disequilibrium between deficit and creditor countries, the White Plan permitted a change in exchange rates only when essential to correct a 'fundamental disequilibrium' in the currency, upon a majority of member votes. White's unit account – the *Unitad* – was equal to $10 worth of gold.

Thus the British effort in the Keynes Plan to place part of the burden of adjustment for deficit countries on the creditor countries was

not accepted by the US. Nor could the idea that surplus countries be penalised in order to force a corrective action in the currency that would permit a deficit country to cure her own deficit be acceptable to the US. The White Plan in many ways recreated the gold exchange system of the 1920s, which the Keynes Plan avoided. The British were on the whole opposed to any restoration of the gold standard or even the gold exchange standard. Having lost hope of ever restoring the old imperialist financial power, it saw in the gold standard a sinister plan to place them under a subservient position. *The Daily Express* of 3 February 1944 declared:

> [I]t should be clearly stated that this country is not going back to gold. Thirteen years ago Britain shook the gold dust off her feet and the change began in our fortunes. Clinging on to gold meant restriction and unemployment among our people. Any move to put us back on gold will result in disaster to those who attempt it!

The US opposition to the British Plan was on the grounds that it would give fuel to inflation, and the *Wall Street Journal* of 8 August 1943 called the British Plan for a clearing union 'a machine for the regimentation of the world'. A small provincial paper in Iowa, sensing a sinister motive in the British Plan to deprive the US of its war booty, warned: 'If we are big enough suckers to swallow the Keynes Plan, we shall be swindled out of everything we have left from the war – and we shall deserve to be swindled.'[4]

To be sure, the clearing union idea, as far as Britain was concerned, was to resolve the contradiction between internal and external financial stability. The gold standard, according to them, had assured external exchange stability but not internal control over monetary and fiscal policy. After the gold standard was abandoned deflationary forces from one country to another developed. What the Keynes Plan aimed at, therefore, was to combine, through the clearing union, a policy of internal price stability as well as stability in the exchanges – 'to obtain the advantages, without the disadvantages, of an international gold currency'.[5] But this was an illusion because it could not be had for the asking.

The insistence on having gold holdings of a country as an important element in determining a country's quotas was considered vital

by the US, since it wanted to establish a new dominance by controlling world monetary and credit resources. Having determined each country's quota, the subscriptions of members would also have to be 25% in gold and 75% in the country's own national currency. In return the members were to receive purchasing rights over other countries' currencies to supplement their normal reserves for balance of payments purposes. They could purchase these drawings by putting in more of their own currency. This would assist the deficit country to 'stabilise' temporary imbalances in their obligations to other countries. The drawing or purchasing of other currencies was called 'scarce currency' transaction, and the aim was to imitate the 19th century gold standard mechanism, which put pressure on both the creditor and the debtor.[6]

But in fact the US could not have revived the role of the gold standard in this form. The experience of the inter-war years had clearly demonstrated that the gold standard could only operate under the conditions of the 19th century, which prevailed over a short period of time in any case. The US itself had at the same time made the gold standard inoperable by imposing the pre-war (1934) price of gold of $35 per ounce, although the prices of other commodities had trebled and even quadrupled, which made it impossible for gold to function effectively for the purposes of acting as money-commodity in internal exchange transactions. This further undermined its role in the international arena as a universal means of exchange, but this was the only way the US could raise the dollar to the level of 'world money' to substitute it for gold, just as sterling had done under the guise of the gold standard. Thus the 'dollar standard' that emerged on the assumed 'gold backing' was a tactic to use and manipulate a gold hoard to attain hegemony. In any case, during the inter-war years and after, the US had effectively 'sterilised' gold from the money stock. The US, however, increasingly found it difficult to hold this former British financial monopoly. Thus, although the US held 80% of all the monetary gold of the world, it did not in fact wish to see the gold standard restored in the old form. It now wielded this gold stock as a political weapon to attain hegemony in the world economy by controlling the exchanges.

The International Monetary Fund

The International Monetary Fund (IMF) was tailored to meet these US demands. The provisions of the articles of the agreement achieved these objectives through the imitation of the gold exchange standard, to substitute the dollar as an international currency. It did this by requiring all countries to fix the par value of their currencies at the rate of 1 ounce of gold = $35. Each country was then allocated quotas according to the White Plan criteria, 25% of which had to be in gold. In this way, the Fund struck a 'historical compromise'. It borrowed some elements from the old British-dominated gold standard, and some from the inter-war gold exchange system of fluctuating exchange rates, in order to achieve the 'flexible stability' of exchange rates. This in effect united two contradictory solutions which had revealed their limitations under the British gold standard, and the competitive fluctuating rates of the inter-war years.[7]

In order to ensure that the dollar would play the role of gold as international currency, the articles of agreement required that the 75% of the quota paid in a country's currency could only be utilised in the event of a balance of payments deficit, in the same way as the 25% subscribed in gold. There would be no automatic credits from any currency which was required. In these cases a country could only have automatic access to its gold (first) 'tranche' (slice). The next 25% 'credit tranche' would equally be available, but only on 'liberal' terms, provided the country was making every effort to balance its deficit. This meant giving the US (through the IMF) supervisory powers over the economies of member states.

The currency most sought by many countries was the dollar, because it was the currency most available at this time. The British sterling did not return to convertibility until 1958, but even then its scope in international spread had been reduced. The released blocked sterling balances were, as we have already noted, immediately converted into dollars. Moreover, the dollar evinced the false appearance of being 'as good as gold', because of the US Federal Reserve Board's promise to redeem green dollars for gold at the rate of $35 per ounce. The result was that the balance of payments deficits throughout the world came to be settled through the dollar unit of account, cancelling debts where this was possible, but otherwise paying the balances in dollars instead of gold. Various forms and

mechanisms of paper transactions were worked out to achieve this purpose. In the first 10 years of IMF activity in this field, 92% of all drawings were in US dollars.[8]

Thus the 'scarcity' of the dollar acquired a premium for its value as an international reserve. Everybody looked for the dollar, and it appeared to evince confidence everywhere it was presented. Even the IMF provision, which was adopted as a compromise to ensure that a persistently 'scarce' currency could have discriminatory action taken against it, was never invoked against the dollar. This was the case, although within 10 years of the launching of the IMF the dollar was perpetually in short supply. The US managed to address these difficulties through a number of *ad hoc* arrangements and measures, measures which nevertheless compounded the problem of the dollar as an international currency. We look at these *ad hoc* arrangements later.

The second provision to maintain the hegemony of the dollar under the IMF articles was the provision prohibiting the competitive depreciation of currencies. This was achieved partly through the par value provisions, but there were other provisions requiring all countries to permit the free convertibility of their currencies for all current international transactions. No country was to be allowed to impose controls on current transactions, although restrictions were allowed on capital movements. These provisions, although not fully implemented, nevertheless became very important mechanisms for applying pressure against weaker and smaller countries as well as neo-colonial Third World countries. The economies of these countries became increasingly subjected to control by the IMF in order to maintain external and internal balance in western countries.

The third important mechanism of the dollar's hegemony and control was achieved through the voting procedures in the Executive Board of the Fund. As we have seen, a country's quota was determined according to its economic and political strength. In many cases, the political supremacy of the country was also equated with the size of its quota,[9] and the size of the US quota was influenced 'by an accounting and political convenience'.[10] Her quota was fixed at $2.7 million and was paid out of the book gain of $2,805,512,060.75 that represented the US devaluation of the

dollar against gold in 1934.[11] Here the US used its *political act* of gold 'sterilisation' to obtain *political control* of the international monetary system, thus placing the IMF in the US Treasury. This quota represented 35% of all the quotas in the IMF at the time. The US quota, based on this historical fraud, in fact formed the basis of the $2 billion of paper dollars and $1.3 billion of gold that served as the Fund's effective resources, since its currency was the only one available for this purpose.

Later adjustments in quotas in 1958 and 1964 modified this dominance but never eliminated it entirely. This weighted dominance assured the US a powerful voice in the Executive Board, exemplified in her insistence at the Savannah Fund meeting in 1944 that the Fund be 'an active monitor of exchange practices' rather than a mere passive body in the international monetary system.[12] Although Keynes at this meeting accused the US of 'slipping back' on her word into the 'old bad ways of thought', White, on the US's behalf, insisted that the only safeguard for the Fund's resources was to suspend the drawing rights of countries which did not convince the Executive Directors that they had surmounted their principal transitional difficulties. This could only be done by a strong Executive Board exercising supervision over the use of resources.[13]

Contradiction Between Liquidity and Reserves

These provisions very soon came into conflict with reality. For the first 10 years up to 1957 there were not serious problems which could not be surmounted. As we have noted, in this period 92% of currency purchases from the Fund to meet balance of payment deficits were in US dollars. This had the effect of reducing the Fund's holdings of dollars to 28% of the US quota, thereby giving the US a gold tranche position in the Fund (including a super gold tranche) of nearly $2 billion. In the years that followed, this strong position was run down, partly due to the fact that many countries continued to use the dollar in repayment of their drawings:

> This was in effect providing financing for the United States by taking dollars off the market and sinking them into the Fund.[14]

This period also coincided with a general 'dollar scarcity', and the

US deficits created by these deficit requirements were seen as the basis for filling the US limited reserve gap that existed up to 1958. Even then this had problems of its own, but as difficulties arose some *ad hoc* improvisations were made to deal with the situation, and this method helped to remove the immediate problems of the dollar as a universal currency. Three main *ad hoc* arrangements deserve attention at this stage.

The first was the injection in Europe of some $26 billion in the form of Marshall Plan aid. Between 1946 and 1952 these vast resources, in addition to US military expenditure in Europe, created considerable dollar liquidity in Europe, liquidity which minimised the demand for the dollar within the Fund. The Fund ruled that a country which was in receipt of this aid could not require the services of the Fund, except in very exceptional circumstances.

The second was the US loan to Britain of $3.5 billion, which Britain used to embark on the enforced convertibility of sterling. These dollars, as we have noted, were liquidated within six weeks in claims, adding liquidity to the system at a time, although modest, which enabled the unblocking of US dollars in the Sterling Area. The released sterling also added supplementary liquidity to the Fund to bolster a US dollar dominated system.

After 1950 there was a drying up of liquidity in the Fund, and a third recourse was devised in the form of a 'standby' arrangement in 1952 whereby the Fund could make advance commitments to a member which had reason to anticipate a balance of payments crisis, but did not anticipate to use the arrangement in the near future, until it became absolutely necessary. This arrangement established a stronger line of defence against the onset of a crisis than if the money was actually drawn. Britain made extensive use of this arrangement in 1957.

By 1958, the weakening of the dollar became apparent. Deficits of a new kind began to appear, meaning that other countries were beginning to export more to the US than she could export to them. This was due to a resurgence in Europe of new production in the former war-torn economies. Having destroyed the bulk of their capital in the wars, they had by now 're-composed' their capital in favour of accumulation. This they did by taking advantage of low wages, which were now possible due to the availability of a whole

reserve army of demobilised soldiers and refugees from Eastern Europe.

All these countries began with currency depreciations from 1949 onwards to bring them in line with their productive capacity: Britain, 30.5% (1949); Holland, 30.1% (1949); Belgium, 12.3% (1949); Canada, 9.1% (1948); West Germany, 93% (1948), and a further depreciation of 20.7% (1949) against the dollar; Italy 63.9% (1945–49); Japan 98.4% (1945–49); France 66% (1945–49) and a further depreciation of 38.7% (1949). It is not surprising that with these devalued currencies, the new growth of these countries should have been export-oriented. So this was the 'miracle' of Europe's new industrial growth, in which the US had no alternative but to assist in order to maintain a 'free' capitalist market in Europe against the new forces of the East.

This export boom gave rise to a drain on gold from the US to those countries, who increasingly demanded gold instead of the dollar token currency in payment for their goods. This development, on the other hand, also assisted these countries to return the convertibility of their devalued currencies into gold or US dollars. At the same time, the development gave these European countries and Japan additional economic strength. It was this changing situation that enabled the IMF to increase the quotas of members to take into account the added strength of the European and Japanese currencies. The quotas were raised by 50%, thereby injecting some $15 billion of liquidity into the Fund to supplement the dollar. The size of Germany's quota was raised. Although this 'convertibility' also enabled US multinationals, as we shall see in the next section and chapter, to begin to remit their profits back to the US, it brought on increasing problems for the US. It should also be noted that this was the year of the signing of the Rome Treaty for a European Common Market.

This drain of gold to Europe from the US created pressure on the official price of gold, which was fixed in 1934 at $35 per ounce at a time when the US held most of the world's gold. It was this scramble for gold that led to the establishment of the London 'gold pool' in 1960 by the US and Britain, and this became the fourth *ad hoc* measure to assist the dollar. The US contributed 50% of the gold to the pool. The aim was to feed gold to the private markets with a

view to bringing down its price and relieving pressure on the dollar by keeping the price at the official rate. The arrangement started in 1961, and was supposed to be self-replenishing in that the consortium of banks which was formed was to share the burden of offering gold for sale on the London gold market. Each central bank was given a quota of gold which it had to provide for sale. Any gold provided in this way could be re-purchased when the crisis was over, and the re-purchased gold would then be distributed among the contributing central banks, again to await another crisis. The pool began to operate in 1962 and bought some $80 million of gold off the market. This reduction helped to stabilise the price, but then the Cuban crisis of 1964 blew up, and in conformity with the historical trend, an unprecedented panic demand for gold re-appeared. Although this too was cooled off with new purchases, the crisis was not solved.

At the same time, following the 'Kennedy Money Market Slide' of 1962 – in which 27% of fictitious capital was wiped off the stock exchanges in the US – the fifth *ad hoc* arrangement outside the IMF was entered into at the urging of the US among the Group of Ten. This so-called General Agreement to Borrow (GAB) committed the participants to provide additional $6 billion of their respective currencies, upon due consultation, to finance concurrently if necessary, maximum permissible drawings from the Fund by the US and Britain. This arrangement bolstered the role of the dollar and to some extent that of sterling as international currencies.

In addition, the Federal Reserve Board launched a programme for the continued external convertibility of the dollar. In order to facilitate this, it established a network of standby credits or what were called 'currency swaps' with the principal trading nations. The arrangement started with a modest $700 million, but later built up to $9 billion, adding to the liquidity required to maintain orderly exchange-markets in the face of increasing difficulties for the US dollar. This arrangement came in operation in 1960 due to the development connected with the 'Kennedy Slide', at a time when there was a sudden demand for gold on the London gold market, leading to its price rising from $35 per ounce to $40. Only the joint efforts of Britain and the US brought this upsurge in gold's value back down, but the development marked a very important episode in the latest US mechanism to control world credit through the dollar.

Chart 1: Gold Production and Private Demand (millions of US dollars at $35 per ounce)

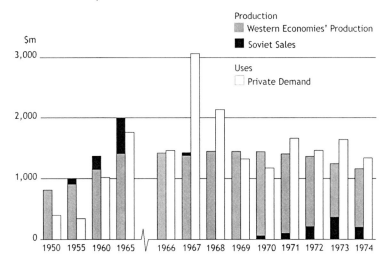

Source: Bank for International Settlements, 1975

The gold pool operated well as long as sales were balanced with purchases. But soon, and particularly after 1964, the attacks on the dollar created an atmosphere for hoarding gold instead of holding US dollar securities. This meant that if other central banks continued to share in the burden of US gold drains they would merely be helping to spread the loss among the other countries. For this reason France withdrew from the pool in 1967. This increased the US commitment to the pool. In November, the British sterling was weakened as a result and was devalued from $2.80 to $2.40, and this triggered off another run on the dollar. In three months the pool released nearly $2 billion of gold on the market, with no possibility of its being bought back. As a result of this run, the central banks terminated the pool and their obligation to supply gold to it. What ensued was a 'two-tier' price of gold, the official $35 per ounce for monetary gold for exchanges between central banks and the free market commodity price varying according to supply and demand and costs of production.

This development re-emphasised the importance of gold as money in a regime of capitalist development in periods of crisis. It proved the fact that gold would still be hoarded as a store of value, as an incarnation of social wealth, despite the fact that the state could de-monetise the metal. The statistics which emerged revealed that from 1950 to 1968, of the additional gold of $23.8 billion, industrial use, luxury goods and the arts took only $5 billion, and an estimated $12.8 billion went into private hoards and speculation. Of this amount as much as $3 billion was consumed in private hoards during 1967 alone and early 1968. US gold reserves declined in the period 1950–70 from $23 billion to $11 billion. Every crisis in the period contributed to this hoarding of gold, crises like Vietnam, the Israel–Arab wars, the Cold War, the Cuban crisis and colonial wars in Africa:

> Many a forgotten man purchased gold coins, gold wafers, gold leaf, and gold nose clips. Those who could afford it began to buy standard gold bars while the more speculative saw in the gold market an opportunity seldom presented elsewhere – a one-sided speculation at some cost to be sure, but with no risk of substantial loss as long as the US stood pledged to maintain a flow on the price and buy gold at $35 an ounce. Before long private demands far exceeded supplies of new gold available for purchase, and a world run on gold was in the making in 1966.[15]

The drain of gold from US reserves to the official reserves of the European and other central banks had taken their toll on the position of US gold. As of 1965, official holdings of gold were distributed as follows: US $14 billion; Western Europe (excluding Britain) $20 billion; and the rest of the world (including Britain) $10 billion.[16] By 1970 European official gold holdings had gone up to about $30 billion, and overall foreign holdings of gold had increased from $8 billion to $47 billion from 1950 to 1970. The US holdings had decreased on the other hand to less than $7 billion.

This decline of US gold holdings weakened the position of the dollar as an asset in the IMF arrangement to provide liquidity because it dealt a blow to the artificial 'confidence' that had been built around the idea that the dollar was 'as good as gold'. We noted earlier the ease with which the US dollar was used by the IMF as the

only currency that was available for purchase by other countries in deficit. This had resulted in reducing the Fund's holdings of US dollars in 1957 to 28% of the US quota, but this at the same time gave the US a gold tranche position in the Fund of nearly $2 billion. This creditor position was whittled down, with the result that by 1963 the IMF's holdings of US dollars had been reduced down to 75%, meaning US dollars were no longer acceptable for other countries' 're-purchases' under the rules.

The US was then forced to negotiate its own standby credit with the IMF, under which it drew on eligible 'creditor' European currencies to coincide with the Fund's repayments by countries that held mainly dollars in their reserves. These dollars were then used by the drawing countries to buy their needed 're-purchases' of German marks, French francs or Canadian dollars from the US. The US drew $1.8 billion from the Fund in this form from 1959 to 1966 through the running down of its own creditor position, and through these means it financed about 10% of its 'liquidity' deficit in this period. In 1962 the IMF financed 25% of US deficit in this way.[17] Even though after these drawings the US remained within its ordinary tranche, her position was weakening rapidly.

With this decline in the role of the dollar as a reliable reserve, it is not surprising that reliance was placed on gold as a reliable reserve as a form of commodity-money. But this did not eliminate the dollar in the sphere of exchange. It continued to play its role as an international medium of payment. Even then the other capitalist countries now accepted additional dollar balances only 'with formal politeness… in accordance with the customary etiquette practiced by central banks'.[18] The role of gold in the US's official ideology declined, and the assumed importance attached to it by the US, when the Bretton Woods institutions were being established. Indeed as we shall see, the US began a campaign to dethrone gold from its role as an international means of payment.

Such attempts did not succeed however because international transactions, and to some extent domestic money transactions, could not be entirely detached from gold. But the bulk of international transactions were increasingly carried out with various saving and economising techniques created by the central banks such as 'gold certificates', treasury bills, sterling bills, euro-dollars,

transfers of dollars and sterling by deposit, as well as the creation of special securities by the US Treasury denominated in marks, Swiss francs and other foreign currencies for foreign central banks.

These devices, which included the rate of interest device and open market operations, were adequate for a time to provide the liquidity required to act as a means of payment for cancelling international balances. It is in this connection that Harrod refers to the dollar as a 'currency of intermediation'.[19]

The problem of gold shortage was a problem for the US precisely because it had put forward the idea of dollar convertibility in order to create international confidence in the dollar. The rush on US gold must be attributed to its declining trade balance, the demand for gold by private hoarders in face of crises, and the need on the part of central banks to hoard gold in their central bank vaults so long as they feared that the US dollar was not strong enough. The increased US military commitments in Vietnam and other parts of the world including Europe increased the deficit burden for the US. This occurred at a time when the US could not, under these conditions of 'limited wars', repudiate its gold commitments like the British were able to do in the two wars, and therefore it became inevitable for the US to lose most of its reserves in order to satisfy this demand for as long as possible and maintain the value of the dollar.

Nor were other options open to the US. Unlike her predecessor, the decision to impose tariffs on a large scale, or to impose exchange controls, or to block balances were out of the question, since to do so would have been to lose her control over the world.

So the US was in a fix. She decided instead to adopt a policy of 'benign neglect'. As the pressure mounted on the dollar in late 1970 and early 1971, matters began to move very quickly against it. Already Germany in October 1969 had re-valued its mark in self-defence, and Canada had returned to a floating rate in 1970. As we have seen, a 'two-tier' exchange system for gold had emerged for the first time. The then official price of $35 per ounce was overridden by a free market price which fluctuated with the collapse of the London gold pool. In May 1971 speculative pressure increased on the dollar. Within three months, speculators converted 'billions and billions' of dollars into yen, marks, Swiss francs, sterling and other stronger currencies. The crisis came to a climax in

early August, and finally on 15 August. On that date President Richard Nixon announced the suspension of gold sales and purchases, inducing other countries to re-value their own currencies. Europe and Japan stopped pegging their currencies in terms of the dollar, and their currencies began to rise against the dollar as a result. The US decided this to be the best 'solution' to the problem and so with it ended the Bretton Woods system, collapsing under the weight of its irreconcilable contradictions.

This then explains why the fixed exchange rate policy behind the gold–dollar myth had to be abandoned. A 'floating exchange rate' regime was substituted, and burdened by the pressure to support the US dollar, the Europeans tried to set up their own currency unit. Starting with the 'Snake' system, they amplified a system of exchange in the 'Basle Accord' of April 1972. In 1973 they set up a European Monetary Cooperation Fund, which formed the basis for the establishment of the European Monetary System (EMS) in December 1978 with a European Currency Unit (ECU) as a 'reserve unit', which in fact went further to complicate the system of international exchanges. It is not surprising that Britain, as of now, still remains opposed to joining the Exchange Rate Mechanism (ERM) under the 1992 European 'internal market'.

The contradiction between the concept of international liquidity and that of a reserve currency – which was itself arising out of bourgeois confusion of these roles of international money – was brought a stage further by the effort by the IMF to create the special drawing right (SDR) as a 'new' international reserve asset with the 'attributes' of gold. The value of the SDR was in fact based on the value of 16 different currencies and merely enhanced the liquidity, which was not in any case threatened as the real problem facing the system was one of the 'convertibility' of the excessively created credit assets – most of them through speculation and the making of money with a minimum of production.

Notes

1. See Gardner, R.N. *Dollar–Sterling Diplomacy*, McGraw Hill, New York, 1969, p.74.
2. *Ibid.*, p.76.
3. Keynes, J.M. *Collected Writings*, vol. XXV, Macmillan, London, 1980, pp.98–9.
4. Quoted in Gardner, R.N. *op. cit.*, p.97.
5. UK Treasury *Proposals for an International Clearing Union*, section v.,

paragraph 20, 1943.

6. Hendrickson, R.A. *The Future of Money*, MacGibbon Still, New York, 1979.

7. Ellsworth, P.T. *The International Economy*, Collier Macmillan, New York, 1964, pp.443–4.

8. Hirsch, F. *Money International*, Penguin, 1969, p.364.

9. Hendrickson *op. cit.*, p.87.

10. Hirsch *op. cit.*, p.368.

11. *Ibid.*

12. Gardner, R. *op. cit.*, pp.257–8.

13. *Ibid.*, pp.259–67.

14. Hirsch *op. cit.*, p.154.

15. Hendrickson *op. cit.*, p.111.

16. *Monthly Review*, New York, vol. 18, December 1966, pp. 22–3 (excluding the Soviet Union, China, North Korea and Eastern Europe).

17. Hirsch *op. cit.*, pp.364–5.

18. Machlup, as quoted by Ellsworth, *op. cit.*, p.449.

19. Harrod, R.F. *Money,* Macmillan, London, 1969, *op. cit.*, p.71.

4

Post-Keynesianism and Monetarism

Keynesianism and Demand

Keynes's main objective in writing his book *General Theory* was to provide a theoretical framework for curing the economic ills caused by the *industrial cycle*.[1] He had pointed out earlier in his *Tract on Monetary Reform* (1923) that a drastic fall in the value of money had destroyed the savings of the rentier class and this had arisen from a general rise in prices. He traced this phenomenon to what he called the 'credit cycle' which in fact was connected with the industrial cycle.

His main concern therefore was to iron-out the wide fluctuations in the prices of industrial commodities, but this had to be done by creating 'full employment', and to achieve this there had to be an increase in the volume of *effective demand*. Keynes's theory therefore centred around the creation and management of effective demand by state intervention.

Although he did not deal with the problem of the industrial cycle as such in his *General Theory* – having laid the basis for this in his *Treatise on Monetary Theory* – he nevertheless indicated that the cause of the crises was due to a decline in the 'marginal efficiency' of investment, meaning a drop in the expected rate of return on investment in relation to the prevailing interest rate on money. This decline was also connected with the uncertainty around future expectations which from time to time prevailed in the money markets. This is why Keynes had emphasised the importance of stability in the value of money as being a prerequisite to reform. In the *Tract* he had declared:

> We must make it a prime object of deliberate state policy that the standard of value, in terms of which they (fortunes) are expressed, would be kept stable.[2]

But Keynes was writing at a time characterised by the prevalence of monopoly pricing. This is why he was complaining about the standard of value being unstable. But he also pointed out that generally low prices are not favourable to industrial entrepreneurs. In this connection he contended that the workers were far better off with relatively lower wages and full employment at monopoly (inflated) prices. In that case higher profits to the capitalist were preferable to unemployment. This was so because the maintaining of high prices for industry's goods while at the same time stabilising the standard of value offered the best policy for creating full employment and increasing effective demand.

In short, Keynes' proposals were aimed at combating the industrial cycle by increasing demand for goods in periods of slump. This was to be achieved by maintaining prices on the *upward* that would give super-profits to the industrialists, for it is from these gross incomes of capitalists that increased investments would arise.

Although at the end of the war Keynes advocated an opposite policy, this was due to the high 'pent-up' demand created by war shortages. In his work published at this time, *How to Pay for the War* (1940),[3] Keynes recommended a severe dose of taxation, rationing and physical controls to bring down post-war inflation. He also advocated a contraction in the national debt built up during the war. The war had created 'full employment', but soon the problems of the industrial cycle re-appeared in the post-war period.

Keynes's theories, developed by his followers in Britain and the United States, were now applied to deal with the management of the post-war economy. One of these followers, Alvin Hansen, focused attention on the income determination theory as the centrepiece in the application of Keynesianism to the US economic scene, because this was connected with three other main components of Keynes's theories of the cycle-investment demand, consumer demand and the concepts of multiplier and accelerator.[4]

Under the policies designed particularly under the Kennedy administration in the early 1960s, a marriage between Keynesian prescriptions and neo-classical theories was adopted. The latter

advocated the 'free' play of market forces, maintaining that higher growth rates could be achieved by these means through the stimulation of higher profits, and an improvement in technological efficiency which could be achieved by enhancing the marginal efficiency of capital, rather than increasing its volume.

The Kennedy 'synthesis' of the two positions was adopted in the policy of traditional stabilisation and measures designed by the Council of Economic Advisers to expand economic potential in the long-run as part of the strategy of combating the industrial cycle. This involved state regulation of the economy and the adoption of two main lines of action to the long-run management of the economy. The first was the application of *fiscal policy*, which was to be directed at expanding effective demand in the economy as well as expanding economic potential generally. This approach emphasised the direct income-generating effects of deficits and surpluses, as well as the stabilisation aspects of the cumulative multiplier expansion process. The second line of approach was the *deficit financing policy* which was to be based on the long-term effects and no longer limited to balancing state budgets on a yearly basis or even over the period of the industrial cycle. Emphasis was placed on arriving at a 'balanced budget at full employment' in the long-run.[5]

Under both these approaches, a growing deficit budget became a necessity, and to that extent became 'legalised'[6] as the instrument of deficit financing was used to increasingly 'whip up' a sluggish economy in order to raise it to the level of full employment and 'full potential'.[7] To achieve this, an increase in government spending was viewed as a direct demand for goods and services. This was because within Keynesian theory, an increase in the quantity of money and credit, brought about in part by increased state credit-creation, was seen as leading to the public buying bonds or taking out additional loans and the acquiring of other credit instruments which had the effect of lowering market interest rates. Such a fall in interest rates was expected to lead to an increase in spending, especially on long and lasting assets such as housing, industrial plants and equipment, as well as other producer durables.[8] This is the only point at which the post-Keynesians saw the relevance of monetary policy on economic expansion, but this was evaluated more from the angle of interest rates than from the angle of 'money supply'.

Furthermore, post-Keynesians regarded a tax reduction as leading directly to an increase in disposable incomes and the 'purchasing power' of consumers and businesses, which strengthened the incentive to spend and hence increase demand in the economy. This in turn raised the net returns on new capital investment. Although such a step could lead to an initial increase in private consumption and investment expenditures, these increases in spending were expected to set off a cumulative expansion in production which would generate further increases in consumption and investment spending and lead to a general rise in production, income and employment.[9]

Thus economic growth policy coincided with the counter-cyclical techniques which post-Keynesianism brought about and the result, at least in the initial stages, was a sustained level of economic growth which was cushioned by increasing monopoly prices. But if the two arms of the post-war policy approaches converged in this way in bringing about a relatively high level of growth in the gross national product (GNP) of most western capitalist states, they also became increasingly counter-productive. The growth in the economy was accompanied with a creeping inflation, so that the policy aimed at countering the industrial cycle came increasingly in sharp collision with the policy of maintaining long-term growth, and this marked the crisis of post-Keynesian recipe as the 1970s approached. A point of stagnation in economic growth was soon reached, but in conditions of high inflation so that a counter-thesis in the form of *stagflation* seemed to bring down the whole policy package framework. This was challenged by *monetarism*, which had nothing substantive to offer to the ills of monopoly capitalism.

Inflation

According to Irving Friedman, the expansionary forces which came out of the post-war US economy created an atmosphere of enthusiasm in which it was expected that the 'Americanisation of consumption and production' would become world-wide in content and application. This was expected to spread prosperity to all countries through 'free trade'. In the event, according to him, the situation turned out differently. He states:

> The inflation growing out of these events could not be short-
> lived. Business cycles would be very different; they would take
> place in [an] inflationary environment. The general levels of
> national prices might be affected by business cycles but their
> trend would be usually upward.[10]

With these developments it was in fact not possible to ignore this
creeping inflation. By 1965 the phenomenon of upward movement
in prices, even in periods of decline, was becoming 'permanent' so
that it became fashionable to talk of 'permanent inflation'. It even
became fashionable to regard inflation as something 'good'.

But it also became fashionable to blame this development on
state intervention in the management of the economy and the
expenditure of 'unearned incomes' created by the state. The generation of credit by the state was also seen as giving rise to the
fuelling and heating of the economy in the direction of inflation.
Yet it was forgotten that state intervention was itself a response
to the capitalist crisis which had arisen out of the earlier slumps.
War-created demand that had led to 'full employment' was seen
as the 'final solution' which monopoly capitalism had sought
to deal with the slump. The need to maintain war-created 'full
employment' is what led to the post-Keynesian and neo-classical
responses which we have just examined. The need to maintain full-
employment could only be achieved if the state intervened to bring
about effective demand in the economy and this was achieved by
the state intervening to 'whip up' sluggishness in the economy
whenever it appeared.

In this way, inflation had become a means of economic
expansion. Debts which the monopolies accumulated became
'manageable' because the value of the debt became 'small' with
the passage of time, although with 'time' interest rates increased
as well. Taxes also, although high, were seen as being no problem
under inflation, because corporations' incomes were rising with
their power to increase prices.

But this manipulation of the economy by the state could not
solve the fundamental problem posed by monopoly capital and its
power to maintain high prices. Instead of prices falling in a recession as before, prices were kept high in order to adjust not by state

action, but by the action of the monopolies themselves in order to 'iron out' the cycle in their own way.

State action in intervening merely went some way in helping monopolies to maintain high prices in periods when they should have fallen. It did this by engaging in open market operations, and later by the manipulation of reserve requirements.

Thus when the economy was veering into a recession the state intervened to maintain employment, but to do this, profits had to be kept high through high prices. Intervention on the money market by the state in order to maintain economic growth was intended to increase credit facilities for state enterprises and for monopolies at a time when interest rates would be high. This suited the monopolies well, since it assuaged their own price policy. This in-built dynamism to increase prices was easily reflected in the high cost imports in Third World countries, adding fuel to internal inflationary pressures, as we shall see later.

Since the whole purpose of the post-Keynesian recipe was the maintenance of prices at monopolistic, profitable levels, its explanations of inflation were bound to reflect a whole series of symptoms, many of which themselves required explanation. On the one hand, post-Keynesians argued that the absolute price level was determined by labour unit cost, but on the other they claimed that the price level was determined by mark-up factors as well as new or unfilled orders. Other non-monetary factors such as the influence of demand shifts and oligopoly pricing were added as additional explanations. Excise duties, which were shifted to consumers, were also added to the problem of mark-ups. The variables determining mark-ups were said to include productivity trends, which allowed producers (i.e. monopolies) to maintain profit shares even though wages were rising faster than prices. Also taken into account were farm and import prices which in their view 'measured other costs'.[11] The new quantity theory variant assumed however a link between money and prices and viewed movements in absolute price levels and inflationary or deflationary pressures as arising from current and past changes in money stock.

These theories of the post-Keynesians arose in part from Keynes's own theory of the 'inflationary gap' developed during the war, but this theory was dropped because, as we noted in the

previous sections, it had focused on an economy where prices were rising because of an excess of aggregate demand over supply. The theory could not deal with the new reality at the end of the war. From 1950 onwards, the post-Keynesians shifted the theory to deal with aggregate demand in *employment* while de-emphasising its impact on price-level movements. As a result they came to accept and adopt the early post-war explanations of creeping inflation as arising from cost-wage-push causes. This arose naturally from Keynes's own belief that a cut in money wages would cause prices to fall by the same amount, and that real wages were determined independently and not influenced by changes in money wages. This was the reason why Keynes had observed them to be 'sticky downwards'. Later explanations of inflation in the early 1960s shifted the emphasis to the position of mark-up prices, sectoral shifts and administered prices.

Yet all these explanations (and explanations they were since there was no agreed theory of inflation) tried to obscure the basic explanation of inflation as lying in the capitalist monopoly power over labour, which was secured by the increasing role of the state in economic management. It is this power which enabled the monopoly capitalist class to exploit labour in conditions of crisis. This monopoly power was maintained in *production*, and the power to *reduce output* in order to maintain high prices was just an *additional* mechanism calculated to give monopolies increased leverage over labour, since it was the labourers on the whole who also provided the market for the commodities. This power did not arise from some transient phenomenon such as advantages caused by rising factor costs or shifts in demand giving rise to monopoly pricing, although these factors were important elements in cost calculation. The control over supply conditions assured monopolies the power to extract higher profits from labour's surplus-value. The resort to higher pricing was a means of addressing some of the crisis conditions in the market which monopoly capitalism faced. Each monopoly tried as much as possible to extract the maximum profit, and limiting supply in order to reap a higher price was one of the ways of addressing the marketing crisis. The real problem was the crisis of *maintaining the value* of existing assets expressed in monetary terms.

But in such conditions *price* competition becomes anathema to all monopolies, for such competition leads to them all incurring losses. It then becomes necessary for all the monopolies, with the assistance of the state, to create conditions to maximise profits, for according to Baran and Sweezy, 'none can wish that the total fought over should be smaller than larger'.[12] The 'price leader' in most cases, according to Galbraith, calculates the price that will best serve the interest of all, 'presumably with some special attention to its own needs.'[13] This is what explains the fact that in spite of the Sherman Antitrust Act of 1890, US monopolies have used these very 'anti-trust' laws to maintain monopoly pricing. In the view of a Supreme Court Judge Robert H. Bork, the anti-trust laws have made it 'easier' for monopolies to divide market shares and, in that way, limit market competition because these laws have acted as an indicator of what degree of monopoly pricing is legally permitted.[14] For this reason General Motors Corporation has for years held its market share just below 50%, for this is the level that was judged to discourage anti-trust problems.

It is true that in periods of 'boom', labour is able to increase its wages, but this is possible only in industries of strongly organised unions. In such unions labour is able to increase its bargaining power and sometimes increase its wages to the level of the increase in productivity. Such gains however do not 'trickle down' to the small industrial enterprises where labour is not so well organ-ised. Here the wages are determined more by 'market forces'.[15] But even in such cases where labour is able to make such gains in wage increases, these are often added to the cost of production and are consequently recovered in the next production cycle. Recent developments, which have led to the deregulation of certain branches of industry, have complicated further the practices of monopoly pricing. Here monopolies have found it necessary to hide such price increases in high service charges, reputation and customer loyalties which are procured by occasional bribery.

The above explanation of the real forces which bring about infla-tion does not rule out other reinforcing factors which give fuel to inflation, including those offered by post-Keynesians. These are, however, partial explanations which do not go to the root of the problem. Shifts in demand do not on their own lead to inflation.

Nor should increased demand lead to the same result. Increased demand under competitive conditions should lead to increased production, which need not result in inflation. Mark-ups also need not *per se* lead to inflation, unless they constitute part of a package of monopoly practices. The *strict control* imposed by a monopoly *on supply* is in fact part of the strategy of monopoly capitalism, for such control assures the monopolies the possibilities of exploiting labour to the maximum since by controlling supply conditions, labour is placed at the mercy of monopoly capital.

The fact that wages might equal increased productivity does not mean that the monopoly capitalist enterprise makes its super-profits from prices. Such a manoeuvre would in fact be counter-productive. Accumulation in that case would arise out of market manipulation. Furthermore, it would not explain why the monopoly enterprise would do its best to recover such wage increases that labour had won. The effort to recover is in fact the result of the need to keep labour in a perpetual struggle to survive and reflects capital's drive to extract higher surplus-value by intensifying technological inputs.

What is said above is proved by *Fortune's* survey of the top 500 corporations for the year 1980. The survey, which was the first of its kind to be held since 1954, revealed that although consumer *prices* had risen *three times* over the 26 years, the sales of the 500 corporations had increased 12 times while *profits* had risen *ten-fold*. In the same period employment had doubled from 8 million to 16 million and the average sales per worker had risen from $17,408 in 1954 to $103,725 in 1980, which in real terms amounted to double per worker.

It can be seen from the above evidence that the higher profits of these corporations did not *originate* in higher prices *per se*, but from *production* itself. As we saw, profits had increased ten-fold as against a three-fold increase in consumer prices. The remaining seven-fold increase had arisen from higher levels of surplus value extraction in the production process from the labourers. This higher surplus-value extraction is evidenced by the fact that whereas employment rose two-fold, profits had risen ten-fold, and this means that the higher wages that might have been gained by labour in these 26 years were no hindrance to the rise of the profits of these

monopolies. For this reason, it could not be argued that the increase in money wages were the *cause* of inflation in the US in these years. On the contrary, a tremendous increase in profits when sales increased six times shows that effective demand was maintained, but that supply was also regulated to maintain the level of the required demand. The increase in wages did not match the increase in the productivity of labour and this is confirmed by the fact that in a single year, 1979, the after-tax profits of these corporations averaged 26%.[16]

In calculating their profits, the corporations take account of the rate of 'expected inflation', which include factors like 'last-in-first-out' inventory costing and various forms of accelerated depreciation to accord with the overall levels of required profitability. In the words of Eiteman, Stonehill and Moffett:

> To remain viable, a company must raise [the] sale-price by a sum of the increase in [the] replacement cost of the item sold, plus the loss in real value of [the] monetary profit expected, plus the increased income taxes which result if [the] actual book cost rather than [the] replacement cost must be used in determining income liability. [The] ability to raise price depends upon price elasticity, for what a business would like to do and what it is able to do may differ.[17]

The re-imbursement of the loss in the 'real' value of monetary profit is another way of 're-imbursing' loss resulting from inflation *by inflation*. The corporation is able to do this because it is able to calculate differences between nominal value quantities and real quantities through the real rate of interest which the actual producers – the labourers – are not able to do on any meaningful basis. By re-imbursing itself the taxes paid to the state, the monopolies avoid paying these taxes out of their super-profits. This explains why, in 1960 for instance, 86% of all taxes paid to the state were by ordinary households against the 14% paid by the corporations. Ordinary 'households' is another way of saying workers and others from the lower middle-classes. These classes are unable to re-imburse themselves of these heavy taxes, which the state uses to maintain the monopoly power of the corporations. Even pay roll taxes are added to the prices by two-thirds of the corporations, so

much that the corporations can truly be said to be the tax-collectors of the state, with corporation tax being disguised as a sales tax.[18]

The swindle is made even worse with the so-called 'capital gains' tax. Realised capital gains are taxed at less than half the normal rates of tax applicable to ordinary income earners from wages and salaries. The theory that justifies this swindle holds that this tax 'relief' gives incentive to the capital saved so that it may 'take risks'. In fact there is no risk involved nor does this kind of capital produce any new wealth. Any risk involved is even borne by the state in research and development. Even risks that would normally be borne by them are recovered through accelerated depreciation allowances, which are applied to land and buildings. What is even glaringly fraudulent is that unrealised capital gains are not taxed at all. These 'unrealised' capital gains are in fact so liquid that monopolies can easily take out loans by using them as leveraged collateral:

> The great power of our great corporations is not their magnificent capacity to produce goods, but the taxing authority inhering in the power to raise prices.[19]

Thus there can be no doubt as to the real causes of inflation. It is monopoly capital's power exercised in collaboration with the state over labour to extract surplus-value. In the modern era, the surplus-value extracted through average profits is not adequate to maintain production. The resort to super-profit realisation arises out of the crisis which leads competitive capitalism to move into monopoly capitalism as a way of overcoming this profitability crisis. Monopoly capitalism enables monopolies to fight off falling profits, as well as to fight off the falling values of money which greater fictitious capital creation increasingly undermines as the production base declines relative to technological changes. Monopoly pricing in part 'overcomes' this crisis, while at the same time intensifying it. This is why the whole high price structure is built into the pricing system as a means of maintaining the value of money in the fictitiously created capital. The *real* profits come from the intensification of technology in its application to labour which produces surplus-value. It is this value which is backed by *real* money which monopoly pricing seeks to *maintain*, while at the *same time* maintaining a certain level of

production to *back up* the heightened levels of fictitious capital. It is this crisis which Keynesianism came to resolve.

But, as we have already seen, a point was reached where post-Keynesianism could not theoretically explain the new situation, created in part by its own economic policies and strategies. A new situation arose where high levels of inflation *co-existed* with high levels of unemployment, which characterised the new period of *stagflation* as we saw. The earlier period in which Keynes had written during the inter-war years had been characterised by high unemployment with low prices. Now it was the high prices which were threatening the capitalist system, and the Keynesians were not providing any new insights as to how to resolve the new crisis.

Responses by such economists as Samuelson and Solow in the early 1960s to create a new 'model' based on the 'Phillips Curve' soon proved equally unworkable.[20] Under the theory, a policy device called a 'trade-off' was proposed under which it was possible to justify the *co-existence* of unemployment and high levels of inflation. It was argued that the workers must 'trade-off' a certain level of unemployment with a certain level of 'acceptable' inflation. If they did not do this, they would instead have to *accept* higher unemployment and this could be at levels which were beyond social and political acceptability, meaning such levels would threaten the very existence of a monopoly capitalist society. The Phillips Curve theory was thus used to justify the economic drift to *stagflation* on a permanent basis. It was utilised to build the theory of *expectations* into the monopoly pricing structure. In this structure, a certain level of unemployment was assumed to exist at a given level of 'equilibrium' (of unemployment!). At this level, an acceptable level of inflation arising out of a given level of controlled wages and demand was to be *anticipated*. This anticipation in turn justified the intervention of the state in the economy to create 'adequate' credit to finance the anticipated economic activity and contracted wages and price increases. Although the Phillips Curve argument was intended to encourage free market conditions, it merely served to strengthen state intervention of the monopoly bourgeoisie.

Thus an anticipated rate of inflation was built into an expected rate of credit-creation by the state, which the monopolies included in their profit calculations in order to maintain the value of money

of their stocks and assets. Prices were automatically adjusted to take account of expected increases in nominal money wages and the expected rate of inflation. This response, while intended to keep the Keynesian approach going, was in fact already an admission of defeat and a concession to monetarist policy at a theoretical level.

With this theoretical tie-up, further effort was made in the mid-1960s to analyse inflation in terms of a disequilibrium model which generalised the earlier Keynesian 'wage-push' theory of inflation. This approach attempted, along with the wage-cost-push explanation, to include monopoly pricing or a 'seller's inflation' explanation under which it was argued that *actual prices*, and especially wage rates, were fixed 'somewhere' between supply and demand price. As such prices and wages were determined 'very often' by *market power* and the *bargaining strength* of the actual participants so that it was possible to have *both* 'buyers'' and 'sellers'' inflation.[21] In this way the exploiter and the exploited were placed in the same position in order to confuse the real issues.

To sum up, it can be seen that the whole post-war period was characterised by a series of new inflation explanations, all of which justified in one form or another the policies of monopoly capitalism in the capitalist countries of the west. As the Keynesian theories came under crisis, a new approach which incorporated a monetarist element inherent in the 'trade-off' policy framework came to the fore. Since the argument was that if the state increased the 'money supply' with a view to maintaining full employment such an act was bound to lead to accelerated inflation, it appeared that the opposite approach would reduce inflation. This was the other side of the Keynesian dilemma, from which it could not retrieve itself. Monetarism appeared to be the 'correct' approach to the Keynesian crisis.

Post-Keynesian Monetary Theories

These developments in the economic strategies and policy instruments of post-Keynesianism were also reflected in their monetary and credit theories in the post-war period. Since the instability in price levels, which were characterised by creeping inflation, made the determination of equilibrium conditions and the quantity of the real cash balances with which to operate difficult to establish,

post-Keynesians applying Keynes's concept of demand for money resorted instead to the use of *nominal* balances or quantities for real quantities. Keynes's demand for money (or demand for real balances) concept which he developed in the *General Theory* was transformed into a concept of the liquidity preference function which determined the rate of interest. In adopting this approach Keynes assumed the level of prices to be given, since these could be *made* to respond to the desired macro-economic levels to avoid the crises inherent in the industrial cycle.

This then explained why Keynes and the post-Keynesians in their *income*-expenditure theories adopted the techniques of nominal balances, for with this approach they could move from nominal to real balances to easily determine the conditions under which market forces would be expected to react. The main policy instrument in the activation of this mechanism was the *market* interest rate, which itself was in fact a nominal rate since its real level was to become evident in the next phase after the policy was implemented. The nominal (market) rate was intended to induce certain activities on the part of economic actors. The real rate was therefore the return to capital (which would have taken account of the depreciation in the value of money), and through this real rate an 'equilibrium' quantity of real balances was expected to emerge.

But while the post-Keynesians were apparently adopting this 'traditional' Keynesian concept, they in fact were increasingly finding it difficult to determine the equilibrium quantities of real balances since these were in movement all the time. The resort to nominal balances increasingly became a necessity for determining macro-economic variables in the economy, along with the use of real money stocks. This approach placed the centre of economic management and the determination of prices, interest rates, and 'money values' in the hands of the Treasury and the Federal Reserve Bank, as we shall see in the next section. The opposing theoretical contention, which held that the real value of the 'money stock' was an endogenously determined variable caused by the interaction between the financial and productive sectors of the economy (and therefore outside the control of the monetary authorities), became increasingly outmoded. The 'free market' conditions for determining 'real' values did not in fact exist, and this was why the

above post-Keynesian approaches had to be married with the neo-classical approach into the 'Kennedy synthesis' as we noted earlier.

The other arm of the Keynesian and neo-classical approaches on monetary theory was the *quantity theory* of money variant. This approach accepted superficially the notion that money demand defined the demand for real cash balances and that this demand was an endogenous variable. It argued that changes in nominal balances generally have an effect on market interest rates, income and prices. However, the theory nevertheless held the view that in transition periods an increase in nominal balances would have a compound effect on interest rates – including a short-run liquidity effect, an income effect and a longer-run price expectation effect.[22]

The quantity theory assumed that the demand for money was quite stable, and that the velocity function derived from this demand could provide a useful link between changes in money and money incomes. This view, in contrast to the pre-Keynesian quantity theory, postulated a stable velocity function of money and credit.

This uneasy marriage between the income and quantity theories became sharply evident with the passage of time. The former focused attention on the discrepancies between actual and full employment output, which made it necessary for them to abstract price level changes while placing emphasis on interest rates as the transmission mechanism in economic policy, while at the same time regarding monetary aggregates as endogenous variables. The latter focused on discrepancies between actual and *desired* real balances, distinguishing between exogenous (nominal) balances and endogenous (real) balances. The former highlighted the full employment surplus as the operational policy variable, while the latter highlighted nominal stock as the operational policy variable. These apparent differences obscured an essential agreement between the two approaches in the conception and use of the money and interest variables which both adopted.

By 1965 these post-Keynesian and neo-classical mechanisms of managing capitalist economies had become exposed to glaring contradictions in their states' stabilisation policies. The use of nominal interest rates as an indicator of monetary policy became ineffective since the rates could no longer be seen to be in line with real rates of interest, which reflected the decline in the value of money due to

increasing inflation. Efforts to minimise the impact of price levels, which this technique in part was intended to achieve, also failed since prices became glaringly high with the passage of time. This also inflicted a blow on the effort to conceal the impact of inflationary expectations on market rates of interest, which had been assumed by the post-Keynesians.

All these developments added together could no longer sustain the post-Keynesians' declared reluctance to distinguish between nominal and real quantities in the economy. In the eyes of the *monetarist* opponents of post-Keynesianism, the income theories of money had obscured the fact that it was the growing 'supply of money' which was behind persistent inflation, and not the explanations advanced by them. Inflation seemed to blow the lid off the Keynesian recipe.

The Chicago School Monetarist Theories

The crisis in Keynesian explanations of inflation and its aggregative tools of management of the monopoly capitalist economies called for a *monetarist* response. This response in fact had as its central concern the overriding consideration of the *maintenance of the value of paper money* in the face of the galloping inflation, coupled with the stagnation which Keynesianism had brought about. Since the central objective of capitalism historically has been the *making of money for the sake of making money*, it followed that what was now required in view of this 'capitalist' attack on money was to secure its historical value with the assistance of the state, instead of trying to expand production *at full employment*. Their basic economic theory was neo-classical in content, but it concentrated on the money side of the production process.

To this end the monetarists re-asserted the self-regulatory character of the 'market place', arguing that for the capitalist economy to be put back on its correct path the state should restrict credit-creation, reduce state expenditure and reduce its intervention in the economy. Since they placed the cause of inflation on the state increase of the 'money supply' (because of its extensive credit-creation), they attached greater importance to the money stock. In the words of the leader of the Monetarist School, Milton Friedman:

> The behaviour of the quantity of money is the senior partner of output, the junior partner. Many phenomena can produce temporary fluctuations; but they can have lasting effects only in so far they affect the rate of monetary growth.[23]

The central proposition of the school was that the quantity of money had no influence on *real* variables in production. The volume of physical goods and services available to the community, its level of employment, and the goods and services earned in exchange for work including real wages were all determined by the society's natural resources and physical, capital and labour supply. In this context, the only long-term impact of money was upon the general *price level*. In this way money could only influence *nominal values*, namely the wage measured in units of money, such as pounds sterling, or the number of pounds that should be paid for particular goods and services. Such influence however, argues Friedman, cannot influence the actual quantities produced, earned or purchased. This is a concerted reply to post-Keynesianism and its incomes approach with its emphasis on aggregative techniques and nominal indicative planning at the macro-economic level.

In this conception, therefore, money is an independent (endogenous) variable. In Friedman's scheme, it can be regarded as one of the five broad ways of holding wealth – money, bonds, equities, physical goods and human wealth (labour power). Each of these modes of holding wealth has distinctive characteristics and each offers some return in money or in kind, including its yield in relation to that of other assets.

The yield on *money* is mainly in kind – a convenience yield which reflects trouble and often costs, which can be avoided if ready money is available. The *real*, as opposed to *nominal*, yield on money depends on movements in the *price level*. If the price level falls, money appreciates and shows a capital gain in real terms which must be added to the nominal yield, while in the more common conditions of rising prices a real capital loss has to be deducted from the nominal yield, and this is the basic concern of Friedman in that the value of money is in that case destroyed.

Bonds, on the other hand, stand for assets which promise a perpetual income stream at a *constant amount*. Like money, their return is affected by changes in *price levels*, but additionally they

are affected by changes in the *rate of interest*. Equities also stand for assets which promise a perpetual income stream at a constant real amount. On the other hand, *physical goods* yield an income in kind which can seldom be measured by any explicit rate of interest. Their nominal rate of return is, however, also affected by the rate of change of the price level which can be considered explicitly.

Human wealth is the discounted value of the expected stream of earned income. It presents a problem because it can be substituted only to a *very limited extent* with other forms of asset holding (e.g. selling other assets in order to pay for training which increase yields). And this, Friedman must admit, explains why *labour power alone* is the creator of wealth which is an independent variable of all the other assumed variables.

The emphasis on prices, which the Keynesians assumed to be a given, reflected the monetarist concern about the impact of inflation on money values. For this reason, the interest rate, which Keynesians emphasised, was not given prominence by the monetarists.[24] Yet it must be obvious that the problem of the weakening of money's value could be placed on money itself. When Friedman therefore reduces the whole problem of inflation to a 'printing press phenomenon', he addresses only one aspect of inflation, that of *money* inflation, which merely leads to a *debasement* of the currency and not the *price* inflation which partially explains the undermining of *value*. In fact Friedman confuses currency *debasement*, which is a problem of the money *standard*, with the problem of *devaluation*, which is a problem of the role of money as a *measure* of value. This is why he argues, simplistically, that inflation 'occurs when the quantity of money rises appreciably more rapidly than output, and the more rapid the rise in the quantity of money per unit of output, the greater the rate of inflation'.[25] He cannot see that in the case of the restriction of output relative to the quantity of money, the restriction element would be a more *important* factor in the inflation arising than the mere increase in money *volume*, although that in itself would also not explain the basic cause of inflation and loss in the value of money. Friedman's statement also confuses the concept of money with that of credit.

The real difference between the post-Keynesians and the monetarists, therefore, appeared to be over the *details* of how to manage

a monopoly capitalist economy, since the monetarists' explanations of inflation also came no nearer to revealing the real issues. Indeed, in placing emphasis on the *quantities* of money stock and supply as the crucial variable, while the post-Keynesians placed greater emphasis on interest rates, the two were concerned with the specifics of how a state deficit in the process of state involvement in the economy *should be financed*, with both arguing that the impact of such a decision would affect how the economy functioned in relation to particular social classes. In short, they were concerned with the *method* rather than the substance of the fiscal and deficit operations.

Thus while the Keynesians argued in favour of state intervention to maintain *production* at something nearer to full employment, while at the same time paying attention to the *financial* classes, the monetarists were interested in *reducing production*, in order to maintain money values if necessary. This is why the monetarists argued that expenditures which were financed either by taxing or borrowing involved the *transfer* of resources from the 'public' to the state and that such transfers affected both interest rates and wealth held in private portfolios. Furthermore, it was argued that the effect of a reduction in taxes on private demand financed through borrowing depends firstly on the extent to which it was viewed by the public as a temporary or permanent cut, and secondly its effect on market interest rates. Once this was taken into account, argued the monetarists, the Keynesian-perceived increase in the direct income-generating effects of deficit financing could be very small and uncertain. On the other hand, they further argued, if the deficit was financed through 'money creation' by the *banking system*, that is if the deficit was 'monetised' by *private* bankers, then the effect on any expansion in the economy would be greater and certain,[26] since such money creation would go to production. This approach, as can already be seen, was to underline most of the Third World IMF-imposed stabilisation policies, as we shall see in Chapter Nine. But as the evidence suggests there, this does not happen in all cases.

In refutation of the Keynesian interest rate emphasis, the monetarists argued that evaluating monetary policy solely in terms of interest rates and credit markets had the effect of obscuring the fact that once money and credit were injected into the system, such an

injection *could* be spent purely on non-productive purposes, and not merely used to acquire bonds and other credit instruments. Furthermore, such an injection could affect the commodities market, especially of durables, without going through the credit market channels. Secondly, it was argued that the Keynesian monetary policy equated money with credit, and this had the effect of emphasising only one way or particular ways in which money was introduced into the economy. Such an approach ignored and overlooked the *continuing* impact of monetary change on credit and markets, which often worked in *opposite* directions from the initial impact, with the result that monetary expansion could lead to *higher* not lower interest rates. Easy money could in such a situation also lead to *tight* credit, and tight money could lead to *easy* credit.[27]

The monetarists, in confronting post-Keynesianism in this way, were therefore calling for a *revision* of the multiplier theory. This would be along the lines of enabling the sequential and quantitative elements played by individual parts in fiscal and deficit financing policy to *separate* out *exogenous* changes in the money stock (which resulted from money-credit changes) from *endogenous* changes (which reflected changes in the demand for money-credit). This, in their view, would make it possible to remove the identification problem in a manner acceptable to the Keynesians, and to provide a definition of a pure fiscal action with restrictions on the growth rate for the monetary aggregates acceptable to the monetarists. This *new compound* approach would assist a proper empirical estimation of the money stock effects of deficits and surpluses in the multiplier exercise.[28]

The main objective of the monetarists, nevertheless, was to use these changes in the way the multiplier was defined and applied sequentially to bring about economic changes which would enhance the value of money-credit instruments. This was the real rationale behind the demand that deficits be financed by *monetising* state debt, but in a manner that reduced full employment, money wages and state subsidies to ailing industries as well as to social services, which in the view of the monetarists, had the effect of increasing inflation and undermining the value of money. The demand that the state should surrender debt to the private appropriators of wealth was, in fact, a *political* demand of this class of the financial

bourgeoisie who were the guardians of the wealth of the entire bourgeoisie world-wide.

It is correct to point out that when the state expands its taxation, particularly through the mechanism of deficit financing, this has the effect of increasing the prices of commodities, including commodity labour power. Deficit financing in this sense has the power of taxation. But such an increase in prices results from *monetary or credit inflation* and to that extent raises all prices to the *same extent.* It, therefore, has the effect of *debasing* the standard of money and not its *value*, since everyone suffers to the same extent. This rise in prices must not, however, be confused with the *price inflation* which the private industrial monopolies engage in. This form of inflation, while raising the price of those commodities where monopolies have used this power, has different levels of impact on different classes depending on the levels of price inflation in each industrial product and branches of production. Moreover, as we have already noted, such a price increase does not affect profits adversely. On the contrary, the whole purpose of price inflation is to increase the share of profits (and through it interest) out of the proceeds of the product. Such a price increase leads to an increase in wages, but as we have seen, such increases are recovered as costs through yet higher prices, which enables capital to recover a *real* return on capital. The real wage, however, remains stable and this is why capital is able to enhance its gains against labour.

This later price increase then results in the *devaluation* of the price of *labour power*. The currency devaluation that results from such a price increase is *one-sided* and does not affect profits, since as we have seen capital is able to re-compensate itself through still higher prices. This devaluation in fact represents an adjustment of the fixed relations in the *inner division* of capital between machinery, raw materials and wages upon which a certain rate of profit is calculated. In periods of crisis or continuing crisis, this relation is disturbed all the time, hence the need to adjust and ensure that the disturbed proportions do not injure the interests of capital. The *devaluation* achieves this adjustment against labour so that capital may reap a high surplus-value from labour. Creeping inflation was an attempt to correct these historically disturbed relations.

In stating that credit-creation by the state leads to high prices which may act as a means of taxation, one has to draw a distinction

between credit as capital and credit as a means of circulation – the former is productive and the latter unproductive. In the same way, not all the credit created by banks is as productive as bourgeois theory assumes. In engaging in the speculative activities of making money without production, banks and industrial monopolies create credit which is not backed by actual production, and it is this activity which, in part, leads to the *financial crisis*. Such credit earned by speculators can appear in the commodities market and also add to inflation.

The fundamental bone of contention for the bourgeoisie that banks do not create credit but *money* is therefore behind the whole argument that state credit-creation is the cause of inflation. It is this same erroneous view which is behind the distinction between 'narrow money' and 'broad money' and it is this failure to see credit as the basis of capitalist production which obscures the creation of fictitious capital, without which the whole capitalist system cannot in fact operate. In part it is the state's regulatory role to control and supervise reserve ratios and the liquidity ratios of the banks that makes it possible for banks to extend credit within limits.

As we have noted, this regulatory power of the state has become even more difficult with the appearance of the euro-dollar and 'offshore' dollars. This over-expansion of credit in the face of declining production is what threatens the entire monopoly capitalist structure, despite efforts to try to control it through various credit devices. The division of 'money' into 'narrow' and 'broad' money – or M1 and M2 – is an attempt to continue the myth that currency notes and forms of deposits are real *money*, when in fact they are instruments of credit.

The bulk of these instruments are not backed by production and commodities, and they are far removed from any monetary connection. But some of the credit instruments are in fact money because they are linked to commodity-money in various forms within and without the monetary system. The fact that gold no longer operates as money within the monetary system but as a commodity has not by any means put a stop to the monetary function of gold or new commodities such as platinum acting as money. On the contrary, the over-expansion of credit has re-asserted the role of these metals as the *only money* into which all credit devices in the form of paper strive to re-convert themselves in periods of inflation and crisis.

Notes

1. Keynes, J.M. *The General Theory of Employment, Interest and Money*, Macmillan, London, 1936.

2. Keynes, J.M. *A Tract on Monetary Reform*, Macmillan, London, 1923, p.2.

3. Keynes, J.M. *How to Pay for the War*, London, 1940.

4. Hansen, A.H. *Business Cycles and National Income*, Norton & Co., New York, 1951, p.493–4.

5. Heller, W.W. *New Dimensions of Political Economy*, Harvard, Massachusetts, 1960, p.vii.

6. Osadchaya, I. *Keynesianism Today*, Progress Publishers, Moscow, 1983, p.259.

7. *Ibid.*, p.260.

8. Thurow, L.C. (ed) *American Fiscal Policy for Prosperity*, Prentice Hall, 1967.

9. US Government, *Economic Report of the President 1963*, Washington, DC, 1963.

10. Friedman, I.S. *Inflation: A World-Wide Disaster*, Hamish Hamilton, London, 1973, pp.88–9.

11. De Leeuw, F. and E. Gramlich 'The Channels of Monetary Policy', *Federal Reserve Bulletin*, June 1969.

12. Sweezy, P. and P. Baran 'Monopoly Capital', *Monthly Review*, New York, p.69.

13. Galbraith, J.K. *The New Industrial State*, Hamish Hamilton, 1967, p.16.

14. Bork, R.H. The *Antitrust Paradox*, Free Press, New York, 1979.

15. O'Connor, J. *The Fiscal Crisis of the State*, St. Martins Press, New York, 1973, pp.19–20.

16. *Fortune Magazine*, 4 May 1981.

17. Eiteman, D.K., Stonehill, A.I. and M.H. Moffett *Multinational Business Finance*, Addison Wesley, New York, 1979, p.447.

18. *Wall Street Journal*, 5 May 1958, p.1.

19. Lundberg, F. *The Rich and the Super-Rich*, Bantam Books, New York, 1969, pp.445–7.

20. Samuelson, P.S. and R.M. Solow 'Analytical Aspects of Anti-inflation Policy', *American Economic Review*, May 1960.

21. Lerner, A.P. 'On Generalising the General Theory', *American Economic Review*, March 1960.

22. Johnson, H.G. *Essays on Monetary Economics*, Harvard, 1967.

23. Friedman, M. *Free to Choose*, Penguin, London, 1980, p.309. For the background to Friedman's views on money and its role in the US economy, reference should be made to the voluminous work: Friedman, M. and A.J. Schwartz *The Monetary History of the United States, 1867–1960*, Princeton, 1963.

24. Bain, A.D. *The Control of Money Supply*, Penguin, 1980, p.309.

25. Friedman, M. and A.J. Schwartz, *op. cit.*

26. Fand, D.I. 'The Post-1965 Inflation in the US', September 1969, p.120.

27. Fand, D.I. *op. cit.*, March, pp.241–2.

28. *Ibid.*, pp. 243–4.

5

The Crisis of Production

Our analysis in Chapter One revealed that the power which capital attains over labour is a historical one achieved, on the one hand, by dispossessing labour in order to pit it against itself as wage-labour. Capital then utilises this labour concretely to expand itself and maintain the system of capitalist exploitation. But this power which capital now seems to possess arises from the fact that it wields *state power* on its side, with power now poised *against labour*, which alone has the living *capacity* to expand the quantity of commodities while they are in production by *transferring* to them *new value* out of their sweat and brawn. This new value is in fact surplus-value, which the capitalist now claims to be profit and the interest arising out of *invested capital*. This, in the mind of the capitalist, looks reasonable, for *labour-power* itself is *bought* in the market place just like any other commodity, be they raw materials, machinery or auxiliary materials. But of all these commodities it is labour-power alone that can turn the others into new products, and hence it alone has the capacity to produce and *add* new value to the expanded product which the capitalist now sells to realise more money.

While giving it new strength, this exploitation of labour by capital finally becomes the cause of its downfall, for the ensuing *struggles* that emerge between capital and labour make it increasingly difficult for capital to realise growing profits unchecked. The check to capital by labour's struggle to increase the *necessary value* on which it reproduces itself leads to the reduction of the surplus value which capital reaps freely. Capital's response, as we saw, is to bring in more machinery in order to reduce the number of labourers and their claim to higher wages (necessary value). The battle becomes a perpetual one of wits and muscle, and it is this battle that finally brings the system down. This battle takes on a sharp form in the Third World, where these struggles between labour and capital

are intensified by IMF and World Bank stabilisation and structural adjustment policies.

De-Industrialisation

What has been said above is in fact already happening, as this analysis has shown. It is already clear that the forces leading to a general depreciation of capital, alongside the devaluation of both capital and labour, have reached irreversible levels. Already, this was self-evident in the 1930s.

The Second World War was fought precisely over the issue of who would survive the crisis. The decline of the industrial hegemony of Britain signalled this crisis. The struggle by Britain to restore its basic industries in the steel and textile sectors, which formed the backbone of its industrial hegemony, merely led to the total collapse of the myth of the gold standard, which had in any case been eroded by this industrial decline. The struggle to maintain the pre-war value of its currency – based on an outstretched credit system – proved untenable as well. It is this failure that compelled the British state to come out more openly to intervene in the money-capital markets, as well as in the industrial sector.

Although the post-war conditions, with the war's 'pent-up demand', made it possible with this growing state intervention to maintain 'full-employment' (making it appear as though capitalism had recovered its ground), the decline was in fact simply compounded as the production-industrial cycles became shorter and shorter. But this 'growth' in the industrial activity of most western capitalist states soon came to face the problems already outlined in the previous chapters. By 1975, British manufacturing was declining so rapidly as to cause alarm in the high circles of British society. One of the leading spokesmen of the British government at the time, Secretary of Industry Anthony Wedgwood Benn had observed:

> The trend to contraction of [the] British manufacturing industry which we are now suffering has gathered force for the last four years. If this trend is allowed to continue, we will have closed down 15% of our entire manufacturing capacity and nearly 2 million industrial workers will have been redundant between

1970 and 1980. During the five years 1970–74 there was a 7% fall in employment in manufacturing in Britain, while it was still rising in most of our competitor countries. In this period, the total number of manufacturing jobs lost through redundancy averaged about 180,000 a year and the net contraction of manufacturing employment averaged 120,000 a year. Only about one in three of the jobs lost through redundancy was effectively replaced by the creation of a new job in the manufacturing sector.[1]

The trend that Benn mentions here was in fact deeper than the figure implied. The contraction through redundancies throughout industry brought to the surface the ongoing struggles between labour and capital. The capitalists blamed the problem on the 'uncompetitiveness' of British goods in foreign markets, which meant that British monopolies were not reaping sufficient super-profits from British labour to be able to maintain production. Yet in this period British manufacturing had a relatively high rate of growth of approximately 4% per annum which, compared to the previous historical experience, was quite high. This is what explained the fact that employment had in this time period (1965–75) fallen by 14%. Profits were made but the *rate of profit* was falling. In the immediate post-war period, British exports had expanded rapidly, taking advantage of the fact that its industry was relatively intact compared to that of its competitors who had suffered more war-damage. Between 1945 and 1960, their volume had grown by 250% relative to the 1938 level.

The re-industrialisation of Western Europe and Japan brought new competition on the scene for British industry, and the new competitors had a more relatively modernised technology than Britain. The organic composition of capital of British industry implied a higher level of employment which required a larger wage bill than the more highly organically composed ones. This is what then compelled the British industrial monopolies to adopt a strategy of reducing the labour component of capital, heighten its exploitation by intensifying existing levels of technological inputs, and thereby raise the rate of profit by reducing the total wage bill. This went on while British multinationals tried to switch their investments to overseas outlets where they could obtain a higher rate of profit than at home.

It is this development that explains Benn's concern about the *de-industrialisation* of Britain. This rapid fall in employment, while explaining the falling profitability of British industry and the industrial effort to raise the profitability rate, also at the same time prepared the ground for the 1972–75 recession which followed in earnest. By 1976, the proportion of the population employed in industry had dropped to 32% of the 1960 level.[2] The contribution of manufacturing to the gross national product (GNP) in current prices also declined as compared to its share in the mid-1950s. The recession clearly proved that the benefits that British industry had accrued in the immediate post-war period – benefits occasioned by the re-organisation and rationalisation of industry, which gave rise to a new wave of mergers and industrial concentration – had exhausted themselves. This rationalisation had enabled industry and manufacturing in particular to grow, despite the later fall in employment. Output per man-hour during 1965–75 grew because of this (3.5%) growth rate, which was higher than during the earlier period of 1955–65 (around 3% annually).

But 1973 marked a new watershed in spite of this general picture. From that year onwards, there appeared a stagnation in the growth of productivity in manufacturing. The organic composition of capital had become too high to permit any increase in productivity and the rate of profit. This, in turn, was expressed as a loss of competitiveness of British industry in overseas markets, marking its final decline. There was a growing 'structural disequilibrium' in which Britain's trading position continued to deteriorate despite its cost and price competitiveness. British industry also found it difficult to raise investment funds within the British banking and financial system since these were increasingly globalised in their operations, creating further difficulties for the British currency through the exchange rate. The Industrial and Commercial Finance Corporation (ICFC), founded in 1947 to provide funding for small- and medium-sized enterprises, increasingly found it difficult to raise equity funding for these enterprises. By the 1970s it was apparent that the ICFC needed a substantial capital base to be able to perform this task, but it was itself caught in the financial speculation that came with the 1973–75 recession, leading to its merger with the Finance Corporation for Industry which was

re-organised in 1981. Faced with this decline and decay, the British Labour government began to think of nationalising the banks in 1976, but this created an atmosphere of fear that led to the Thatcher monetarist 'revolution' which re-asserted the supremacy of 'money' over industrial production as such.

This trend had also affected the profitability of major industries in other OECD (Organisation for Economic Cooperation and Development) countries. A report compiled by a 'Group of Independent Experts' for the OECD showed that the profitability of the major OECD industries had rapidly declined. This has led to the sapping of US investments overseas as well. The huge budget deficits of the US were being financed primarily by high interest rates on domestic savings and high-cost capital inflows into US money and bond markets from overseas. The steady decline in net investments income from abroad (due to the rising interest

Table 1: Trends in Overall Productivity* of Major Western Countries

Country	1960-73	1973-76	1977	1978	1979	1980
	Average annual change (%)					
United States	2.1	0.0	1.9	0.1	0.5	-0.4
Japan	9.1	2.4	3.9	3.8	4.2	3.1
Germany, Fed. Rep. of	4.5	4.8	3.0	3.0	3.3	1.1
France	4.7	3.1	1.3	3.3	3.4	1.0
United Kingdom	3.0	1.0	0.7	2.0	-0.2	-0.3
Italy	5.7	0.7	0.8	2.2	3.7	2.6
Canada	2.5	0.8	0.4	0.0	-1.2	-2.6
Belgium	4.3	2.8	0.9	3.0	1.0	0.6
Netherlands	4.0	2.8	2.2	2.1	1.3	-1.0
Sweden	3.3	0.9	-2.7	1.0	2.1	1.0
Switzerland	2.9	0.6	2.6	-0.3	1.8	1.3

* Real gross national (or domestic) product in relation to civilian employment.

Source: Bank for International Settlements, 'Fifty-First Annual Report', Basle, June 1981, p.34

payments on debt) was also sapping the robustness of the US position in the world economy as a result.[3]

These figures reflected a trend that began in the early 1960s and continued unabated into the 1970s. The rising interest rates reflected US Treasury's concern about the need to maintain the 'money' character of US state debt which was necessary to finance this production, since the taxes from corporations and personal incomes were inadequate to meet the costs. Moreover, because of this decay, a burgeoning 'tax revolt' was underway through the 1970s, with the US state estimated to be losing as much as $30 billion a year in 1973 and as much as $50 billion in 1979, building up a huge 'underground economy'.[4] By 1986, tax avoidance was as large as $100 billion. But these high interest rates coincided with the interests of the banks and large corporations, who began to invest their own surplus funds in US Treasury bills and bonds since they could not engage in productive investment.

Table 2 clearly reveals an overall decline in the productivity of all the capitalist states as well as in the rate of investment of new productive capital in industry. This dismal picture represents the fundamental contradictions of the capitalist system, as we noted.

Table 2: Average Annual Rate of Change in Real Private Non-Residential Fixed Investment (%) of Major Western Countries

Country	1960-73	1973-79
United States	5.4	3.1
Japan	14.0	2.2
Germany, Fed. Rep. of	4.6	2.7
France	7.5	1.1
United Kingdom	4.3	1.6
Italy	4.9	-1.6
Canada	5.8	4.5
Belgium	5.7	1.3
Netherlands	4.6	1.7
Sweden	4.9	-1.3
Switzerland	5.8	-1.8

Source: Bank for International Settlements, 'Fiftieth Annual Report', Basle, 9 June 1980, p.55

The flow of foreign capital into the US in search of high interest rates also coincided with the needs of the US economy and the US Treasury as the main guarantor to world capitalist exploitation. The inflow came in handy to assist US corporations, while the US state for its part utilised most of the locally created, fictitious capital for its economic, political and defence activities. The US state debt became increasingly interwoven with foreign capital inflows. This was shown by the fact that since the 1970s the foreign component of state debt had become an increasingly important element in financing the US budget.

By January 1985, the US had become a net debtor nation for the first time since the 1920s. In this way, the fate of this weakened US finance-capital in its global operations, with declining productivity and profitability, was being tied up *intimately* with the fate of the economies of all the countries of the world under the US hegemonic defence umbrella. The incoming savings of other countries were being utilised increasingly to meet US defence budgets and to make the US politically safer, at least for the time being. J.F. Smith has observed:

> The huge financial inflows from abroad since 1981, attracted by high interest rates, have permitted the Reagan administration to finance its defence build up without imposing any real hardship on the American people.[5]

This defence build up, as we noted in the earlier chapter, was itself a reflection of the decay of American capitalism and represented a decline in the leadership role of the US economy in the world economy. The US corporate structure that had been globalised since the 1960s was itself coming under the pressure of this de-capitalisation, which was under way in most countries of the capitalist world.

To be sure, the US corporation was itself becoming 'hollowed',[6] as the US economy was itself becoming de-industrialised. For the United States, 1965 had already marked the period of its loss of competitiveness in world markets with the re-emergence of European and Japanese economies as solid competitors in world markets. This early loss of leadership also signalled the weakening of its currency, the dollar, which, through gold, had constituted the standard of money for the other currencies of the world. It

managed to maintain its hegemony in the financial and monetary fields only with the *ad hoc* arrangements it entered into with the banking and financial systems of other western countries. This leadership, which was maintained in this way, gave way however with the 1971 repudiation of the gold exchange standard upon which the dollar had been based. The US economy increasingly came to rely on deficit trading and financing in order to maintain its position in the world economy.

Despite this, the US economy still maintained the traditional industrial sector as the mainstay of its economy, for it is this sector that formed the basis of the monetary and financial system. But the decline, nevertheless, set in. From the real gross national product growth of 4% between 1950 and 1960, it declined to 2.8% in the 1970s. Productivity per work also began to fall as Japan and Germany began to take up the US markets. Even the Third World so-called newly industrialising countries such as South Korea and Taiwan, which were in any case US economic satellites, were becoming more productive.

The response by the US and Britain to this decline at home was to increasingly export their capital overseas, with a view to exploiting the relatively cheap labour in these foreign countries. Most of the new capital floated on the London Stock Exchange went into non-manufacturing corporations whose investments went into foreign acquisitions such as Rio Tinto Zinc and Consolidated Gold Fields, which were both financial houses involved in financing and developing mining (especially in South Africa, Zimbabwe, Zaire and a number of other Third World countries). Vast amounts were also floated for trading activities connected with 'invisible' earnings.

The US for its part tried to wade off its uncompetitiveness by exporting investments for manufacturing *outside* the US itself. It shifted production to 'offshore' bases, which went on under the general term of the 'globalisation' of industry. This industrial 'migration' took the form of looking for a 'site' overseas where it could locate its plant and, using local labour, produce and then ship back to the US products for sale in the home market.

A number of corporations took this path rather than go under! A US monopoly product-manager at Caterpillar remarked, 'What is the alternative? If our major concern is whether we're gonna be

around next year, we'd better make a dollar.'[7] The cheaper goods it produced offshore enabled it to 'net' $198 million in 1985 on sales of $6.7 billion. This was a remarkable 'turn-around' for a monopoly that had made a loss in 1982.

The 'globalisation' took different forms of the 'export of jobs'. Apart from finding a site and constructing a factory for production, it also took the form of entering into arrangements with former rivals and competitors in these foreign countries to jointly produce, with added technology from US corporations.

It is these developments which explain why a huge US corporation such as General Electric would spend some $1.5 billion in 1985 to import products into the US which it then sold under the trade label GE.

Almost all its consumer electronic goods were being made in Asia, with the result that by the end of the summer of 1986 it planned to shut down all its colour-tv plants in the US. It was also buying all its microwave ovens from Japan on the same basis, while planning to go 'offshore' for its air conditioner production in 1987. Eastman Kodak was also buying its camera-recorders and videotapes from Japan, along with its midsize copying machines.

This de-industrialisation within the US has compounded the earlier export of manufacturing capital and now has added the shifting of fundamental technology, management functions, and even the design and engineering skills that would have ensured the monopoly of the US over certain forms of technology. The cost structure of industrial production, which is in fact connected with the decline of industrial profit and the craving of fictitious capital to maintain the 'money value' of credit, has turned large research and development expenditures into negative investment. The large amounts of money spent on the innovation of car production by the 'big three' car manufacturers in the US have not stopped over one-third of all car sales in the US going to Japanese car manufacturers. It is estimated that of the $1 billion auto-sales in the US by foreign (i.e. Japanese) manufacturers, some $2.8 billion was 'lost' to the US economy in terms of production, trade, insurance, transport, mining, plant construction and financing.[8]

The loss of manufacturing also implies the loss over the monopoly exercised over technology to other monopolies. The US

corporations are finding it particularly difficult to keep track of the new techniques, particularly the latest innovations in the field of software. Faced with the reality that despite its vast overhead research and development expenditures in the microchip technology, Japan had managed to take control of over 40% of the world market in microchip sales, the US corporations have had to find various ways of linking up with their Japanese competitors in order to make sales both on the world market and in Japan itself. Motorola – the second strongest US monopoly in software – has, for instance, had to link up with the Japanese Toshiba Corporation – Japan's second microchip manufacturer. Over the five-year period of 1986–91, Motorola offered to swap its most sensitive and precious technology in return for both Toshiba's less sophisticated one and its help with gaining a foothold in the Japanese market. In exchange, Motorola agreed to buy Toshiba memory chips stamped with its name. If Motorola wanted to produce the memory chips themselves, then they had to get Toshiba's design and production technology on the basis of a joint venture world-wide.[9]

Thus, unlike the earlier methods of 'second-sourcing' and design-licensing deals, the loss of industrial hegemony is making it possible for new forms of internationalisation of capital to emerge. The new arrangements involve equity participation, joint ventures, technology sharing and even the coordination of marketing and product development strategies. Although secretive deals are still made to ensure control over certain processes, there is a steady loss of control in the long-run. This is compelling supermonopoly drives by computer companies to help them exercise a joint monopoly globewise. For instance, Siemens of West Germany and Philips of Holland are working on a joint mega project costing $1 billion and backed by their governments, with the aim of 'catching up' with the Japanese in next generation memory chips by 1990. Thomson of France and Italy's SGS are also working out a joint venture for the same purpose. This has not stopped Siemens finding another link with Toshiba and the US's General Electric to develop a so-called standard cell library for semi-custom chips. These new arrangements are eating away national anti-trust and anti-monopoly laws, making global inter-networking a necessity within which capital can operate.

The Growth of the Service Sector

As de-industrialisation has proceeded, so has the role of the service sector widened. This may be seen as a sign of progress beyond industry, but in reality it represents a stage in the decline and fall of capitalism. This trend of the decline of manufacturing and relative growth of the service sector was more evident in the British economy as early as the 1960s. By 1971, while trade in manufactured goods fell significantly, growth in services remained more or less constant, despite the fact that industry was by then being granted substantial state subsidies and generous tax cuts during the preceding decade. By the 1980s, the growth in the service sector had risen tremendously relative to the manufacturing sector.

In the United States, the service sector was also already becoming significant as early as the 1950s. By that date, services already accounted for one-third of foreign direct investments. But by the 1970s, there was a qualitatively new significant shift towards the sector at the cost of the extractive industries. The *composition* of the investments changed from transportation, communication and public utilities towards trading, finance, insurance and diversified services.[10] Between 1977 and 1985, the stock of foreign direct investments in services almost doubled from $60 billion to $111 billion, and the share of services in the total stock of investments rose from some 20% to 43.7%.

The shift of Japan and the Federal Republic of Germany has also been very significant in the same direction. Although the two countries are considered 'late comers' to direct foreign investments, they are at the moment among the largest investors in the service sector behind the US and UK and are ahead of Switzerland and France, who are regarded as 'traditional' investors in this sector. Table 3 shows the positions of a number of countries in their shares of direct investments in services.

It is noteworthy that Japan has the greatest share of investments in other countries in this sector. She has had a significant shift from 29% in her stock of direct foreign investments to 52% in 20 years, while West Germany has moved from a bare 10% to a sizeable 47%. This shows that those countries that are currently regarded as having a broader and dynamic industrial sector are still in fact moving *faster* into the service sector than the US and UK. This, if

Table 3: Stock of Foreign Direct Investment (FDI) in Services, Selected Home Countries, various years (value and percentage)

Country of currency	Year	Value		Percentage
		Total FDI	FDI in services	Share of services in total FDI
United States of America (billion dollars)	1950	11.8	3.8	32
	1957	25.4	7.8	31
	1966	51.8	163	32
	1977	147.2	60.4	41
	1985	254.7	111.2	44
Japan (billion dollars)	1965	1.0	0.3	29
	1970	3.6	1.4	28
	1975	15.9	53	35
	1980	36.5	14.0	38
	1985	83.6	43.3	52
Federal Republic of Germany (billion deutsche marks)	1966	10.6	1.1	10
	1976	49.1	20.0	41
	1980	84.5	36.2	43
	1984	145.4	68.0	47
Netherlands (billion guilders)	1973	43.6	53	12
	1983	119.9	27.2	23
Canada (billion Canadian dollars)	1973	7.8	2.4	31
	1980	25.8	6.8	26
	1984	41.7	12.0	29
Australia (billion Australian dollars)	1978	1.4	0.7	47
	1983	3.4	1.6	47
United Kingdom (billion pounds)	1971	93	2.2	24
	1981	45.5	16.2	36

Source: United Nations Centre on Transnational Corporations, based on official national sources

anything, demonstrates the rapid decline of the profitability of modern industry as a back-up to money capitalist relations in almost all the countries of the capitalist world.

The drift from hard manufacturing to services in most western economies is shown clearly in the emerging blurring of lines between production and services. The shift is most evident in the emphasis on trading, which was characterised most clearly in the growth of advertisements as part of the effort to fight off the realisation crisis in the 1960s and 1970s. Data for West Germany shows that for the year 1984, out of a total of 5,792 foreign investing corporations and individuals, 1,718 (30%) were in services and three-quarters of these were in trading and holding companies. In the United States, in 1982 out of the 2,245 corporations surveyed, 889 (40%) were in services and more than half were engaged in trading. Furthermore, many of these units engaged in trading were *small* in size relative to earlier, larger industrial corporations. It was also noted that the emphasis of these new service companies was on trading in information-data service 'industries'.

The importance of the service sector is also illustrated in the levels in employment generated by this sector. Since 1970, the United States has seen most of its new jobs being generated in this sector. Between 1981–82, when the recession was at its highest, 80% of new jobs were in services. By 1987, service enterprises in the US were paying 70% of all the workers in the private sector of the economy. Worse still, the Department of Labor in the United States was forecasting that out of every 10 jobs created between 1987 and 1995, nine would be in the service of the economy.[11] This clearly showed a deterioration in the productive sectors of the capitalist economies, despite the tremendous boost in the technological base. This was also a clear sign of decay and old age. Labour productivity was falling at a time of great strides being made in the introduction of new techniques, including the introduction of computer-integrated manufacturing, but little real profit was being generated.

Decline of Equity Capital

The decline in the industrial sector is also noticeable when one looks at the workings of the money-capital markets in relation to the size of the fictitious capital created in the credit markets going into actual production. This form of fictitious capital is called 'equity capital', as opposed to other forms of debt. It has become ever apparent that since 1973–75, the levels of fictitious capital going to industrial

investment have declined significantly. This in many ways has to do with the already observed fact of stagflation, which became a permanent feature of the period. The old belief that inflation was 'good' for development turned out to have been a falsehood of the highest order. Common stock of many corporations on the stock exchange was at the time seen as a good hedge against inflation, and this helped to increase the sales of industrial debt to the investors. This was to some extent possible because the corporations were able to pass on the inflation to the workers. By the mid-1970s, this game could no longer be played, as we saw.

This explains why 1975 also became the year when the sales of equity stock peaked. After that year, levels began to slide, as the figure below clearly demonstrates for US industry. From this date onwards, retained profits as a major savings mechanism in the growth of equity also began to decline. Since the capacity to borrow

Chart 2: Credit Market Debt Outstanding and Market Value of Outstanding Equities, 1960–85 (dollars in billions)

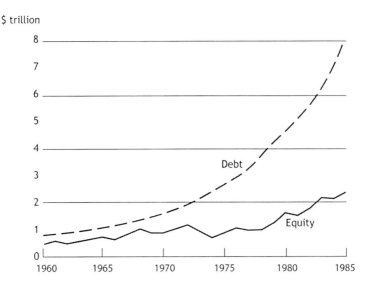

Source: Kaufman, 'Interest Rates, the Markets and the New Financial World', p.108

in the money capital market depends on the foundation of equity capital raised from profit (retained profits), its decline also undermined the very mechanisms of the money capital market, as we see in Chart 2.

But this development in fact manifests a deeper problem. As we noted earlier, the drop in the rate of profit of major industries in the capitalist economies was bound to affect the reproduction of capital since industrial capital found it increasingly difficult to pay interest on money capital. Indeed, the very mechanisms of increasing the corporations' profits from higher levels of labour exploitation, as also manifested on profits' reliance on inflation, meant the outer limits of capitalist exploitation were increasingly coming into sharp focus. High rates of inflation pushed interest rates on capital to very high levels. The interest rates demanded by money-capital increased as interest rate perspectives of market participants became sensitively influenced by previous cyclical rate peaks. This made money capital nervous as it sought short-term returns on loans, which in turn undermined the long-term production of enterprises.

This development led to the increasingly poor performance of industrial bond prices, which further went on to widen the negative gap between the production cost and market value of institutional bond holdings, since these bonds formed the backbone of industrial production. This negative gap also added to the drop in the quality of new corporate bond issues.

As Table 4 shows, beginning around 1974 there was a sizeable shift in the ratios of investment of pension funds in industry as compared to investment in debt, from $7.7 billion in 1971–75 to $26.80 billion in 1981–85. Whereas in 1960 almost 70% of pension funds were invested in industrial bonds, by 1985 only 25% were so invested, while 75% were invested in short-term money market debt which in turn also increased the interest rates of money-credit on debt.

Furthermore, it was noted that whereas speculative debt had ballooned to some $7.1 trillion in 1984, equity capital represented only $2.0 trillion. This shift from investible capital to speculative capital was also reflected in the investment strategies of the industrial corporations themselves. Contrary to the belief by supply-side economists that a lessening of taxes imposed on the corporations

Table 4: Average Annual Net New Investible Funds of Private
Pension Funds (dollars in billions)

	1966-70	1971-75	1976-80	1981-85
Equities	4.56	6.28	8.32	9.48
Debt	1.34	7.74	21.53	26.80
Miscellaneous	0.74	1.45	2.20	1.38
Total	6.64	15.47	32.05	37.66
Equities as percentage of total	69%	41%	26%	25%

Source: Kaufman, 'Interest Rates, the Markets and the New Financial World',
p.168

increases the equity capital available for further investment in
industrial manufacturing, the evidence that has piled up since the
introduction of Reaganite–Thatcherist monetarism has shown the
contrary to be true at the present juncture of the capitalist crisis.

The evidence from German corporations brought out in a book
by the German economist S. Welzk has revealed that as these corporations have made higher profits arising from tax deductions and
tax loopholes, they have progressively invested less new capital
into new plants and machinery while more of the profits have gone
into speculative stocks on money-capital markets. This was in sharp
contrast to the earlier observed fact that whereas German industry
was, in the 1970s, the highest taxed on its capital profits and dividends, it had in that period also been the leader in productive capital formation among western European economies. It did not have
inflated depreciation allowances at the time. But the study revealed
that apart from the tax deductions which the Kohl administration
granted to German industry, the corporations had also exploited
a loophole which had long existed but never been exploited to
the same extent of building tax-free 'reserves' to cover future pensions and other unforeseen liabilities. They used this loophole to
create large reserves from their profits, so much so that this, as of
1986, accounted for 30% of all corporate capital (which equalled
shareholder equity).

Working in a climate of high interest rates on money, these corporations pumped these large 'reserves' into debt paper on the
stock exchange since they were able to make 'profits' from interest

income higher than that from enterprise. Such incomes from interest on money also exceeded the costs of interest. Whereas in the 1970–79 period German capital formation (from equity) had increased by 49 billion marks, and productive investment had increased in real terms by more than this figure (57 billion marks), in the period 1982–86 the net capital formation had increased by twice this amount to 105 billion marks. Actual productive investment had dropped to 25 billion marks while job creation had stagnated.[12]

From this Welzk had concluded that the German 'boom' was a sterile bonanza for finance-capital. He observed that the bulk of the funds 'saved' from productive investment had gone into 'off-shore' operations of German corporations via tax havens through which they had escaped German taxation. They had invested in US Treasury bonds, which financed the US deficit budget as we have already observed. Whilst in the US this increase in the import of foreign capital was helping boost its economic performance (and this performance was mainly in the service sector in which the information and financial activities predominated), these huge investments in US bills were also helping to finance the US defence budget.

Thus the tax reform brought about by supply-side and monetarist political pressures was assisting the de-capitalisation of capitalist industry. The tax reduction of 1981 in the US in the 'double taxation' did not increase investment funds. On the contrary, increased depreciation allowances went further to undermine capital formation. It added to the craze to leverage capital and added also to the merger and 'hostile take-over bids' that became fashionable in this period. The rates of savings dropped in the same period.

These hostile take-over bids and acquisitions were a reflection of the non-viability of a number of corporations. Non-profitable corporations were forced by these mergers and acquisitions to 'restructure' but in a manner that rendered them not productive but 'buyable'. It was the drive to deregulate industries which also helped unleash the drive to short-term gains from investment. In the take-over bids, hostile bidders made offers of intention to take over the corporations to the shareholders directly, over the heads of management. The attractive offers in most cases induced the shareholders to accept the higher price and make a quick profit.

But the financing of these take-over 'buyouts' were themselves being undertaken by investment banks by selling 'junk-bonds' to the public in speculative stock market activity. Between 1980 and 1986, it was estimated that some $75 billion high-yield, high-risk 'junk-bonds' were issued over the six-year period. About half of that amount was directly related to the financing of the take-overs and defensive corporate restructuring that was being forced on industry by money-capital.[13] This 'strategy', which was began by a US Wall Street Investment firm, Drexell Burnham, has taken on the character of 'merchant banking' in which a few multimillionaires, abetted by an equally wealthy class of corporation executives, had by 1987 brought US industry into a highly leveraged and old-fashioned 'asset-stripping' state. Many of the take-overs were relying on 'inside trading'. The Boesky scandal clearly revealed the parasitic impact of money-making in capitalist production. In the US the total take-overs were growing daily. The *Mergers and Acquisitions Magazine* counted 936 mergers completed in the first three months of 1987 alone. These totalled some $31.8 billion compared to 807 acquisitions worth $33.4 billion in the first quarter of 1986. In Britain, where financiering reached peak levels with Thatcher's continued sale of state property to individual shareholders, mergers and acquisitions reached a high level in 1986. There were a record 1,323 take-overs, worth a total of £325 billion, which represented two-and-a-half times the levels achieved in 1985. A record 11 bids were valued at £31 billion. The promoters of these bids earned a record £3,850 million in 1986, more than double the earnings in the previous year.

Thus corporations suffering from profitability crisis were being cornered by money-capital and acquired yet higher debt-creation. To defend themselves, the corporations also resorted to debt-creation in order to restructure themselves into 'lean and mean' organisations. A commentator remarked:

> To protect themselves against this type of take-over, companies have begun large-scale restructurings of their own, whereby they assume significant amounts of additional debt in order to shrink their equity and increase the price of their stock.[14]

Under these circumstances, capitalism seemed to have exhausted its productive potentiality. All the productive capacities that the new technologies were making possible seemed to undermine it instead of reviving its continued existence.

Notes

1. Bacon, R.W. and W.A. Eltis 'Too Few Producers', *Sunday Times*, 14 November 1976.
2. Brittan, S. 'De-Industrialisation Revised', *Financial Times*, London, 26 January 1977.
3. *International Herald Tribune*, 17–18 December 1983.
4. Smith, J.F. *The Coming Currency Crisis*.
5. *Ibid.*, p.20.
6. *International Business Week*, 3 March 1986.
7. *Ibid.*, p.56.
8. *Ibid.*, p.58.
9. *Ibid.*
10. Wichard, O.G. *Survey of Current Business*, February 1981.
11. *International Business Week*, 3 March 1986, p.69.
12. Welzk, S. *Boom Without Jobs*, 1987. See also *International Business Week*, 26 October 1987, p.9.
13. *International Herald Tribune*, 29 May 1987, p.14.
14. *Ibid.*

6

The Crisis of Wage-Labour

The fall of money capital is a dual process. On the one hand it has implied the fall of profit and its source surplus-value. This is seen by the capitalist as a decline in the productivity of 'capital', which in fact is a fall in the productivity of *labour*. On the other hand, it implies a fall in wage-labour, which has also arisen on dual account. On the one hand it is seen as a negation of labour-power by machinery on the *technical*-productive side, while on the other hand it is a reflection of the fall in the actual wage or price of labour on the *value*-maintenance side.

In fact the duality is only apparent. The fall in the productivity of labour is a reflection of the declining profitability of enterprises as a historical process. This, in turn, has led to the intensification of the exploitation of labour by increasing the level of machinery in order to *reduce* labour's share of the product. This is considered necessary in order to raise the rate of surplus value as a means of enhancing the rate of profit of industrial enterprises. This action reduces the relative level of wages in relation to surplus value. It raises surplus labour time while reducing necessary labour time, a mechanism which is reproduced on the value side through monetary and credit movements through prices and, in this respect, monopoly pricing and currency devaluations help to reduce the share of labour power in the productive process, as we have already noted.

The above process in the end leads to the negation of wage-labour since falling productivity and falling profitability must undermine capital's capability to employ and sustain labour in the production process. Wages drop to levels which can no longer sustain, maintain and reproduce the working force as the traditional industrial production declines and de-skills the captains of industry as well as replacing them with a *financial speculative aristocracy*. These are assisted by the 'Young MBAs' (Master's of Business Administration)

engaged in programme trading on financial markets to perpetu-ate fictitious capital beyond production. The working-class is de-classed through a process of de-industrialisation, and female and child labour are brought into its place on an increasing scale in 'flexible' engagements which are temporary in character. The factory is replaced by robots and automated processes, and in places the labour force is actually 'assisted' and 'aided' to starve to death, as is happening in many Third World countries.

What is said above is in fact already apparent and has been ana-lysed, but our task here is to try to bring the threads together. We have already seen that in the case of that part of the world called the 'Third World', the introduction of capital, which sought access here as a means of combating the falling profitability of enterprises around 1880–1914, led to a brutal exploitation of the labour force. The proletarianisation of the labour force took the form of economic and non-economic means. Coercion and violence were applied together with the force of economic laws. Capital was made profit-able by the exploitation of the unpaid labour of the family which supplemented the wage of the worker. In time, the value of labour was increasingly devalued through a process of lowering the already low wage levels, forcing the working force to fall increasingly on village and family labour for its reproduction. The bottom line was soon reached with mass starvations added to by environmental destruction caused by cash cropping, fertiliser use, over-grazing, desertification and, overall, 'environmental bankruptcy.'[1]

In the developed capitalist world, the process of de-industrial-isation was increasingly leading to mass unemployment, coupled with wage cuts. The critical point was reached in the watershed period of 1973. Faced with the prospect of unemployment, the workers were forced to accept pay cuts or face actual poverty in the slums. Whereas in 1973, the median household income stood at low levels, by 1985 in the US it had dropped by another 8% in those years. In the 1960s, money wages were increasing at a gross rate of 4% a year, which after inflation rose by only 2%. During the mid- and later 1970s, pay rises were surpassed by the rate of inflation, with the result that pay increases were in fact negative. If this was in doubt, by 1986 the average worker's real wages were reported to have dropped 'back to their 1969 levels'.[2] Even the monopolies

themselves were conceding that an average US family in the mid-1980s had to accept a standard of living below that which had been achieved by their parents.[3]

The deregulation of industry and the financial system led to the illusion that there was more job creation under the 'free market' conditions that had been set in motion by monetarism. In fact, as we noted earlier, the new 'jobs' were in the service sector. In the US 25 million such 'new' jobs were created between 1970 and 1986. Between 1981 and 1982 alone, 11 million service sector jobs were said to have been created. By 1987, service sector employment provided 70% of the total employment in the US. Even then, many service sector jobs were not counted as they still lay 'buried in the figures for manufacturing employment'.[4]

What was important was that service sector jobs were poorly paid. The wage gap between the manufacturing and service sectors was as high as 11%, which was made worse by the fact that services offered shorter working hours because they were mainly part-time. Even in the engineering and data processing industries, which were assumed to offer high wages and salaries, the 'expansion' here was from a very narrow base. Thus with the service industries, the workforce was increasingly being moved into low-paying jobs with the prospect of lowering existing standards of living.

This under-valuation of labour as a global and generalised phenomenon in the capitalist, 'socialist' and Third World countries is a signal of major developments in the existing social and economic systems. The tendency towards the negation of wage-labour is manifest in the fact that it is becoming *costly* for the worker to be employed. 'Flexible employment' policies are making it difficult for the family to maintain itself on the going wage. In the US, single mother family units are on the increase with growing impoverishment. The female head of the family found that being unemployed on welfare was better than being employed. Wages were inadequate to offset the benefits of unemployment, which themselves were miserable. At a $6–7 wage per hour in employment, she could not pay for childcare while she worked. In short, in order to live and maintain her baby, it was more profitable to be idle *in poverty* than to attempt to work.

The increasing shift to female employment, apart from the free skills that women have in the 'female dexterity' in handling of minute

information products like microchips, also reflected the fall of male wage-labour. Increasingly it was becoming ever more difficult for a family to live on the wage and salary of the long applauded male 'bread-winner'. As a result, it became ever more necessary for the wife to take up employment as well, at much lower wages, for the family to survive. According to a 1986 study by the Joint Economic Committee of the US Congress, a 30-year-old male earned (in current dollars) an average of $25,253 in 1973. This average wage had dropped to only $18,763 after adjustment for inflation, which represented a 25% drop in earnings. The Committee observed as a matter of fact:

> Clearly, if only the father worked in an average young two-parent family in the 1980s, there would be a drastic decline in family income as compared to 1973.[5]

But even with the wife working, the Committee noted that the average total wages would still be 3.1% below 1973 levels. The decline would have been three times greater overall if wives had not taken up employment. The *International Business Week* further observed:

> The conclusion is unsettling: Many American families now must put two people to work to match the living standard that one person could have provided in previous decades... the average family is working harder just to stand still.[6]

An American economist noted: 'Today, you need two people working to make what is considered a middle-class standard of living.'[7] This development has forced families to sink into deep debt to supplement their survival at the very time when big corporations, and even states, particularly in the Third World, are also going into debt to maintain themselves. The systems are clearly eating themselves up in this parasitic situation, a situation that is highly exploitative of the working family and peasant communities in the world. What has been said above is also characteristic of the situation in the 'socialist' countries. The loss of the profitability of state enterprise in general leads to continuous efforts at 'reform', and the opening-up to western capitalist markets. The latter is driving these countries into deep debt with western banks, which is affecting the standards

of the working-class. Poland has been the clearest weakest link of these countries.

This explains then why in the US and UK the number of women in employment has risen by leaps and bounds. In the US for instance, the overall labour force had grown by 28% between 1973 and 1980, to more than 115 million people. Of these new 33 million jobs, three-quarters were female labourers striving to maintain single-family units or to supplement their men's devalued wages. Single women now head 16% of all households in the US on average, as compared to 12% in 1973. The percentages are much higher among oppressed racial minorities (and groups), especially among black people. Even then sex-discrimination still remains in a majority of employment avenues, producing as a gap as wide as 40% in the wages paid to men and women. The sex difference has become a major factor, which capitalism is exploiting with ever increasing zeal to preserve itself.

The above picture has produced a vicious circle of evils for the working-class. Overcrowded housing, poor health, a lack of child-care for working mothers and isolation in slums have all become barriers to a better life, as wage-labour is increasingly undermined. From unemployment a real shift to pauperism is self-evident, with 20 million people in the richest country in the world – the US – categorised as living in poverty in the 1980s. A 'floating' employed force, a demoralised unemployed force and a labour force abstaining from low-wage employment (in fact, an 'unemployable' labour force), all illustrate the high watermark of a fallen wage-labour system. The 'magnet' of unfilled jobs is no longer pulling millions into the labour force to work. In these circumstances, the observation by a US economist on this point is worth noting:

> When you have a part of the society that has been pauperised, then you have also made them unemployable.[8]

The spell of doom around wage-labour is also reflected in the parasitic efforts which monetarism has tried in order to turn workers into 'capitalists'! In Britain this move was connected with the plunder and sale of state property to private interests, which in turn were turned over to speculation on the financial markets. This is what characterised hostile take-over bids, raids and acquisitions

involving such quaint techniques as shark repellents, show stoppers, poison pills, sweetheart deals and green-mail raids. The employee share-ownership drive brought in some 8.5 million people into speculation activity from 1979 to 1986 – 20% of the British population. Twenty-five per cent of the American population were reported to be 'owners' of shares.[9] But most of these shares where in fact bought for speculative purposes and sold as soon as share prices went up. By 1987 it was becoming apparent that this was so, as Nick Goodwin's comments illustrate:

> Privatisation offers-for-sale have attracted large numbers of people who do not appear to stay in the market. They have happily stagged the issue and sold on the first day of dealings. Such are the people who have been well served.[10]

In fact the drive to get workers to become capitalists was being undermined by an even greater fraud and robbery of the working persons' pension funds; their last survival resort. Even here the process of the negation of wage-labour proceeded with equally exploitative zeal. The financial sharks found that they were making almost nothing by trying to turn midgets into capitalists, and instead they saw value in 'raiding' their pension funds, not only to earn fat fees on the transactions, but first and foremost in order to turn these funds from productive to speculative purposes. Goodwin states:

> As stock brokers are fined for not clearing unsettled bargains, they are realising that the paperwork involved in selling 500 shares for a small private client is the same as for trading five million shares for a pension fund. The profit on the latter is much higher.[11]

This latest 'raid' on pension funds is in fact the second such attack on the reserve-living-funds of labour. For a long time now pension funds have provided one of the major pillars of the so-called institutional investors in the economies of most capitalist economies. These funds had at this stage gone to industry.

With the monetarist attack on equity capital that has developed over the past eight years, pension funds have also been under pressure to de-equitise and instead 'securitise' themselves. The methods

used in this new attack have been to try to invest pension funds into fixed interest stocks in order to earn higher interest rates on money than have prevailed in the last few years. In the case of the United States, 75% of pension funds had been shifted and invested in debt stocks in this way, compared to the less than 25% that went into productive investment.

In the same way, in the case of Great Britain, pension funds have, apart from the government's gilt-edged securities, formed the foundation for the globalisation of British securities. Since the removal of the distinctions between banks, brokers and jobbers, the management of pension funds has come more and more in the hands of the new financial sharks called 'financial conglomerates' – a merger of banking, brokerage, corporate financing and jobbing or 'market-making'. This has led to the so-called 'diversified financial services fund management', which is the short-hand description of combining speculative market-making with discretionary investment management.

This development has placed these huge workers' pension funds in the hands of the speculators, who are using them to liquidate productive industries through the take-over bids which we referred to earlier. Some of these take-overs, called 'Shotgun weddings', have resulted in the use of pension funds – which on the New York Stock Exchange account for over 45% of all quoted shares – to finance the purchase of 'junk-bonds', which are relatively high-yielding stocks with a high risk. In a 'green-mail raid', the existing stockholders in an industry become the real losers and since the funds used in such transactions are in most cases pension funds, it is the pensioners who are in the final result financing the 'busting' of industries, because it is they who have to pay the premium on the redemption of the predator's share which inevitably is paid out of their funds.[12]

A further technique called 'poison pills' is being used as a defensive weapon to fight off take-over bids, with devastating consequences for the pension funds. The technique is used to issue a special class of preferred stocks which are available in the case of a hostile take-over bid through a third party acquiring more than 20% of the company stock. The manoeuvre is to make 'buy-back' rates so high that such a hostile bidder would have to pay a very high premium to acquire the company:

These defensive moves of share repurchases and poison pill tactics have enabled US companies to buy back more than a billion of equity annually, sometimes more than the amount of new shares issues on the market. Again in-house pension funds have been used to buy back existing shares within the same company.[13]

The technique has been used for the 'in-house' employee buyout of the British National Freight Consortium (NFC) into private ownership. The British government had failed to sell the state-owned consortium to the private sector. The NFC then decided to sell the company 'out' to the workers at £53.5 million. The workers of the consortium, together with the companies' pensioners, paid some £6,187,500 for 82.5% of the equity, while the government paid £47 million of the £53.5 million, which was in fact the amount due to the workers in pensions, which had been under-funded. This gigantic fraud was seen as a success story for a policy of private ownership of the company by the workers, but which was in fact the unloading of the industry from the state which wanted the workers to maintain a monopoly capitalist structure held in place with the pension funds of the workers themselves.

In the US the so-called Employee Stock Ownership Plans (ESOPs) were being hatched for the same purpose. Beginning in 1985, a number of corporations – starved of equity – were offering workers a percentage of the stock in the company, which was then eventually sold to them through a trust. In one company, the workers 'owned' 70% of the stock, but they did not have any voting rights on the board. A union official remarked:

> The company stamps its cartons with a big 'D' and 'employee-owned'. But most people realise that they don't own anything. They're just paying the bill for these big management people to own the company.[14]

This technique of using pension funds as basis for speculative investment was becoming counter-productive. In the US it was reported that the private pension system had found itself in turmoil due to the fact that many companies were taking the largest 'surplus' in their pension funds for their own use. Since these

funds were insured by the state Federal Pension Benefit Guaranty Corporation as a means of subsidising the private monopolies, pressure was mounting on the state to pay up whenever losses occurred. As a result, the insurance corporation was reported to be $4 billion in the 'red', largely because the country's 'struggling' steel and heavy-equipment manufacturers had dumped their liabilities 'on the government's doorsteps'.[15]

The guarantee corporation, which had insured the pensions of some 38 million workers through employer-paid premiums, was increasingly faced with such claims, and this was itself affecting the financial system and the 'confidence' around it:

> The nation's nest depends on voluntary private pensions. A loss of confidence in the entire system would be devastating. Policymakers should act soon to reassure workers and pensioners that their retirement benefits will be there when they expect them.[16]

Thus it was becoming patently clear that the whole monopoly capitalist system was hanging on a fallen equities market, which itself had depended to an increasing degree on pension-leveraged pension paper that had no material basis whatever. With no prospect that the industrial process would be rejuvenated to provide back-up for the workers future, there appeared to be no real 'security' for the workers.

The process of the negation of wage-labour was in fact the last straw for the capitalist system, upon which the whole process depended. The capitalist credit system depended on the availability of surplus value with no equivalent, and this in itself established the capitalists' claim on the future labour of the worker. With the process of de-industrialisation and de-materialisation which the current monetarist policies implied, no such future claim on labour was possible, for it was the capitalist system itself and its inherent contradictions that were creating the negation process, as we have seen throughout this analysis. Capitalism could not exist under the possibility that the workers could become capitalists themselves, for to do so they would need other workers to exploit in order to maintain the system. The workers could not make better capitalists than the capitalists themselves. No such prospect existed any

longer, and this signalled capitalism's demise, and the emergence of a new society in embryo: workers' self-management without capitalists and without surplus value.

Notes

1. Timberlake, L. *The Crisis in Africa*, Earthscan, London, 1985.
2. *International Business Week*, 27 April 1987, p.44.
3. *Ibid.*
4. *International Business Week*, 3 March 1986, p.69.
5. *International Business Week*, 27 April 1987, p.44.
6. *Ibid.*
7. Quoted in *ibid.*, p.44.
8. Barry Bluestone, quoted in *International Herald Tribune*, 30 September 1987.
9. *Observer*, London, 25 October 1987, p.68.
10. Nick Goodwin in *ibid.*, p.69.
11. *Observer*, 27 October 1987, p.68.
12. Tandon, V. 'Americanisation of Security Industry and Pension Funds', mimeo, London, 1986.
13. *Ibid.*, p.30–1.
14. *International Business Week*, 15 April 1985, p.54.
15. *International Business Week*, 23 February 1987, p.32.
16. *Ibid.*

7

The Making of Money Out of Speculation

We can now see that the existence of money-capital based on the industrial process of production is rapidly coming to an end. As we saw in Chapter One, unless industrial capital is able to pass through the various stages of production and circulation in which money-capital exists as money, productive, and commodity capital, it becomes immobilised. But since the capitalist production process begins as money and ends as money in expanded form, it appears that the very aim of capitalist production is *money-making*. That is why Marx observed that to the capitalist, the process of production appears as a mere unavoidable, intermediate link, a necessary 'evil' for the sake of money-making. In the end, when the capitalist is unable to produce, he tries to 'make money without the intervention of the process of production'.[1]

As this analysis has already shown, the process of capitalist production and value maintenance of money-capital arises with a monopoly. The power which finance-capital attains of making profits with increasing monopoly pricing ultimately undermines *both* production and value. At such a point, with heightened inflation that went with stagflation, both production and value seemed to come to an end. The bourgeoisie were quick to see the truth of this development and Irving Fisher noted this in the context of the early 1970s:

> Inflation seems to make business men interested in buying and selling commodities rather than manufacturing them.[2]

The capitalist is unable to produce because capital exists only as a *claim on future labour*. It exists objectively merely as money-capital.

It can in reality reproduce itself only as *new labour*. But, caught up in irreconcilable contradictions, it tries to get rid of labour in order to reproduce itself as money in the process of buying and selling. What has been happening since the mid-1970s has been the intensification of de-industrialisation, as we have seen. This has also been accompanied by the craze to buy and sell. But since no production is expanding, the buying and selling has increasingly taken the ultimate form of buying and selling money!

This development has come out sharply in the US economy, which has hitherto been regarded as the leading capitalist economy. Between 1982 and 1984, speculative capital in the form of debt grew by an enormous 14% annually, bringing the total speculative capital to an estimated $7.1 trillion at the end of 1984, rising from the $2.4 trillion recorded in 1964. Debt in general grew at an annual rate of 13% during the 10 years which ended in 1969, and by 11.1% in the following 10 years to 1979. Although it slowed slightly in

Chart 3: Nominal Gross National Product and Credit Market Debt Outstanding 1960–85 (billions of US dollars)

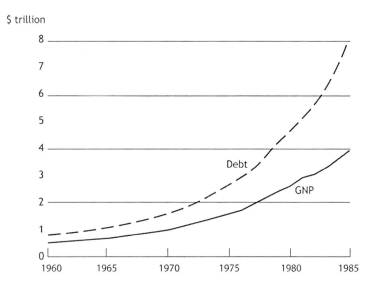

Source: Kaufman: Interest Rates, Markets and the New Financial World, p.28

1982, it began to pick up rapidly to 14% annually. The result was that the creation of debt or, in short, the making of 'money' out of money, began to distance itself with an even greater movement from material production, as reflected in gross national product (GNP) statistics.

Compared with the $7.1 trillion debt market and speculative money-capital, nominal gross national product recorded a total of only $3.7 trillion in 1984 – as Chart 3 shows – compared to the earlier period. Thus the debt market exceeded material production, as expressed in the GNP, by a ratio of 2:1. The ratio in 1974 was 1.7:1 and 1.6:1 in 1964. As we noted earlier, 1984 recorded equity-capital investment of only $2 trillion compared to speculative debt amounting to $7.1 trillion – a vast gap of $5.1 trillion![3]

These statistics and recorded figures, according to international capital's foremost expert in financial management, Henry Kaufman, greatly *underestimate* the extent of speculative capital in the form of debt. He refers to the vast 'hidden debt' for which, in his opinion, no aggregate data is available. This hidden debt is put away in credit–debt instruments such as futures, options, interest-rate swaps, currency swaps, credit guarantees by banks and insurance companies, as well as 'lines of credit'.

In addition, he refers to debt growth disguised in accounting conventions which permit the 'netting out' of assets and liabilities. This is because borrowers of credit–debt, financial intermediaries, and other debt market actors employ greater leverage of debt to capital than can be discerned from balance sheet accounting. This leveraging increases the level of liabilities to assets, which is the other side of de-capitalisation of production by money-capital. We shall return to some of these issues later.

Financial Deregulation

The drive to deregulate financial processes and institutions was in fact connected with the above developments. The drive to deregulate started in 1973 onwards out of forces emanating from the 1960s. This drive increasingly led to a monetarist demand to deregulate banking and financial institutions. The drive was also connected with the effects of the euro-dollar market and 'offshore' banking. As we also noted in Chapter Four, whereas Keynesianism emphasised

employment (and hence production) and income generated from it as being the crucial elements in determining GNP, the monetarists, who came to dominate economic policy-thinking in the US and Britain as well as in other western countries from 1979 onwards, saw the money supply as the crucial variable. It is this drive to turn the tide against *productionism* and labour that explains the deregulation of financial institutions around 1979 onwards.

Since it was asserted by the monetarists that state credit-creation was behind the burgeoning inflation and the subsequent loss of the value of money, private credit-creation by banks was seen as preferable since it was more likely to be in accord with the actual demands of the economy. This argument ignored, however, the real causes of the declining rate of enterprises' profit, which itself had led to the increasing intervention of the state in credit-creation and productive activities through its monetary and fiscal policies.

Thus deregulation of the financial system came to mean that interest rates ought to be used more to guide state credit policy, beginning with the *Treasury Accord* of October 1979. This became the practice, despite the monetarist pressure to place the emphasis on money supply. From now onwards, the interest rate structure became particularly volatile since it was used on a day-to-day basis to try to make sense of the over-expanding paper market that was claiming recognition as 'money' with a possible claim on future labour.

Monetarism had thus the effect of shortening the impact of interest rates on the economy. The growth in the 'money supply' did not respond to small changes in interest rates. The volatility reflected this pressure of monetarism to impart money's value to a growing sub-structure of private credit instruments by giving a value in the interest rate, and this was bound to have effect on long-term interest rates. This led to the development of variable interest rate financing, which responded and had an effect on new, innovative marketable securities.

This policy in turn led to the growth in a variety of private credit instruments, with a specific interest rate structure which was responsive to an aspect of the crisis of the production–credit relations and structures. Such variables as inflation, the level of interest rates, the level of commodity prices, the effects of taxes,

technology, internationalisation, and legal effects were all taken into account in working out the different credit instruments which, as we will see in Chapter Nine, ranged from such new innovations as negotiable collectible debts (CDs), floating rate obligations, euro obligations, zero coupon bonds, Government Guaranteed Marketable Assets (GGMA), mortgage appreciation securities, variable rate mortgages, financial futures, bond options, money bonds, and bonds bearing warrants *to buy additional bonds*.

Deregulation meant first and foremost the dismantling of the limits that had been imposed on the interest rate structure; under the Regulation Q legislation introduced after the 1929 money market collapse in the case of the US. These regulations had placed a ceiling of a 4–5% rate of interest on the deposits held by banks. With the advent of creeping inflation, which gave rise to continued interest rate increases to maintain the value of money, and as the interest paid on stocks and government bonds rose above the levels set by these ceilings, voices calling for deregulation were heard at the very time when monetarists were also attacking Keynesianism. This pressure to dis-intermediate deposits from banks to market-credit instruments commanding higher rates of interest led to state-supported measures to re-strengthen banks, contrary to many of the accusations of the monetarists. This was an attempt by the state to maintain 'narrow money' to avoid a crisis of 'liquidity'. But it did this by also broadening its debt.

The intervention by the US government to stem the tide of dis-intermediation to this extent took the form of raising the minimum denomination of US Treasury bills from $1,000 to $10,000. In so doing it hoped to confine the dis-intermediation of deposits into US Treasury bills only to the rich, with those depositors holding less than $1,000 being forced to keep their meagre savings in banks. This action of the government, instead of stemming the tide, in fact added fuel to the fires of dis-intermediation. The measure set in motion a new credit instrument called the *mutual fund*, which was used to *pool* small savings into large *bundles* of $10,000 which were then used to purchase US Treasury bills.

The emergence of mutual funds therefore effectively checked the role of commercial banks' participation in the 'new' savings deposits, which increasingly found their way not only in US Treasury

bills but also into other credit instruments, which began to multiply to take advantage of this movement into stock exchange paper. In this way, banks increasingly became agents for selling US Treasury paper as the US budget deficit built up through these borrowings. US government debt rose from $235 billion in 1960 to $285 billion in 1970 and $715 billion in 1980, reaching $1.5 trillion in 1985.

The removal of interest rate ceilings from small deposits was at the same time accompanied by further measures by the state, measures which added to the protection of credit market operations. Following the 1929 crash, the US government had in 1934, also under the Federal Deposit Insurance Corporation, insured deposits up to $2,500 (equivalent to about $20,000 in current terms). With deregulation, this ceiling was raised to $100,000 which had the effect of shifting US government protection of deposits from *individual* small depositors to *institutions* which, through a system of mergers, obtained *full* insurance protection for their deposits. This action gave further strength to the drive towards the private credit market, of which state fictitious capital creation was itself part. It weakened the direct link between borrower and creditor through banks, since the final risk taker was the state through the insurance mechanism.

This development is what led to the so-called *securitisation* of credit obligations. This arose because the new financial processes and institutions that arose in the wake of deregulation did not wish to be bound to particular borrowers. They preferred to 'disengage' from the link as soon as they had lent to the borrower, and this was facilitated once more by the state. In the US the institutions made their new loans available to borrowers through a 'packager', who bundled these disparate loans together into a publicly protected marketable security.

In this way a 'private' loan made by a financial institution to a private borrower was turned into a publicly or state-protected 'property'. One of these packaged marketable securities that emerged in the US was the GGMA, which was guaranteed by the US government. Banks, which were now weakened at their base by this drift of depositors, became the major agents of selling securities on behalf of clients, including corporations. This further undermined the equity base of the corporations, who also began the game of security buying and selling.

This development strengthened, instead of weakening, the role of the state in financial markets since it became the sole guarantor of all speculation. Its securities and bills rose in price as interest rates on treasury bills escalated, with a dampening effect on equity shares and other shares in the real economy. This is what explains why US Treasury bill sales increased tremendously while US corporations bonds fell, as we noted earlier. In the same way, US government and state agency-guaranteed securities had a higher valuation than those which did not have state support, unless they were very high-rated marketable securities.

These developments were already foreshadowed by the 'May Day' New York Stock Exchange reforms of 1 May 1975, which led to the abolition of fixed commission rates on US securities market operations. This step, which was already pointing toward deregulation, gave further strength to securities market dealings. This was followed by London's 'City Revolution' or the 'Big Bang' of 27 October 1986, which abolished the distinction between 'jobbers' and brokers on the London Stock Exchange as well as dismantling the minimum commission scales which had operated hitherto. A Financial Services Act was also passed through parliament which apparently passed over the powers of regulation of the financial markets to the institutions concerned. But this legislation in fact gave the minister concerned powers of authorisation of these private institutions. Thus deregulation and 'privatisation' meant the creation of new state-monopoly capitalist ventures to replace the old ones.

Technology and Finance

The rapid growth in speculative stock market paper could not have advanced without the increasing intervention of new technologies in financial markets. Indeed the second leg to deregulation and the 'Big Bang' was the rapid mechanisation of share dealing on the stock exchanges of New York, Tokyo and London. These new and sophisticated electronic dealing systems began to provide computerised information and settlement systems for the smooth operation of the exchanges.

In London, the stock exchange in 1980 developed an information distribution system, TOPIC, whose function was to carry

share price information to the subscribers of the system. It began as a data system of 300 pages, but by 1986 had grown to an incredible 5,000 pages of share price information covering, in addition to company announcements, overseas share prices, foreign exchange information, traded options and financial futures information. It also developed a computerised system, TALISMAN, which by 1986 was settling deals between stock exchange dealers each day amounting to 20–25,000 deals.

Its other service, SEAQ – Stock Exchange Automated Quotations – was intended to be inaugurated in 1986. Its main function is to provide a screen-based system able to offer up to 3,500 security prices to competing market 'makers', who would themselves be able to input their own prices from anywhere in the UK and Ireland, removing the need for a physical presence on the trading floor of the stock exchange. The most active stocks would each have at least 16 market-makers, with other large brokers and dealers prepared and able to buy and sell direct to clients if they could offer a better deal.

Due to the rapid expansion of the financial markets, London was planning the introduction of yet another electronic financial system. Called TAURUS – Transfer and AUtomated Registration of Uncertified Stocks – its function was to raise the automatic creation and registration of securities traded on the stock exchanges of the world to an even higher level. By 1989 it was expected that TAURUS would 'de-materialise' UK- and Irish-registered securities by abolishing the physical holding of share certificates as evidence of possessing a share in the credit-money market.

TAURUS would cut out further paperwork by streamlining the administration and settlement of shareholdings. Shares would be held in uncertified form in securities accounts, which would be computerised and kept with the share dealer and with centralised registration at the stock exchanges. Settlements of accounts would also be by means of computerised book entries, rather than by physical delivery of the stocks. This development shows how far removed the present credit system has become from material production, evidence of the desire by capitalists to substitute the production of goods for the 'manufacture of money'.

Globalisation of Financial Markets

We already noted the increasing internationalisation of banking side by side with the development of the euro currency and off-shore banking. The developments in the new financing techniques that have emerged over the last five years have however brought about a qualitatively different form of internationalisation, which has been correctly referred to as the 'globalisation' of financial markets.

This development has been brought about and itself affected by technological developments in the communications and financial fields, the innovative instruments in credit-creation, and the 'securitisation' that has come about with it, as well as by the deregulation of financial institutions and processes that have occurred and are continuing to occur on world scale.

This development has led, as we have just noted above, to the blurring of distinctions between traditional banking and the new kind of investment banking interested mainly in buying and selling securities. With it the depositor–borrower relationship is also fast disappearing.

The emergence of global financial markets has meant the spread throughout the world of US, European and Japanese banks in new areas to back up new operations overseas or in acquiring foreign securities, which has intensified competition between traditional banking, which is fighting to retain some of its old functions while trying at the same time to diversify in new areas, and the new investment banks. In the same game, old brokerage houses are also fighting to turn themselves into banking institutions of a new type. This is also forcing foreign governments that wish to take part in these new developments to open up their markets or 'perish'. In this way many Third World countries are being forced by this globalisation-cum-privatisation to sell their public enterprises and liberalise in order to take part in this new 'trade' of making money in secondary operations without production:

> The impetus of this revolution is coming from two principal sources: the increasing slippery nature of capital because of electronic technology, which makes information just as accessible to a trader in Paris, Tokyo or the Bahamas as it is on the Wall Street;

and financial deregulation, a worldwide trend that is old news in the United States, but which is gaining momentum in other countries.[4]

This is turning financial speculation into a 24 hour activity. Securities trading shifts from the New York and Pacific exchanges to the Tokyo exchange within three hours of the closure of the former after seven hours of trading, and in Tokyo the trading continues for another five hours before the Paris, Amsterdam, Frankfurt, Munich and London exchanges open in Europe. Here the trading continues for some seven to eight hours, before the New York exchange opens again. This round-the-clock trading enables speculators to achieve less volatile returns by diversification and thereby assures a more 'stable' money value to securities:

> Twenty-four hour trading in the major currencies makes it possible to deal on finer terms and at lower risk than would be available to anyone who shut up shop at London's closing time… A liquid 24-hour market enables customers to complete transactions at the timing and price of their choice, without having to take overnight risks on currency or interest rate movements.[5]

Such fluid trading also enables the shifting of debt paper over a relatively larger material base which, at a national level, is increasingly shrinking with the continued slide in equity investments. Thus this global equity trading is merely a technique for shifting risk rather than expanding production. This also applies to the Japanese banks which, with the slowdown in the Japanese economy in recent years and increased competition in the home banking industry, are also diversifying into speculation in overseas financial markets, and by so doing using their trade surpluses and the weak US dollar to attain ascendancy in financial markets. Table 5 shows that out of the 25 leading international banks, 10 are Japanese.

This rapid expansion in global financial markets has been accompanied by the increasing sale of paper issued by governments, especially the US government treasury bills. As already indicated, the level of state involvement in the economies of most western countries has increased, and the latest financial innovation has just fed on this rather fruitful business for speculators. This explains

Table 5: The 25 Largest Transnational Banks (1985)

Rank			Assets less contra accounts	Total deposits	Number of employees
1985	1978		(Millions of dollars)		
1	3	Citicorp, USA	167,201	104,959	81,300
2	8	Dai-Ichi Kangyo Bank, Japan	157,659	124,169	21,125
3	11	Fuji Bank, Japan	142,128	109,316	15,836
4	12	Sumitomo Bank, Japan	135,388	108,116	14,486
5	13	Mitsubishi Bank, Japan	132,939	102,421	15,075
6	5	Banque Nationale de Paris, France	123,081	101,977	59,294
7	14	Sanwa Bank, Japan	123,008	98,671	15,766
9	1	BankAmerica, USA	114,751	94,211	80,000
10	6	Credit Lyonnais, France	111,458	95,210	54,870
12	21	National Westminster, UK	104,677	93,533	92,000
13	18	Industrial Bank of Japan, Japan	102,770	89,398	5,601
14	7	Société Générale, France	97,627	82,274	44,172
15	4	Deutsche Bank, FRG	95,751	87,583	48,851
16	19	Barclays Bank, UK	94,169	79,629	105,900
17	22	Tokai Bank, Japan	90,423	73,686	13,748
18	24	Mitsui Bank, Japan	88,501	71,188	11,331
19	10	Chase Manhattan, USA	84,865	61,353	46,450
20	41	Midland Bank, UK	83,886	75,778	78,590
24	36	Bank of Tokyo, Japan	78,194	62,200	14,000
25	9	Dresdner Bank, FRG	76,403	48,163	33,098
26	25	Tajyo Kobe Bank, Japan	74,499	58,326	14,194
27	26	Manuf. Hanover Trust, USA	74,339	46,261	32,218
30	79	Hong Kong and Shangai Banking, Hong Kong	68,816	61,591	46,000
31	34	J.P. Morgan, USA	67,611	39,845	13,506
32	38	Royal Bank of Canada, Canada	67,233	61,132	36,430

Source: UNO: CTC Reporter (No. 23 1987)

Share of employees outside home country	Foreign Network (Number of entities)				Share of foreign assets
	Total	Developed market economies	Developing market economies	Centrally planned economies	
48	231	69	160	2	49
4	48	24	21	3	-
2	37	21	16	-	-
21	45	25	18	2	-
5	53	24	25	4	-
8	128	58	63	7	22
25	41	17	22	2	-
19	184	62	120	2	35
6	103	58	43	2	-
11	29	21	7	1	54
-	38	22	13	3	-
22	89	38	40	11	32
8	67	33	32	2	
27	188	82	104	2	60
4	37	19	16	2	-
2	49	22	24	3	-
39	108	41	65	2	-
9	69	45	22	2	70
64	101	44	54	3	-
-	42	34	7	1	-
3	27	14	10	3	-
11	67	38	27	2	36
76	55	24	26	5	-
32	87	38	49	-	47
13	96	39	57	-	36

why the deficits of the US government, in particular, have become such hot issues throughout the world since most of the financial speculation has involved raising funds in foreign financial markets for the US Treasury. Indeed, one of the factors that has pushed Japanese banks and brokerages into the US financial markets in Wall Street – and its transformation of the yen into an international currency – has been the selling and buying of US Treasury bills by these institutions. Trading on the Tokyo financial market in US Treasury bills has expanded rapidly. It is estimated that the daily turn-over in US state debt on the Tokyo exchange totals some $2 billion on a normal working day. In April 1987 the total sales for the month equalled $173 billion.[6]

With pressure mounting from foreign dealers to participate in the Japanese state bonds, Japan itself has been selling large amounts of government securities, and this also has contributed to the deregulation and internationalisation of Tokyo as an international financial market. Originally the Japanese Ministry of Finance operated a dual system for issuing government bonds, using a tender system for short-term bonds and a fixed syndication system for long-term bonds. The Ministry had severely limited the participation of foreign financial houses in these delays through these methods. The Ministry has now agreed to extend the tendering system in order to widen the area of foreign participation.

In Britain, the sale of British government debt in the so-called gilt-edged securities has also increased tremendously. The removal of exchange control restrictions in 1979 led to a rapid inflow of foreign funds into the London securities market. But whereas the turnover in UK ordinary shares increased from £56.1 billion in 1983 to £73.1 billion in 1984, the trade in overseas government and municipal securities increased from £219 million in 1979 to £2.1 billion in 1984. Over 4,000 of the 8,000 securities quoted on the London Stock Exchange were fixed-interest securities, most of which were government gilt-edged paper. The volume of daily sales has nearly trebled to an average of £3.5 billion.

Previously, gilt-edged securities were structured around the Bank of England's direct dealings with a half a dozen jobbing or trading firms, but dominated by just two firms – Wedd Durlacher and Akroyd & Smithers – with a combined capital of £100 million. They

sold the government gilts on to the stockbrokers who had access to the largely British-based institutional client base. This has changed with the 'Big Bang'. The Bank of England deals with 27 dual-capacity market-makers with a combined capitalisation of £600 billion, 14 of which are either American or Swiss and Canadian. These 27 dealers are committed to a *continuous* two-day market-making 'in fair or foul markets'.[7]

A limited auction system has been introduced to supplement the existing 'tap' system of issuing £1 billion short-term gilts under auction. Under the tap system the government fixes the prices but takes the unsold lots of paper back 'on the shelf', allowing the lots to trickle back onto the secondary market in blocks of varying sizes on a 'tap basis' as and when the Bank feels the market is ripe. Although this has the advantage of fixed price, it does not assure the government a regular source of cash. Now under the auction system this will change:

> Auctions will provide a full flavour and benefit to the government of greater competition among the financial intermediaries, namely lower interest costs and wider distribution of its debt.[8]

Thus although it does not have the 'luxury' of a fixed price, it nevertheless 'at least assures the Treasury the cash will be there'.

This development has not only increased the capability of the state to raise debt in the money market, it has actually made the state gilt-edged securities the 'heart of the London market'. In this way, it contributed to turning London into one of the three modern financial centres of the world, with the pound behind the US dollar and the Japanese yen.

The Futures and Options Market

This increasing globalisation of financial markets in an atmosphere of the *de-materialisation* of credit instruments would in fact be impossible without the 'back-up' provided by the futures and traded options market. Faced with unstable interest rates, which have increased the volatility of credit instruments, the futures and options market is seen as a *hedging instrument*. Likewise, faced with unstable interest rates, which have also increased the volatility

of credit instruments, the futures and options market is seen as a hedging instrument intended to facilitate risk management. These instruments are supposed to add to the liquidity of the money markets overall and to help reduce volatility and the distortion of the stock markets. But a futures market contract in fact offers nothing material or concrete. It merely *promises* to deliver or buy or sell at some distant future date a contracted commodity or credit instrument. In short, a futures and options contract sells or buys a promise *of a promise*.

As a financial innovation, a futures and options contract is convenient because it can be put together in place more quickly without the complexities of production or proprietary rights. Furthermore, the skills required to promote financial innovation of this kind is minimal. It does not require the years of experience required in proprietary contracts. Such *deskilling* of managerial capacity is made even easier with the electronic equipment available nowadays, as we have referred to above. Furthermore, futures also help to convert part of the traditional fixed interest investment into commodity-like transactions, some of which do not have the savings investment characteristics that underlie money flows into the securities market. This in fact is the same process of de-materialisation of the monetary and credit system, which also reflects itself as a process of deskilling of the productive and traditional financial managerial personnel.

The growth of *financial products* and the relative decline of commodities, according to a *Financial Times* survey, has altered the balance between market players. In turn the growth of the futures and options markets have also altered the nature of the markets' users, and it was only a matter of time before they began to exert their own clout so as to fashion the industry the way they want.[9] The biggest players in this market are big security houses and banks. They need large liquid markets in which they can trade cheaply, at any time, from any major financial centre around the world. Hence the globalisation of financial activities, which became ever more intertwined in a network of global parasitism. In the United States, there were by 1986 five index futures contracts, eight different options on cash settlement indexes, and two options on index futures, all of which traded on two exchanges. There are 20 stock index futures

which were pending approval and more than a dozen non-stock index futures which had been proposed, including a consumer price index, housing starts, additional currency and metals indexes.[10]

In London, the London International Financial Futures Exchange (LIFFE), which was opened in 1982, has rapidly expanded, particularly after the 'Big Bang', to take account of these developments. The Bang has given LIFFE a strong domestic base from which to sell its products to the rest of the world. By developing its own set of contracts, it has become relatively independent of the Chicago exchange contracts. The London Stock Exchange has also at the same time given strength to the development of the traded options market. The exchange has set up an Options Committee and Options Development to see to the development and further consolidation of this market of future credit instruments. The idea is to eventually link up the market in LIFFE to those in traded options.

Despite the tremendous growth in these hedging instruments – which appear to confirm the 'privatisation' of financial markets – the whole of this parasitic structure is dependent on the structure of state debt, as we have noted above. This merely reconfirms what has already been said concerning the increasing role of the capitalist states in the economies of these countries, and particularly the increasing deficit financing of the US government. In 1984, for instance, of the $6.1 billion transactions in US government bonds on a single day, $4.5 billion were in treasury bond futures.

The futures market in the major currencies of the world has also expanded rapidly in the US stock markets, a fact that has given the US considerable leverage in raising credit from other countries around the world. In 1984, futures markets in five major currencies other than the dollar averaged a daily volume of $2.7 billion. If the futures are combined with note issues, the daily transactions in US debt totalled $16 billion in the first half of 1985. This represented close to 80% of the cash transactions in outstanding government issues with maturities over five years. Trade in currency options alone increased 800% since 1983, the year in which they were first offered. The average daily open interest in options on government bond futures was $20 billion in 1984, compared to $5 billion in 1983, their first year of being traded.[11]

In London, the futures market was said to have become an 'integral part' of the gilt-edged paper of the state, and was also said 'in

some ways' to be 'a better reference point for price levels than the cash market'.[12] But London's own futures market was also dependent on the US Treasury bond market, as London found out through actual experience in discovering that it could not develop an international futures contract without a link with US state bonds. The link was through the Chicago Board of Trade and the Sydney Stock Exchange, with linkages to the Tokyo Exchange which too was being fungibly tied to the issue of Japanese state securities as well as a euro bond future contract, also tied to the US dollar. It is this development which, according to the *Financial Times*, will mean 'US T-bond futures are traded fungibly virtually around the clock'.[13] Such a development, it points out, will enable dealers to 'open a T-bond position in London and close it in Chicago later the same day while essentially paying only one set of transaction and margin posts'.[14]

It is this development which capitalism has undergone since its rise, a development which appears to undermine the very basis of capitalist production and its reproduction and hence one which signals its fall. The hedging against risk – Keynes's 'fourth cost of production' – based on a multiplication of credit instruments increasingly detached from the productive base only leaves the state legal tender as a possible measurement of capitalist money 'value', to which 'privatisation' leads. But this merely intensifies the capitalist crisis which must ultimately lead to the crash of international finance-capital.

The Socialist Countries and Financial Markets

The USSR and the countries of the former socialist world market have since rejoined the capitalist world with a consequent impact on the workings of the financial markets. Socialism, as we came to know it, was constructed in the Soviet Union from the 1930s. The system was based on centralised planning and centralised resource allocations. While the 'law of value' under the New Economic Policy (NEP) applied to a wide range of economic activities, Lenin emphasised that this was necessary only to revive trade and that the proletariat had to 'cautiously and gradually get an upper hand' over petty proprietorship and capitalism. This was achieved with the equalisation, over time, of the prices of commodities with their

values through the streamlining of the financial system and prices of commodities in the famous 'scissors crisis'. Increasingly, socialist planning took charge of socialist exchange in which money was nominalised in all its functions, including the function of the store of value. Its use remained because of the need for the proletariat to maintain a political alliance with small-producers operating in cooperative units, but these were increasingly being turned into state farms with the aim of creating a unified socialist exchange where money would become a voucher or a certificate for the allocation of resources, just as Marx had seen it.

This process came to an abrupt end with Nikita Khrushchev's coming into power. Khrushchev immediately denounced Stalin and initiated a debate on the need for 'economic reform'. This debate has never ended and has recently been picked up with a new vigour by Mikhail Gorbachev. Khrushchev called a conference on the law of value and the 'majority' of the participants invited to this conference had concluded that 'Stalin was wrong' in having limited the law of value in its operations. By inference the whole socialist planning system was brought into question.[15]

When the reforms were introduced both under Khrushchev and Leonid Brezhnev, profit was re-introduced as a 'regulator' in exchange and as these reforms got into difficulties there were attempts to impose further bureaucratic measures to control the operation of profit in the economy. Under Gorbachev, it is now a clear economic policy to utilise profit as a basis of the 'socialist' economy and to encourage enterprises to run their activities independently of Communist Party interference. Any enterprise that fails to make profit is now declared bankrupt and such an enterprise has the power to sack workers in such a case. New forms of wage slavery are being introduced under the so-called workers' 'collectives', under which workers are exploited in a system of *collective contracts*. Workers are paid a collective wage which they then distribute among themselves according to the work performed. This is another form of piece work which Marx exposed in his *Capital* as a system which the bourgeoisie used not only to prolong the working day and intensify the exploitation of labour, but also as a means by which they could decrease average wages.[16]

The Soviet attempt to do away with socialism and re-introduce capitalism through the back door is nowhere more well-illustrated

than in its attempt to use its gold production on the financial markets to bolster and uphold capitalist production on a global scale. Beginning in the 1960s, the Soviet Union has collaborated with western governments and banks to ease the pressure on the dollar and sterling as well as other currencies. In 1960, after the Sharpeville riots in South Africa, the London gold dealers and other financial speculators feared more political disruptions were bound to occur and since South Africa was the main gold supplier on the world market at this time, supplying three-quarters of the world's gold, the prospect of increased political unrest led to a rise in the price in gold, which in turn put pressure on the main reserve currencies. The USSR, instead of letting the crisis take its toll on the capitalist financial markets and providing supportive revolutionary strength to the people of Azania, counteracted the fall in the value of currencies by releasing its own gold to 'calm the markets'. This quietened the markets, at least for a period.[17] Similarly in 1965 when the 'gold pool', which had been constituted to relieve pressure on the dollar and sterling, dried up, the USSR obliged the capitalist markets by pouring in $550 million in gold. Fred Hirsch, the former editor of *The Economist*, observed:

> Without the Russian sales of the mid-1960s, which were needed to pay for the huge imports of North American grain to make up for the calamitous failure of Krushchev's agricultural policy, gold reserves in western official hands would have fallen. And on at least two occasions (autumn and again two years later) the prospect of these sales came at a critical time when private gold speculation might otherwise have burst out of control. In this sense the prospective breakdown of [the] monetary system of the capitalist West was averted by the actual breakdown of the farming system of the communist East.[18]

Thus the combined effect of both economic mismanagement and the need to reinforce the world capitalist market, into which the USSR wanted to re-enter, necessitated this new Soviet gold policy on international money-capital markets. Because of this new development in the Soviet revision of socialism, the capitalist system on world scale was given an additional lease of life. As Susan Strange has noted:

And even the Soviet Union in the late 1960s could no longer be sure that an epidemic economic depression in the capitalist world, whether followed or not by widespread revolution, would be to its political advantage.[19]

This means that, from an economic aspect, the Soviet Union turned politically counter-revolutionary. The economic aspect in Soviet gold policy also came out clearly in the events connected with the Cuban crisis. In 1962, the Cuban missile crisis created a 'war scare', with a consequent rise in the price of gold. Here the Soviet Union cashed in on the price rise, selling its own gold stock to make a 'quick kill' of a few million dollars on the financial markets. It chose to sell $50 million of its gold in one go, and in the opinion of Fred Hirsch this was the reason why the 'war scare' was so 'easily repulsed'. He adds:

> It is doubtful that Khrushchev took time off to order this (sale) as part of his deal with Kennedy; more likely the sharp-eyed Russian gold managers merely took advantage of the gold price of $35,18.[20]

It is this policy of combined political opportunism and economic advantage that has made Soviet gold production a top official secret to the public but one not so secret to its collaborators, who have since the mid-1950s handled around $450–600 million of its gold sales in the western financial markets. This also explains the now well-known collaboration between the USSR and the South African De Beers and Anglo-American conglomerates in the shape of a cartel managing world diamond and gold sales.[21]

The present reforms in the USSR aim particularly at encouraging the investment of western capitalist ventures in the USSR through joint ventures in which profits are shared. Many Soviet monopolies are also being encouraged to invest in other countries in joint ventures and tripartite arrangements with a view to sharing profits. This in turn has made it ever more necessary for the Soviet ruble to be made internationally convertible, so that it too can be 'marketed' and speculated on international exchanges and Soviet paper sold on these exchanges. In order to 'qualify' to enter these markets, it has already begun its own financial deregulation, which will enable

Soviet banks and new financial houses to set up financial markets in Moscow for raising debts for Soviet industry. It is also a well-known fact that many Eastern European countries are now deeply indebted to western banks, a factor that has fuelled the crises in their economies. China and Hungary have already set up stock exchanges and these developments are bound to intensify the crises of international financial markets. It will also increase the political opportunism of these former socialist states, who will abandon their role as a support base to national liberation movements and working-class struggles throughout the world. Today, they are more interested in business than in revolutions.

Notes

1. Marx, K. *Capital*, vol. 2, pp.51–2.
2. Friedman, I.S. *Inflation: A World-Wide Disaster*, Hamilton Hamish, London, 1979, p.149.
3. Kaufman, H. *Interest Rates, the Markets and the New Financial World*, Taurus, New York, 1986, pp.35–6 and p.63.
4. *International Herald Tribune*, 3 April 1987.
5. *Financial Times*, 27 October 1986, p.26.
6. *International Herald Tribune*, 22 June 1987, p.9.
7. *International Herald Tribune*, 14 May 1987, p.12.
8. *Ibid*.
9. *Financial Times*, 19 March 1987.
10. Kaufman, H. *op. cit.*, p.107.
11. Kaufman, H. *op. cit.*, p.41.
12. *Financial Times*, 19 March 1987, p.10.
13. *Ibid*.
14. *Ibid*.
15. Nove, A. *Soviet Economy*, George Allen Ellwin, London, 1986, pp.305–6.
16. Marx, K. *Capital*, vol. 1, Progress Publishers, Moscow, 1977, pp.516–23.
17. Strange, S. *International Economic Relations of the Western World 1959*, Vol. 2: International Monetary Relations, RIIA, 1976, pp.73–7.
18. Hirsch, F. *Money International*, Penguin, London, 1969, p.26.
19. Strange, S. *op. cit.*, p.300.
20. Hirsch, F. *op. cit.*, p.299.
21. *The Financial Gazette*, Harare, 22 November 1985.

8

The Crash of Financial Markets

We can see that what has been discussed and analysed in the previous chapters is a very fragile system of economic and social relationships on a global scale. The volatility of the financial markets is not the cause of this fragile situation. It merely reflects the contradictions of capitalist production as it has evolved over the last two hundred years. It is this historical evolution that has brought about these recent developments. The recent build-up in financial instruments merely adds to the fragility of the system and intensifies the crisis. The futures and optional contracts, upon which the financial structure is now balanced, themselves add to the volatility of the system, although they are supposed to alleviate its problems. In the words of Kaufman:

> While their purpose presumably is to reduce risk, not all trans-
> actions are perfect hedges and not all arbitrages work as antici-
> pated. This type of volatility tends to enlarge asset and liability
> positions and. thus increases the need for improved risk-control
> management.[1]

This clearly is a new vicious circle, for such improved risk management is itself undermined by new credit hybrids intended to help control further risks! It is this financial 'groping in the dark' which has led to 'new' theories about stock management by stock 'technicians'. An 'Elliot Wave Theory' has been advanced which tries to predict the behaviour of stock prices and interest rates along certain 'waves', while other technicians have been devising a 'sentiment measurement' scale and other 'internal market dynamics' to deal with the volatility. But these gimmicks cannot help arrest the 'gyrations' of the markets, because they emanate from *deeper causes* within the productive system.

The financial markets have become increasingly nervous with political developments and economic data reports. The reported illness of the US president and his political discomforts lead to immediate reaction on stock exchanges throughout the world. It was this which led to the regular occurrence of the so-called 'triple witching days' which crop up every quarter when stock holders try to 'square their positions'. These are days when stock index futures expire and options with options on the underlying shares also 'take positions'. These options, as we noted before, have shrunk in size with the decline in equity shares. There are also 'random days' when a sudden change in investment mood or the release of surprising news (economic or political) cause violent market movements.

These 'random days' have occurred on at least two occasions, if we leave out the 'Black Monday' crash and the developments connected with the 'October Crack'.

On 11 and 12 September 1986 and again on 23 January 1987, reports of frenzied trading and plunging market prices, which ostensibly were triggered off by computers with minimal human involvement, caused tremendous alarm among politicians and the financial oligarchy around what could happen if such events were to lead to the total collapse of the financial system. In January, the Dow Jones average had dropped by more than 114 points in little more than one hour, which was considered spectacular in the circumstances and was seen as likely to lead to more state regulation of financial markets.

The response to the triple witching days is looked at in terms of the need to have *more* trading time so that the markets may be able to 'cope' with the pressures of index adjustment, since the volumes of traded paper increase with such expirations. This must add more volatility and more sensitivity to the whole financial credit structure, leading to the real possibility of a crash.

This volatility of course reflected the shrinking economic base of most capitalist states, including economic satellites in the Third World, not to speak of the crisis faced by the so-called socialist world. The huge global financial activity based on the 'securitisation of assets' also reflected most of all this process of de-capitalisation that had been under way. The crisis was beginning to touch the very structures and institutions said to be aimed at

reviving the system for a 'private' productive new era. The strains in these new financial institutions began to show in one of the major American investment banks on Wall Street, that of Salomon Brothers. In an 18 October 1987 report carried in the British paper *The Sunday Times*, a day before Black Monday, it was revealed that this huge financial house had decided to fold up and reduce its staff in London due to the high cost of operations. This firm, which had grown from a brokerage to an investment bank, had between 1982 and 1987 tripled its staff to 6,500, growing by 40% in 1986 alone. It had done this, in the words of the paper, at a time 'when bankers could make money merely by holding securities and watching them appreciate [in value]', between 1982 and 1986.[2]

But by mid-1986, the 'raging bull market' began to slow down, and with it the 'delusions of grandeur' which capitalism had begun to see as reality began to set in. Salomon's brisk profits on its global operations, despite 'buoyant revenues', fell from 23% in 1983 to 16% in 1986 in the same year that its operations were growing 40%. The expansion was taking place on a narrow profitable base. Salomon's own 'equity' share prices fell from $59 in April 1986 to $30 in September 1987. All this was happening in an atmosphere of pessimism on Wall Street, which had been the leader in unleashing new financial wealth over the previous five years.

The Friday before Black Monday, the Dow Jones average had slumped 198.36 points in what was regarded as 'unprecedented' for a single day. The activity was also said to be the 'finale of a shattering week' that had seen three consecutive days of heavy stock-selling resulting in the index of 235 points.[3] This drop was severe even when compared to the 'peak' of the index in August 1987, a development that had convinced 'many that the bull market was over'.[4]

The October Crash

Indeed, the crash was on time. On 19 October 1987, Black Monday, the stock market came tumbling down under the weight of value-less paper. Within a few hours, $500 billion 'worth' of various papers were wiped off the values of the stocks and shares on the New York Stock Exchange alone. The Dow Jones 30-stock average index lost 508 points, 23% of its value, on a volume of 604.3 million shares in

six and a half hours 'of pure fear'. This marked the end of a phase began five years before of pure speculation, which had weighed industry down. In this phase, according to the *International Business Week*, 'Investors, seeking ever-higher returns, bought paper backed by paper backed by paper', creating a new financial 'wealth' for the few amounting to some $2 trillion.[5]

This slump on Black Monday added to the earlier 'loss' suffered between August and October. On 25 August 1987, the Dow Jones average had peaked at 2722.42 and at the closing bell on 19 October 1987, a total of $1 trillion of equity value had been wiped off the exchange.[6] Half of this amount, as we have seen, went down in a few hours during Black Monday. Thus between August 1982, when the bull market began, and August 1987, when it 'peaked', the value of equity holdings had tripled to $3.3 trillion, creating $2 trillion of new 'wealth'.

Panic erupted and spread to the other stock markets, since the new financial world was an interlinked, globalised market working 24 hours a day. The panic in the US had led to the storming of brokerage offices, fistfights in trading pits, and reported shootings and suicides. Telephones of investment banks and brokerages had jammed, and many computer terminals had gone dead as they could not unravel the confused instructions to sell and buy, sometimes the same stocks over and over.

Now the panic spread to Tokyo, which was the next exchange to trade. Here, within a few hours of the closing of the New York exchange, share prices dropped by an 'unprecedented' 14%, wiping out $400 billion in 'capital'. In Sydney, where the theatre now shifted, shares dropped a clean 25% 'before staging a modest comeback'. In Hong Kong, where shares had already fallen because of the fear that the US dollar would weaken once more before the New York crash, the exchange 'simply shut its doors'.[7] The chaos now spread to Europe, which had been asleep only a few hours before. London lost $170 billion on the Tuesday morning. The Financial Times Stock Index (FTSE) dropped by 250 points on the Monday alone. By the weekend, it had dropped a total of 507 points, wiping off 22% of the value of stocks. In Tokyo, the Dow Jones and the Japanese index Nikkei had on the Monday risen and fallen 'in a dutiful minuet'.[8] The index dropped 15% at first and then lost an

additional 5.2% within the day. With this 'minuet', Japanese investors became 'very anxious' about the New York market and the US
economy.[9]

In Hong Kong, where the exchange had closed on the official
explanation that the closure was intended to 'protect investors',
there were accusations that the exchange chairman was doing this to
shield his friends and relatives. When the exchange opened a week
later, 'pandemonium erupted', with angry investors 'besieging' the
market. Those whom the chairman was accused of shielding were
reported to have borrowed to buy stocks before Black Monday and
were said to have been over-extended financially. With this mood
in Hong Kong, investors 'rushing to meet margin calls at home,
[called in] their money from neighbouring market[s] – worsening
crashes in Taiwan and Singapore'.[10]

As the week ended and investors tried to pick up the pieces, a
Black Monday Part II erupted a week later in New York. On the
New York exchange the Dow Jones took another dive of 157 points,
which represented an 8% value loss. This was on 26 October and
it dashed the renewed hopes arising from the slight improvement
seen during a week of stock market recovery. Every one looked
bleak, suffering under the widening 'two deficits' of the trade
account and the state budget. Outsiders concentrated their attention on the budget deficit, as if it was this deficit that had 'caused'
the crash. We will return to this point later.

Black Monday II had another lesson. During the previous week's
crash, fingers had been pointed at the computers as having 'started'
the panic. It was noted that, at least as far as New York was concerned, electronic trading had accounted for 30% of the value that
had been wiped out on the exchanges. But with Black Monday II,
there was no such connection to the computer panic. In fact, hidden
behind this new 'invisible hand' was a yet bigger and more fundamental issue, which this new electronic civilisation had sought
to solve. Unlike the old use to which the computer had been put
of carrying out electronically what was done manually, the device
of the new 'invisible hand' had sought not only to save effort in
manual activity, but to *replace money*. This was why attention was
focused on computers.

This new 'invisible hand' manoeuvre was achieved through
the so-called 'dynamic hedging' or 'portfolio insurance' which the

computers or programme trading were supposed to imitate. The real matter at issue was the creation of a 'value' back-up to the valueless trading of paper on the stock exchanges. Before this, back-up was provided by the commodities market, but this market had also been de-materialised by a long historical process of 'forward trading' and 'futures' markets, which were supposed to be linked to the real production of value. As the gap between fictitious capital and material production widened, the gap was replaced by a 'promise to deliver' as the basis of the new paper that was increasingly churned out on the exchanges. The new 'dynamic hedging' was intended to overcome the problem of value maintenance without the need for full material backing.

The 'hedge' was done by establishing a 'portfolio insurance', which was a form of arbitrage. In existing circumstances, it was an 'index arbitrage'. Both these strategies involved computer programming, as we have seen. The new programmes thus *combined* share dealing, which is enabled by the centralised computer systems at the stock exchanges, and futures trading, which has its own centralised computer trading in the major commodities and futures markets. What the new system of 'insurance' and 'hedging' does is to *rapidly* buy and sell *contracts* to deliver a package of stocks included in an index. This index is normally the Chicago Standard and Poor's 500, and the contracts are 'sold' *at a fixed price* with a promise to deliver at some future date.

In fact, this is a fictitious manoeuvre because there is no intention to deliver such stocks. Instead the portfolio 'insurers' later buy and sell the same contracts that cancel the obligations! As to the insurance part, no insurance policies are issued, nor are premiums paid by these money managers to protect the investments. All that is done is to 'guarantee' their clients that if the stock markets *fall*, they will *not lose any money over a period of time*, and that should they rise the clients will capture 'a good share' of any such market rise! All this is not based on any material security or collateral, as it is called in law. It is merely based on the *hope* that things will operate normally and shares will remain fairly well within the arbitrage margins of pluses and minuses.

Thus index arbitrage is an attempt to assure investors of the solidity of the 'value' behind their shares. This is basically enabled

by the *simultaneous* buying and selling of the same investments. The computer programmes merely take advantage of the momentary price discrepancies in the markets. To achieve this, computers do the monitoring of *both* the value of the 500 Standard and Poor stock index and the price of the future contracts *based on the index*. The two transactions move in unison, but there is always a discrepancy arising from the difference in yields on stocks and other investments. At the pre-Black Monday levels of interest rates, futures prices were normally slightly higher than stock prices. The arbitrage insurer could then make a profit on this transaction and invest it in US Treasury bills and still be comfortable with the transactions. Thus the whole thing in the final analysis depends on the backing the insurance receives from state debt. This must consolidate the lie in the minds of the bourgeoisie that it is the state which gives value to money, despite the fact that this is said to be taking place under 'private enterprise' brought about by deregulation and 'privatisation'.

Behind the Crash

The Black Monday crash has given vent to numberless 'explanations' as to what caused the crash, as can be seen from the above accusation against computers. Other accusing fingers have been raised at such phenomena as deficits and the high levels of interest rates. Those who argue that it was the high interest rates that were behind the crash assert that the movement towards these rates was an indication that inflation was creeping back into the economy, which was a danger to the value of stocks. But this archaic argument ignores the fact that high interest rates were always assumed to be connected with high monetary values. Moreover, the deregulation that has taken place aimed at doing away with state ceilings on interest rates, as we have seen.

Those who argue that it was the deficits which 'caused' the crash also forgot that it was the same budget deficit that explained why interest rates were high in the first place, which also explained why foreigners would buy US equity shares to make the US the world's biggest debtor nation. US corporations were able to raise increasing amounts of capital in foreign markets while very much unaffected by the fact that US trade and budget deficits were increasing at the

same time. The amount of euro bonds issued by US corporations has increased from the $7 billion issued in 1983 to the $35.1 billion issued in the third quarter of 1986. The deficit also did not affect the ease with which US corporations were able to 'swap' their foreign-raised money from one currency to another. In 1986, US corporations issued about $1 billion in equities overseas (outside Europe), compared to $28 billion in 1984. American Express was able, in the same year, to raise and swap 20 billion yen into $109 million, which were then swapped into eight different currencies.

The fall in the value of the dollar could also not be seen as contributing to the crash in any direct way. This is because the very depreciation of the dollar was decided on as a means towards the narrowing of the US trade deficit. US exports did not necessarily rise nor did foreign imports decline measurably. Moreover, the very fact that the US dollar depreciated made US dollar investments in foreign currencies very attractive for speculators. While the bull market allowed many Americans to reap high profits on the American exchanges, it was those Americans who invested in foreign currencies who made the greater gains. About 40% of the returns made on these investments were accounted for by the low level of the dollar.[11] These speculative activities tended, if anything, to strengthen the dollar, which was detested by the US Treasury.

Some insights of the real cause and factors underlying the crash have also been advanced by a section of financial journals. For instance, in a special issue of *International Business Week* of September 1985, a number of factors were mentioned. Some of the elements mentioned include the fact that the system had moved into the speculative use of debt and other forms of leverage which had burdened and under-capitalised the financial system. The other element raised was Reagan's deregulation drive, which had undermined government control over credit-creation. This allowed many 'upstarts' to enter the financial field and heighten its speculative activities. This new situation had improved the access of capital to those who did not deserve it and at the same time shifted the risk from those who didn't want to bear it to those who did, at least in theory. The globalisation of financial markets was also seen as a factor in the over-expansion of the 'casino society', as well as arbitrage hedging. A survey conducted by a magazine *Futures* revealed that

90% of all institutional investors in futures and options contracts were doing so for speculative purposes only. It concluded:

> As a result, huge sums of capital are sloshing around the globe now in ways that even the new scientists don't comprehend. And despite a long stretch of fabulous profitability, the [Wall] Street's capital has expanded far less robustly than the markets it must support.[12]

This gives a glimpse of fundamental factors like the fall in the profitability of productive capital against the raising of financial capital or money, which is a problem we have been tracing in the analysis in this work. But looked at in this way, it does not explain why this occurred at this very moment, since the authors of this article look at this as a bad 'omen' for the capitalist system.

Another factor mentioned in the article is the fact that the authors find the fault to be lying not in speculation *per se* but in the inadequacy of, what they call, 'genuine liquidity'. They want the state to demand stiffer capital requirements for dealers and stricter margin rules for their customers. This, they argue, would put 'more real money under all those mountains of IOUs'. This is why they blame the 'options insurers' for having spread their activities too thin. 'The spreads between the value of stock-index futures and options contracts and the value of the underlying securities widened to the point of theoretical absurdity [under the new financial regime]', they point out.

Indeed, all the elements mentioned above as contributory factors to the crash are important to note. The two concerning profitability and the lack of liquidity are more important to examine in the context of this analysis. They confirm Marx's analysis of the concept of money and credit. In fact, they go to expose the one-sided function of money and credit in the capitalist system upheld by bourgeois theoreticians. This analysis has always overlooked the fundamental importance of money-capital in the operations of the system. Specifically, they tried to obscure what lay behind money's role as an element in the exploitation of labour. Credit could only function in its role as a means of payment so long as the productive system was seen to be continuous, and so long as labour could be made to produce. Any interruption or fear of interruption was enough

to make the holders of money-credit paper run on banks to collect *real money* in place of the various credit instruments being held by the capitalists. Speculation is endemic to capitalism and credit-creation, but this in itself cannot explain a crash. It merely intensifies the crash at critical moments. What really explains the crash is the fact that the bulk of the 'wealth' created on the exchange has no material equivalence in the form of material wealth. This means that the capitalists were making money not out material production, which satisfies people's needs, but out of money itself.

With deregulation and the new innovations brought into the financial dictionary in the last five years – as a development intended to 'free' monetary activity from 'big government' – it became possible under the de-capitalisation of industry to try to further substitute old credit instruments for newer devices. This accounts for the emergence of technological innovations such as computerised options insurance, which was supposed to provide security and liquidity to the system.

But with the thinning of the productive process such security has hung in the air. Thus the demands of a new financial system to be free to make more credit money without production, and the demand that such credit-creation be 'backed' by fresh security and liquidity (itself no more than computerised programming), have built up into a crisis situation. What was behind this drive was the craving to accumulate money, the very purpose of capitalism. The response by the Federal Reserve Board and other central banks to 'inject in' more liquidity after the crash merely assuaged the demand for real money. But what was injected was not real money but merely more credit money created by the state, hence the continued nervousness.

If anything the injection merely added to the credit pyramid, which became more complex and more shaky in awaiting another crisis. Half of what had been built up in the last five years as new 'wealth' was wiped out in just a few days. Yet the craving to make more money before the next crisis did not diminish. Marx was right when he said of that the mantra of the bourgeoisie – 'Accumulate, accumulate, accumulate' – was the law of capitalist existence. But now the accumulation of social wealth cannot be assured as it is undermined by the very mechanism of fictitious capital. Wealth

conservation now is of paramount importance and is critical to future accumulation.

For this reason it cannot be said, as has been argued in some quarters, that the craving to make and accumulate money is a 'disease' like alcoholism. This 'argument', put forward in a recent newspaper article, goes to expose further the shallowness of bourgeois thought:

> How much money is enough? How can people who earn more than $1 million a year need money so badly that they are prepared to break laws to get even more? There are obvious reasons: a craving for power, to name one. But what most of us overlook is the fact that some people actually get 'high' and 'hooked' on money in the same way that others become addicted to alcohol, cocaine and other drugs. An injection of money can make people feel instantly secure, victorious, strong, loved, proud and sexually attractive. Money becomes the antidote to a feeling of insufficiency.[13]

The author then goes on to argue the necessity of accepting that those addicted to money should be categorised as having a disease – a kind of *moneholism* – because to do so would help cure the malady, just as accepting alcoholism as a disease has helped addicts to face their problem. This, according to the author, has led to a reduction of the problems of alcoholism.

This trivialising of reality has to be faced. Capitalism generates an economic environment which compels people, on the pain of becoming workers or peasants, to accumulate. It is a 'healthy' capitalist pre-occupation to accumulate, and such activity includes the need to speculate, to destroy other people's livelihoods and to steal other people's labour and wealth. The bourgeois state itself is at the centre of this activity, and if it was a question of merely calling people *moneholic*, the bourgeois state would be the first to deserve the 'disease'.

The analysis has shown that such activity is, nevertheless, not an endless economic activity. We can see that accumulation is possible so long as surplus value is being produced, and this is the very basis of accumulation. But accumulation has to take place in a money form whose value is assumed to be that of commodity-

money. This though cannot be maintained at a such a level in any of the money-credit instruments necessary for the maintenance of the credit system (and without which capitalism cannot function). Thus capitalism has to strike a deal – as it were – between accumulating gold and accumulating value in the form of book-keeping units of account called money. The capitalist opts for the latter, for in fact he has no choice in the matter since it is a historical process he has to accept. He does this on the understanding, however, that from time to time, he can convert some of these credit units into real money, hopefully, just before the next crisis comes round the corner. This becomes the craze for all capitalists, a craze that, in fact, represents the *central contradiction* of capitalism undermining capitalist production.

To this extent gold acts as the pivot of the monetary and credit system, including banking. It plays the role of money as a store of value. Under it, this is maintained but with the modification that gold will not be adequate to meet the demands of all wealth holders. Those who are very wealthy and 'lucky' accumulate most of their loot in jewellery, gold, silver, platinum and any other form of commodity considered 'valuable'.

The less wealthy and unlucky capitalists have to content themselves with holding credit paper, including state credit paper. Thus gold becomes negated as money because it is in fact not adequate to hold *all private wealth*. Credit is also partially undermined to the extent that it has to act as an instrument of accumulation of private wealth, but since with the inadequacy of profit no such value can actually be accumulated and hoarded, those who hold credit paper have nothing in their hands. Those who have managed to hoard their wealth in gold also suffer the same fate since their gold no longer represents any *future claim on labour* because the gold they hold cannot be reproduced in the form of commodities with which to exchange it. Gold thus becomes a barren hoard which cannot renew itself. It becomes a simple commodity that can be used on public buildings and street pillars of the future, as Lenin once remarked.

In the meantime, those who believed that their investment in state bills would be safe are also presented with a clean bill of 'nil' commodities which no state paper can produce. State credit and

private credit thus collapse, though not because of being *too little* like gold, but *too much*. Credit remains a viable instrument so long as it is divorced from the rate of profit and interest. It is no longer money-credit, but a means of issuing vouchers for the needs of individuals on the basis of disposable time, rather than labour-time.

A Science of Chaos?

The sensitivity and volatility of the financial markets have created a doomsday feeling among financiers and speculators about the capitalist system. There is nothing to assure them that the vast financial wealth which they have created can be sustained and maintained in a stable environment. Besieged as they are by a wave of violence around the most of the world – especially in the Third World, whose material production upholds most of the financial papers – they begin to see *disorder* and *chaos* as a natural phenomenon. The old, uni-linear sciences of progress are giving way to a sense of non-direction and non-vision.

It is this atmosphere that has given rise to a new 'science' of chaos, which has been hailed as one of the three major scientific 'breakthroughs' of the 20th century beside the quantum and relativity theories![14] Bourgeois scientists now assert a total loss of faith in predictability: 'No matter how much we know, how powerful our computers, and how sophisticated our models, much about the world remain unpredictable and chaotic.'[15] This is the conclusion from the natural sciences.

But it appears that desperation affects the social sciences as well. Since no economic and political theory can explain much of what is happening in the world's economy and politics, even here the belief that chaotic behaviour is the norm is beginning to gain ground. Recent financial market disruptions have also added to this mood:

> Economists are beginning to apply the techniques of chaos theory to the especially intricate and self-conscious brand of disorder displayed in financial markets. After the explosive movements of the last month, some researchers believe that chaos theory may be particularly appropriate to the stock market, notorious for creating trends and then violently defying them.[16]

153

As applied to economics and financial management, the science of chaos would try to seek and search for 'underlying patterns' of a kind that have been discovered in a variety of seemingly random systems. These 'non-linear dynamics' would then try to make sense of these random occurrences, such as those connected with the effects of budget deficits and price movements, establishing new rules to guide action on the stock exchanges.

Such a development in fact shows that the end of capitalism is historically in sight. A science of chaos is tantamount to an admission of the senility of the system. A 'science' of chaos is a non-model and begins by admitting the failure of all models which have hitherto appeared to work. Chaos as a 'science' is, therefore, only capable of producing a non-theory and a non-model. No system can sustain itself in such a situation. It must collapse and with it a new society must emerge, a global community, based on human solidarity and not for profit, a society in which exploitation and class divisions are abolished.

Notes

1. Kaufman, H. *Interest Rates, the Markets and the New Financial World, Taurus,* New York, 1986, op. cit., p.41.
2. *Sunday Times,* 18 October 1987, p.83.
3. *Ibid.*
4. *International Business Week,* 2 November 1987, p.28.
5. *Ibid.,* p.22.
6. *Ibid.,* p.25.
7. *Ibid.,* p.34.
8. *Newsweek,* 2 November 1987, p.25.
9. *Ibid.*
10. *Ibid.*
11. *International Herald Tribune,* 25 November 1987.
12. *Fortune Magazine,* 21 December 1987, p.124.
13. *Ibid.*
14. *Ibid.,* p.126.
15. *Ibid.*
16. *International Herald Tribune,* 23 November 1987.

9

The Crisis of the International System and the Third World

The analysis of the preceding chapters has revealed the internationality of finance-capital and its ramifications all over the entire globe. These ramifications are nowhere more blatantly felt than in that part called the 'Third World'. The detractors of Marx's theory of capitalist exploitation – including their modern variants, the 'neo-Marxists' – have argued that Marxist 'orthodox' categories of analysis cannot explain today's social relations, particularly when it comes to 'social formations', in which 'pre-capitalist' elements still dominate. To some extent Rosa Luxemburg lent credibility to these attacks when she tried to trace the sources of capitalist surplus value realisation as lying in these 'non-capitalist markets'.[1] Marx for his part was forthright in pointing out that capitalism right from the beginning emerged as a world system. He had declared:

> No matter whether commodities are the output of production based on slavery, of peasants... or of communes... of state enterprises... or of half-savage hunting tribes, etc, as commodities and money they come face to face with the money and commodities in which the industrial capital presents itself and enter as much into its circuit as that of the surplus value borne in the commodity-capital, provided the surplus value is spent as revenue; hence they enter into both branches of circulation of commodity-capital. The character of the process of production from which they originate is immaterial.[2]

Thus it is from this theoretical framework and that which was provided by Lenin on *Imperialism: The Highest Stage of Capitalism* that we can comprehend the mechanisms of exploitation of finance-capital in its international operations in the Third World.

Indeed, what has been presented in this book up to this stage has presupposed all economic activities in the Third World countries upon which they depend. We say depend because these relations, institutions and structures upon which international finance-capital is sustained could never have been built up nor nurtured without the labour and other material resources of these countries. The colonialisation process, which still continues to exist on the African continent in South Africa, Azania and Namibia was, and still is, very much at the base of the mechanisms of international finance-capital controlled from the main centres of monopoly capital. The initial political struggles of the peoples of the Third World that led to the political independence of most of these countries have not interfered in any material way with these relations and mechanisms of exploitation. On the contrary, the crisis that faces imperialism has made the international financiers intensify these exploitative relations and mechanisms.

Neo-Colonialism and the Crisis of Finance-Capital

The struggle of the people of the countries of the Third World, which aimed at putting a stop to finance-capital's exploitation while working towards the hopes they entertained for their development, were, however, soon dashed because within these social relations that finance-capital had established on a global scale was the transformation of the social structure of these societies. This transformation had given strength to the new agent forces created to service finance-capital. These social forces were the comprador bourgeoisie. The forces that could have been described as 'national' bourgeois were overwhelmed not only by the continued relations of domination and mechanisms of exploitation but also by these comprador agent forces that fattened themselves on the proceeds of the exploitation. These proceeds – super surplus value and super-profits – which were created within their countries were used not for the development of the societies away from finance-capital, but for the aim of reinforcing finance-capital's exploitation on a global scale, and this is what weakened genuine efforts by a number of Third World countries to create a national economy within the ambit of the existing international system. It turned out that no room existed for such attempts and these efforts were turned to good account by

international finance-capital. Those who have attempted to obscure these mechanisms of imperialist domination by over-emphasising and over-dramatising the role of 'national', 'domestic' or 'merchant' capital in the African situation in particular and the Third World in general have only themselves to blame.[3]

To be sure, the very economic development 'plans' which many Third World countries worked out to 'develop' their economies were shaped within the theoretical frameworks of 'modernisation', which meant modernisation along western-cum-'socialist' lines. Many of them were based on IMF and World Bank projections of economic resources.[4] These 'plans' in fact never envisaged 'national' resources as being the basis of such 'development'. They took as their starting point the need to 'attract' foreign 'investment', as if international finance-capital required such gimmicks; its very existence was based on such investment! As a result, the 'plans' came to represent no more than projects worked out with the IMF and World Bank to 'solicit' foreign loans, grants and aid.[5]

Nevertheless, all these 'development plans' reflected the democratic pressures of the peoples in Third World countries for advancement and the need to tackle the problems of poverty and deprivation which history and colonialisation had brought about. Rapid industrialisation and the expansion of manufacturing, together with agricultural development, were a recurrent feature of such programmatic projections. This led governments to adopt import-substitution strategies which, at first, were assumed to lead to integrated agricultural–industrial complexes with 'backward and forward linkages'. These were assumed to lead to a modernised rural life with monetised rural production and a developed small-scale sector, a sector which could service not only rural areas but also the urban economy (given that many local entrepreneurs were unable to raise the large amounts working capital needed to engage in relatively large-scale manufacturing or semi-processing). Many of these 'plans' also looked upon the 'diversification' of an economy as being vital. They assumed that this would make the agricultural sector, which was dominant, not only the 'fulcrum' of rural development, but also the basis of employment creation, income generation and enlargement. They were also seen as the basis of social and cultural development, which would have given

rise to broad democratisation and the participation of the popula-tion in the development of human and material resources.

All these 'progressive' objectives of 'modernisation' came to nothing however, not because the leaders were hypocrites and corrupt (although many of them were and this added to the prob-lem!), but because the achievement of these objectives would have complicated the adjustment *mechanisms* which international finance-capital was in the process of devising to *minimise* the recur-rent crises in the economies of the industrial imperialist economies. These adjustments were under way, beginning in the mid-1960s as we have already noted in the previous chapters. The strategies of development devised by Third World countries under the direc-tion of the World Bank to bring about the industrialisation of their economies based on import-substitution turned out to be the very mechanism of adjustment which the US-dominated multilateral imperialism required. These mechanisms required European, Japanese and other capitalist monopolies to restructure from their bilateral colonial and semi-colonial markets into multilateral ones which would compete on equal terms *on a world scale*. This strategy required these countries to introduce themselves into unfamiliar economic enclaves of their erstwhile enemies and to some extent into a hostile environment.

On the other hand, as part of this adjustment and in order to *defend* their export markets, the former colonial monopolies 'offered' the new countries investments to 'substitute' their former exports (which were the imports of the colonies) with assembly plants as a means of 'industrialising' the countries by engaging in local manu-facturing. The new competitors also saw an advantage in wanting to gain entry into the new countries by 'offering' to 'industrialise' the country in order to 'create employment' and 'save foreign exchange', which would otherwise have gone to importing industrial goods! This gave the monopolies an opportunity to offload their old plants and substitute new ones fitted to the new competition.

Thus import substitution, which was also desired by the leaders of the new countries, turned out to be a new form of monopolistic competition in a changing economic-political environment, both for the new countries and for the new and old monopolies in the neo-colony. It turned out to be an adjustment mechanism for the industrial monopolies in the new countries and in the metropoles.

These adjustments included not only finding new outlets for investment (which were being offered to them by the new countries in the shape of tax relief and tax 'holidays'), but also in the form of new sources of raw materials, ancillary materials and food products. These outlets and sources had to be protected and defended against 'communism', hence the crucial importance of the US multilateral defence umbrella under NATO, which saw to the emasculation of the new states and their confirmation as neo-colonial enclaves.

Since the new giant competitors did not control any particular country, the competitive mechanisms they adopted had to be 'flexible' and able to respond to different environments. This meant that the new monopolies had to adopt strategies of being everywhere and 'nowhere', meaning they had to maximise their profits at points of strength and minimise their losses at points of weakness in order to obtain a satisfactory (i.e. competitive) super-profit. Furthermore, none of the new competitors was in control of the conditions of competition for any length of time, which heightened and intensified competition in a situation of recurrent crises. The adjustment process had, therefore, to be *ongoing and ceaseless* on all fronts. This in itself also sharpened the tools of competition and adjustment able to adopt and respond to the changing environment. This also introduced and, at the same time, added to the volatility of the international system.

It is this environment in which the new states of the Third World found themselves. This was a rapidly changing environment without any stability in economic activity, geared purely to consolidating the 'development' required by the monopolies in their own ceaseless game of competition and adjustment for survival. In this game, the weak lost and the strong gained – the weakest of all lost most just as the strongest gained most of all. It was a game of elephants and sharks in which the 'grass suffered' and the smaller fish got eaten and digested by the sharks.

This is what explains Africa's plight: being the weakest in the imperialist chain, the continent on which the last two colonies exist and the last bastion of imperialist enslavement.

The Failure of Third World Development

The Import-Substitution Industry

It is in this international context that the 'strategy' of import substitution failed as a basis for *national development*. It only suc-
ceeded as an instrument of transnational incorporation, for
import substitution was seen by the monopolies as a strategy of
internationalisation in their joint-venture approach throughout
the world. Through this mechanism, the monopolies were able to
export their capital in different *forms*: as *money-capital* on which they
earned interest; as *machinery* (or technology) on which they earned
profits, dividend fees, or charges; as *ancillary and raw materials* from
their diverse bases, and on which they earned profits or received
differential rent; as *goods*, whether durable or consumer, on which
they earned commercial profit; and as *personnel* to manage the joint
ventures and or act as engineers for the machines and technology
they imported, on which they recovered their working capital in
the form of salaries. It was to these elements of the total imported
finance-capital, to which 'national' capital or domestic resources
were mobilised and *added*, which made up international finance-
capital.

Such a combination of resources, techniques and modalities of
operation enabled transnational corporations not only to operate
internationally but also 'flexibly', and this enabled them to fit into
different competitive environments, including the 'national' development corporations in which they were able to operate and still
retain their monopoly (as has happened in most so-called national
industries based on import substitution).

In conformity with the need to adjust and accumulate greater
profits, the transnational monopolies used the import-substitution
structure to undermine any possible effort to create independent national industry since the machinery they exported to these
industries was one intended for their competition against their
monopoly adversaries at home and other countries ('inappropri-
ate' technology!). Such technology did not 'create employment',
nor did it 'save foreign exchange' since the cost of the imported
technology and machinery increased in line with all the prices of
manufactured goods in industrialised countries. In time the spare

parts and imported raw materials also became 'too expensive' to
sustain any domestic production since the raw materials were
imported at exorbitant cost, though the prices of Third World raw
materials were going down. This was because once raw materials
were in the hands of the transnational monopolies and the commodity exchanges located in London, Chicago, Paris and Rotterdam,
they were 'priced' differently to take into account the operations of
financial and insurance markets, including the cost of speculation.

For this reason, the neo-colonial strategy of 'integrated
development', which aimed at creating 'backward and forward'
linkages within the domestic economy, was itself *integrated* within
the structure of transnational corporate activity and *linked* both
backwards and forwards, horizontally and vertically to the international market. Agriculture continued on the old traditional markets
mentioned above.

Thus with industry and agriculture de-linked in the Third World
economy, there remained little internal market to talk of nor any
'internal' economic or financial mechanisms to sustain any form
of development. These were all unquestionably linked to the main
economic centres, which dictated the terms on which resources
could be exploited (including the rates of profit and interest) in all
countries of the Third World and elsewhere. It is for this reason that
none of the policies or strategies of development could have worked
in accordance with the needs of the people in these countries.

The example of Brazilian import substitution will go to show
that these mechanisms of control and exploitation of international
finance-capital are not specific to Africa or the post-Second World
War Third World states in general. A.G. Frank demonstrates and
confirms the thesis given by Normano in 1931 of how US capital
took advantage of Brazil during the First World War by attempt-
ing import substitution to strangle its national development. In
the inter-war years, Brazilian industrialisation had expanded
from 3,000 units in 1907 to more than 13,000 in 1920. As the main
metropolis recovered from the war, this development was turned
around to serve the restructuring of the metropolis, especially
the United States. The negative features that have characterised
the second industrial development effort of most African and
Asian countries came into play: inflation; devaluation; first an
increase, then a decrease in the terms of trade; and finally, external

financing. The foreign financing of coffee production brought in foreign exchange, but this money was used to import foreign goods which undermined Brazilian industry and economic development.[6]

The price support programme initiated by the Brazilian government gave strength to inflation and domestic demand, and this attracted foreign monopolies which came into Brazil to produce in competition with Brazilian firms. The devaluation and deflation that followed in the wake of the adjustment again made it cheaper for US companies to come in and buy up Brazilian installations on the cheap. With this development, Brazil began to build up an external debt, which had to be serviced at great cost. What happened in the 1920s and 1930s was repeated at a higher level in the Brazil of the 1960s and 1970s. Normano observed that what had frustrated the national development of Brazil were affiliates and subsidiaries of the 'top thirty' US mass-producing monopolies, who were using the 'native capital' of Brazil as 'foreign investment' through the local branches of foreign (US) banks. Today, this picture is repeated and worse still in the relatively weaker African countries.[7]

To illustrate the African situation, Tanzania is a good example. Tanzania was one of the three East African states that were incorporated into a colonial regional market, with Kenya and Uganda, having been a German colony before the First World War. After its political independence in 1961, Tanganyika, as it was then called, embarked on a strategy of import substitution of three industries, that of fertiliser, cement and petroleum refineries. The fertiliser plant was supposed to revolutionise agriculture and cement was supposed to give strength to industrial construction, while the oil refinery was to provide the energy. But the substitution 'industry' turned out to be a mechanism by the former importers, now 'manufacturers', to increase their imports. The fertiliser plant, which was located in the port town of Tanga, was highly capital-intensive with technically advanced equipment used. This required expertise from outside and regular spares from the suppliers to maintain it. Despite the fact that most of the raw material inputs could have been procured domestically, the firm – managed and maintained by the foreign monopoly – decided on importing almost all the sulphur, phosphate rock, liquid ammonia, nitric acid and potassium

salts needed in the production process. The only raw material provided locally in Tanzania was the water and local menial labour.[8]

Cement was another classic case of Tanzanian import substitution. The import-substituting company was also foreign-controlled and owned, with the government holding a bare 10% of the shares. At first, it rejected the idea of import substitution, contending that it had sufficient cement capacity in Kenya to supply the Tanganyika market. When the Tanganyika government demonstrated that there were other companies interested in doing the job, it 'offered' to do it. It signed a management agreement with the government and made all the decisions on investment and the location of the plant. It decided to locate the plant away from the main centres of the raw materials which were available in the country and imported an over-capacity plant. It rejected the use of local raw materials on the grounds that they were 'unsuitable' due to 'technical specifications'. When Tanzania decided to 'nationalise' the factory by taking over 51% of the shares, the former managers were asked to continue managing production since no Tanzanian had been trained to run the industry. In essence, nationalisation made no difference to the running of the enterprise. Despite government guidelines, which required the use of labour-intensive technology, the managers insisted on a more capital-intensive technique since it was this technology which assured them higher profits, lower labour costs and control over the production process. While the 670 employees whom the factory employed took 20% of the total earnings of the industry, the top 15 experts and managers were brought in from outside and their salaries, which were repatriated almost wholly, accounted for 25% of the total wage bill (and 3–7% of the total cost of production). Overall, the 'industry' imported 75–80% of the total inputs that went into production. This resulted in a great foreign exchange drainage to the country, money which was supposed to be 'saved'.[9]

What added to this monopoly structure *within* the African neo-colonial situation was the provision by the state of *tariff protection* for these joint-ventures engaged in import substitution. The tariff protections gave the monopolies a border security against foreign, usually also, monopoly competitors. So protected, the monopolies never complained about the smallness of the domestic market because they saw this market as part of a global

network joined together by the flexible arrangements of the *trans-nationalisation* of finance-capital. These tariff protections then gave the import-substitution joint-ventures leverage to *increase* internal prices and *restrict output*, where necessary, to reap super-profits in the neo-colony. This power to increase prices without competition added to the external monopoly prices, which were injected into the domestic prices through their own exports of goods and capital, as we have seen, and this, in great measure, explains the *tendency towards inflation* within Third World countries.

In this respect, a study of tariff protection in Tanzania revealed that even normal tariff protection expressed in tariff percentages or quotations did not sufficiently reveal the *effective* protection, which in many cases was higher in reality. This protection was more pronounced in tobacco, matches and beer industries. In Kenya, a similar phenomenon was observed by the International Labour Organisation (ILO). Sugar had a much higher effective protection of 172% above that provided for (100%).

Perhaps it is this phenomenon which also explains the very high monopoly structure in Zimbabwean industry. According to estimates of monopoly structure in Zimbabwe, more than half of the 6,000 industrial products produced by Zimbabwean manufacturing are under the control of one monopoly industrial enterprise, while over 30% of the products are produced under 'oligopolistic' conditions, that is under the monopoly control of two or three industrial concerns. Put together, it can be seen that something in the region of 80% to 90% of all Zimbabwean manufacturing is under one form of monopoly or another. It is this monopoly power, which is guaranteed by state tariff protection, which enables these monopoly industrial enterprises to charge increasing prices while at the same time being able to reduce output to create political pressure within the country. Such tariff protection also encourages the maximum use of the existing industrial plant without any motivation to introduce innovations and new techniques suited to domestic demand conditions. Monopoly pricing is, therefore, built into the domestic industrial economy, and inflation, which is imported through the mechanisms already mentioned, adds even further to the tendency towards permanent inflation within a domestic economy.

From the above, it can be seen that the programmes of economic and social development envisaged by African governments could

not be met. Local savings through local branches of foreign banks were also used by the same companies, who brought in very little foreign investment to back up their activities, activities on which they earned tremendous (repatriated) profits. Local savings were turned to good account by foreign import-substitution monopolies, particularly now that they were regarded as 'national' industries.

Agriculture

The other resources which were mobilised by African states from *export crops* went towards financing this exploitative strategy. The entire development strategy in agriculture was centred on export-oriented production which was supposed to earn the foreign exchange to pay for the modernisation of industry and agriculture. But the prices of these export crops continued to decline relative to the prices of the imported goods required for import substitution and consumption, leading to a deterioration in the *terms of trade* of all African countries. The factors that contributed to this deterioration were again externally induced (putting aside the natural and minor internal causes).

These external factors, to be sure, were connected with the recurring cyclical industrial and financial crises of the major industrial countries. These cyclical crises were in turn caused by declining profit levels, technological conditions and declining asset values, which caused inflationary pressures in the economies. It is these crises which compelled *technological intensification* in certain fields, and this then compelled the shift in the demand patterns for certain raw materials into synthetic materials. Internal pressures within their own countries also led to demands to produce some of these commodities domestically. This resulted in protectionism, undermining the exports of Third World countries in the very areas in which they were assumed to have a 'comparative advantage', not to mention the protectionism against Third World manufacturers.

Money, Prices and Interest

The increase in the prices of industrial products imported by Third World countries had a double effect: they added to internal inflation and reduced the value of Third World currencies. These two elements induced yet two other effects both directly and indirectly:

they led to the rise in interest rates in the industrial countries, while both the high industrial prices and the new high interest rates made it imperative for Third World countries to borrow extensively to repay the higher prices and higher interest rates in a cumulative way. Every new increase in interest rates *automatically* increased the old Third World debt, without any negotiation! To these factors must be added the two oil price hikes of 1973 and 1979, which themselves were part of the manoeuvre by the US to bolster its currency against its competitors with a view to drawing in their savings to finance its deficit budget, as we have seen. Thus the limited foreign earnings from the agricultural sector were not only over-exploited by the import-substitution industrial sector, they also bore the brunt of the external debt that arose from the reforms and other sources. Agriculture, on the other hand, was benefiting little from industry.

It is the above developments which explain then why Third World agriculture and export crops could not provide a solid basis for the modernisation of their economies, if ever such a thing were possible. These developments could also not have led to a *diversification* in the production pattern of these countries since almost all continued to produce single export crops whose prices and volumes declined in conformity with the above factors. An example will illustrate the point. Ghana and Ivory Coast are producers of cocoa, among others. In 1959, African cocoa producers exported 560,000 tonnes of the crop, for which they earned $409 million. In 1963, the same countries and others who had entered crop production exported 738,000 tonnes – a 40% increase – for which they received $371 million, i.e. 10% below the receipt of 1959, but for a greater quantity. Today, the cocoa-importing monopolies are already producing a much cheaper synthetic cocoa which will put to waste all the cocoa fields in these countries, making it necessary for the cocoa fields to be uprooted. There was no possibility that the world market could accommodate any other diversification in the production or any profitable employment from it.

Overall, according to various international organisations, countries of the non-oil exporting Third World countries faced tremendous losses in their export earnings as a result of these developments, as well as suffering from the rising prices of manufactured goods exported by western industry, which on the unit value index rose from 100 in 1975 to 122 in 1978 and 160 in 1980.

According to UNCTAD (United Nations Conference on Trade and Development), the total losses suffered by these countries between 1961 and 1970 amounted to $350 billion. The IMF estimates losses of 23% for the entire period between 1974 and 1981. The monetary adjustments of the US caused by the inflation of the late 1960s and mid-1970s – which led to the de-monetisation of gold, US dollar devaluation and the currency floating of the major currencies – had also led the country to increase its interest rates on credits from 7.25% in 1975 to 11.75% in 1978, 15.24% in 1979 and 21.50% in 1980. Other western banks followed suit, although at slightly lower levels.

The Third World countries forced to resort to the euro currency market (petro-dollars in US and European banks) found they had to pay the higher Inter-Bank Lending Rate in London (LIBOR) of 9.20% in 1978 and 16.63% in 1981. With the floating currencies most banks also resorted to floating interest rates in order to maintain their value. This added to the rises and fluctuations. The World Bank estimated that every rise in the LIBOR of 1% automatically

Chart 4: Debt Servicing – African Countries

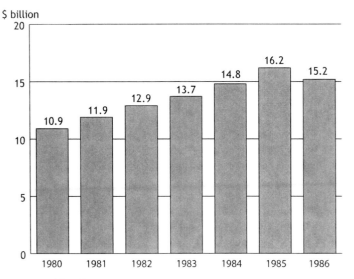

$ billion

Source: World Bank

added $1.8 billion to Third World debts around this time. The IMF also estimated that every increase of 1% in interest rates on world money-capital markets entailed an increase of about $3 billion in the interest to be paid by all non-oil exporting countries on their external debts in this period.

It is clear that the above interest rate and debt structure had nothing to do with the internal economic policies of Third World countries. As a result, a number of African countries found their foreign debt-servicing ratios (external debt-service payments as a percentage of export earnings) highly unmanageable, even within the hitherto prevailing levels (which were themselves high). A few examples will illustrate this point. Algeria, which in 1975 paid 8.7% of its export earnings servicing debts in 1975, had its ratio increase to 23.9% in 1981; Zambia in the same period increased from 10% to 24.4%; Uganda from 4.5% to 24.4%; Gabon from 5.5% to 15.1%; Morocco from 5.8% to 28.0%; Guinea from 14.8% to 24.6%; and Malawi from 7.9% to 18.4%. Chart 5 below illustrates the general African debt and servicing picture.

Chart 5: Growth of Debt – African Countries

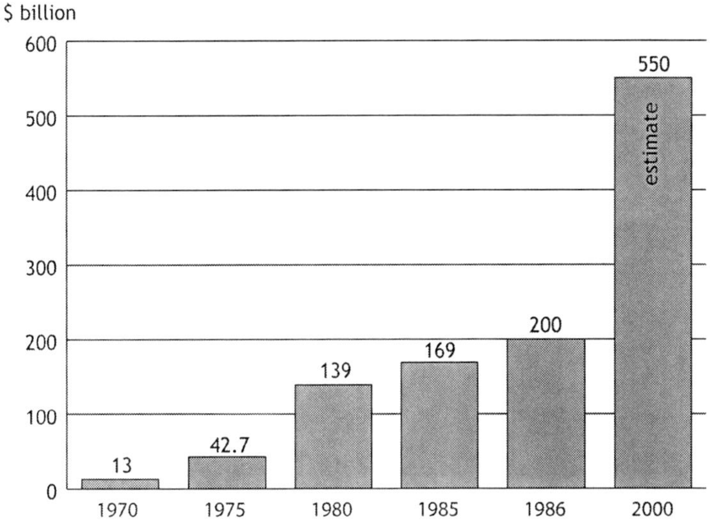

$ billion

Source: Economic Commission for Africa

With their low level of development, the end result was that African countries were encumbered by heavy external debts, putting a stop to any further development. Indeed, it can be said that the debt burden was itself a reflection of the negative impact international finance-capital was having on African development overall. The debt was evidence of the parasitic character of international finance-capital, which had brought about this *negative development* in African countries. By 1982, Africa's external debt had ballooned to some $134.4 billion. This figure had almost doubled by 1988, when it was estimated to be $250 billion.

Monetarism and the Third World

If economic development was almost impossible under these circumstances, it was clear that Third World countries could not control their own resources. It is clear they could not even maintain monetary and financial autonomy to regulate their development or carry out any meaningful adjustments in their internal economic relations and structures. It was quite clear that one of the fundamental reasons for this 'weakness' was the fact that Third World countries were 'open' economies, dependent in differing measure on the world market. African countries were even more vulnerable in this respect since they were the economies most 'open' to western supply and demand pressures and adjustments, an openness which was *increasing* rather than declining with the passage of time.

This 'weakness' and openness was nowhere more blatant than in the monetary and financial field and will, later in the analysis, come to explain why African governments came to change monetary policy in response to international pressure.

Many of the central banks that were established with political independence, with all the sovereign trimmings of a monetary authority, found that they could not, given this openness, use most of the monetary and financial instruments to regulate their economies. The reasons for this were obvious. *First*, African countries had no independent currency of their own. Their currencies were convertible into foreign goods and other currencies only through one or a basket of foreign currencies, something called the 'pegging' of a currency. African countries had all their currencies pegged in this way to major international currencies, whether the dollar, the franc

or the special drawing rights (SDRs). The West African Monetary Union (WAMU) and its West African Central Bank operate within global credit limits set by France. The same applies to other countries with currencies pegged in a similar way.

Second, African currencies so pegged have fixed exchange rates for their currencies vis-à-vis the major currencies to which they are tied. Thus any changes or strains in the exchange rates of the major currencies affects the African currencies almost directly. This means that such pressures in the metropoles as unemployment, labour strikes or inflation have an immediate impact in African countries.

Third, since, as we have seen, African economies are very externally dependent on either one or two export commodities to the very countries with which their currencies are pegged, there is almost no direct linkage between the productive (real) and the monetary (value) sectors of their economies, since these variables are controlled from external sectors. This also explains the cause of the lack of developed financial intermediaries and near-money devices in African economies such as deposits, certificates, bills and bonds. Because of this lack, the mobilisation of domestic resources becomes a difficult if not impossible task.

Fourth, this narrowness of the real and monetary base and the volatility of export earnings expose African countries to pressures from dominant external sources, sources which take advantage of these weaknesses to exploit an already weakened situation. This, in sum, explains the utter unmanageability of the ongoing African crisis.

According to a 1980 IMF study by L.M. Goreaux, cyclical movements in the economies of the developed capitalist countries explain much about the fluctuations in primary commodity prices of Third World countries. The study points out that each one percentage point change in the business cyclical index of these countries gave rise to an adverse impact of 2.2% in Third World country prices, and this is what explains the *tendency* for primary commodity fluctuations and declines.[11]

Monetary policy instruments such as the bank rate, open market operations, reserve ratios and liquidity ratios became unworkable for most African countries, right from the beginning of their independence. The *bank rate* – which acts as a re-discount rate on bills and other forms of paper, or the rate at which a central bank lends

Table 6: Exchange Arrangements of African Countries

Currency pegged to	No of countries
US dollar	9
French franc	14
S.D.R.	10
Other currencies	4
Other currency baskets	7
Other	4
Total	48

Source: IMF

to commercial banks on suitable securities – was made ineffective by the fact that financial intermediaries were undeveloped. This is also why commercial banks came to hold government treasury bills in large quantities as lenders to government, which in turn made them unresponsive to monetary policy. In short, due to their holdings of government bills commercial banks became too liquid to be controlled meaningfully. Even in its role of acting as a discreet way of setting rates for banks' savings and lending rates, the bank rate had limited value. Furthermore, in conditions of a very high rate of inflation, the effectiveness of interest rates on savings was limited as such rates became negative in relation to the rate of inflation. The device of interest rate adjustment through liquidity controls was therefore in the main unworkable, with inflation becoming an increasingly 'normal' condition in most Third World countries.

The *open market operations* technique was also inoperable for somewhat similar reasons. More importantly however, this was because government securities – which central banks would have used to influence economic activity by enlarging or reducing the 'money supply', i.e. credit, or influencing rates of interest – were being held in large quantities by commercial banks and institutional investments such as pension funds, insurance and securities funds. There was also no money and financial market of which this technique could take advantage. The fact that positive interest rates were undermined by inflation mitigated against the general public's purchasing of government bills in any case, with those that did so on either sentimental or patriotic grounds soon surrendering them as the central banks guaranteed their repurchase

at par before maturity. In Sierra Leone in October 1981 for instance, commercial banks held the equivalent of 81.7% of all government treasury bills outstanding. When the holdings of other financial institutions were added, the proportion of treasury bill holdings by banks and financial institutions increased to 90.9%.[12]

The *reserve* technique was said to be more operable as a substitute for the open market operations technique because of its 'potency' in an African situation. But a closer analysis based on experience in Africa also revealed that its effectiveness was undermined by the aversion to risk of expatriate banks and also, to some extent, by 'national' commercial and development banks to lending to agri-culture and small-scale industry. Since these same banks also held a high quantity of government bills – which would be the instrument by which the government could manipulate them – they instead found themselves extremely liquid on the strength of government securities. The result of this was that the use of the reserve technique – which would have required the banks to hold a certain amount of cash relative to deposits (with a view to influencing the availability of credit to the private sector, among other things) – became inef-fective when applied. Some governments such as Ghana and Sierra Leone tried to rectify this problem by raising the legal minimum reserve requirements, but the commercial banks reacted by refus-ing to take deposits because they did not pay, preferring to hold the more liquid government treasury bills!

The fundamental weakness was the fact that the central banks themselves did not have any mechanism for controlling their own reserve ratios or liquidity creation since they did not hold gold. Since they in turn held the major currencies to which their own currencies were pegged or the treasury bills of those countries – particularly those of the United States – as the reserves of bills of monetary stock, they found that they themselves were being regu-lated by the central banks of those countries. The result was that the reserve holdings of African central banks became part of the 'funds' and credit instruments manipulated and regulated by other central banks in their open market operations and reserve ratios. In such a situation, it would be a near miracle for any African government to be able to regulate its own money supply since in effect this was being regulated from outside as part of the international 'money supply'. But these central banks of the major countries had also, as

of 1979's US Federal Quantitative Accord, lost relative control over the 'money supply' to private bankers.

Left with no other viable technique, African central banks and governments resorted to *moral suasion*, but this was only possible where 'good relations' existed between the government and local branches of foreign bankers (who were in any case controlling credit and liquidity on the international markets). Failing persuasion, the governments instead resorted to *direct controls*, direct orders and commands to the banks to direct credit to certain 'priority' areas. Initially, these 'priority areas' included agriculture and small enterprises but of late, due to adjustment policies, these 'areas' have boiled down to the importation of government 'priority' supplies such as medicines, oil, and government and military supplies.

The failure by the commercial banks to provide credit to the productive sectors other than the trade and export and input sectors led governments to re-appraise their role, with many deciding to 'take over' more economic activity than they could effectively manage. This, in turn, increased the state budget deficits brought about by earlier infrastructural development projects, with the result that government spending became self-reinforcing. In short, the very mechanisms of the international economy required increased state intervention, which also suited local bureaucrats well because it increased their benefits and privileges while creating avenues for patronage for politicians to provide 'jobs for the boys'. This in many countries meant joining the army or parastatal boards and provides a basis for formulating a *law of African neo-colonial development: statisation and militarisation*, a law that explains the tendencies towards *re-colonialisation*.

This is a law of neo-colonial economic necessity. It arises from economic relations internationally. It also explains the dilemma of African states around maintaining their independence when faced with a growing crisis. Since the real social forces of change on land and in towns could not be availed, the lack of money-credit needed to generate productive activity beyond the minimum required by international markets led to these forces deteriorating markedly in rural areas. Indeed, this was reflected in the pervasive reluctance of commercial banks to extend credit to these forces even from the deposits they had obtained from their cash crops.

Governments from time to time tried to force the banks to increase credit to these sectors by keeping the amount of government bills they could hold to a minimum. But this proved unproductive and indeed counter-productive since this also undermined governments' ability to raise funds for their own economic activities. Because of increasing inflation, the public itself was unwilling to buy government bills. For this reason state debt to the commercial banks continued to expand, something reinforced by declining tax revenues. The central banks were obliged in these circumstances to buy government bills, only for commercial banks to complain that the central bank was using their money in the form of reserve deposits to engage in commercial-bank business. The central bank then in turn abandoned these purchase restrictions, enabling commercial banks to finance government debt and deficits to the satisfaction of all concerned: the commercial banks, the central bank and the state! With low interest rates on the bills (a fact which also helped to reduce debt servicing by the state of its deficits), the deposit business declined even further, giving way in some countries to non-formal (underground) deposit and savings systems. The international system was increasingly coming into confrontation with productive social forces.

The Case of Zimbabwe

This is a typical problem which many African countries faced. Relatively developed systems, such as those which prevailed in Zimbabwe, Ivory Coast, Egypt and Kenya, were soon also facing the same problems once they embarked on broad programmes of economic development. Racist Rhodesia was able to avoid all these pressures by driving the majority of the population in 'native reserves' to be used as a source of cheap labour, which kept costs down and enabled it to develop its financial structure. But independent Zimbabwe, faced with the same democratic pressures to bring about socio-economic development, soon found itself under similar pressure within a few years of its hard-fought independence. The Reserve Bank of Zimbabwe (RBZ) increasingly found that its more developed monetary policy techniques were being challenged by the pressures of development projects and state existence. The techniques used by the RBZ at the beginning of independence were

discount rates, open market operations, variable reserve ratios, variable liquid asset ratios, moral suasion and selective instruments of credit control. During 1979, the Smith rebel regime had borrowed extensively to fight the liberation war, creating a large deficit on the government budget of ZWD$502 million, which was only counter-balanced by an inflow of foreign assets. During 1980, 'broad money' (M2) rose sharply, which partly repaid the deficits of the previous years, as well as claims against the private sector.[13] The significant development of 1980 and 1981 was that there was a shift in budget deficit financing from external to internal sources, and this internal source was the banking sector. Whereas in 1979 government borrowing from the banking sector had amounted to 42% of total bank holdings, in 1980 this had already increased to 51%. The holdings of government securities by financial institutions – finance houses, building societies, Post Office Savings Bank (POSB), insurance companies and pension funds – rose from ZWD$74.8 million to ZWD$276.6 million in 1980. This raised claims against the government in 1981. In that year, the growth rate in the economy had topped 14%, which led to increased borrowing from the private sector and especially the agricultural sector. These increases in monetary expansion, which were consistent with this high level of economic activity, were only maintained by bringing the country's foreign reserves down to a bare two months' worth of exports by the end of 1981.[14] In order to maintain that level of external reserves, the government was already by this time being forced to resort to foreign short-term borrowing. To sustain these large budget deficits and to encourage private savings, the RBZ increased the bank rate from its 1963 level of 4.5% per annum (p.a.) to 6% p.a. and then to 9% p.a. in 1983 – thus doubling the 20-year rate. There was an expansion of consumer demand reflecting this economic activity and what could be described as the historical 'pent-up demand' of the African population, which for the first time had access to an increased level of income. This was particularly so for those from the middle strata who now obtained regular incomes from the state and private bodies. New higher reserve and liquid ratios were set for the banks, but these were beginning to produce the symptoms which characterise other African and Third World situations: a clear contradiction between state fiscal policies linked to development needs on the one hand, and monetary policy, which controls money and

credit needs as tied to international reserve and liquidity ratios, on the other.[15]

This became clearer by 1982. The fiscal policy aspect, which had injected tremendous activity in the economy in 1980 and 1981, began to ebb. The balance of payments worsened in 1981, and by January 1982 the IMF was asked by the Zimbabwean government to look into its economy under the provisions of Article IV of the IMF Articles of Agreement. A loan of ZWD$140 million was asked for, but since the IMF insisted that the exchange rate of the Zimbabwe dollar was too high and needed a 30% devaluation, there was no agreement at first. However, by September 1982 Zimbabwe's external reserves had fallen to US$8.6 million from US$13.5 million at the beginning of 1982. Having no choice, Zimbabwe accepted a standby agreement under which it at first devalued the dollar by 17% with a limited float, which resulted in an effective devaluation of 20%. At the same time, government expenditure was reduced by ZWD$200 million in the capital development sector of the economy. Soon thereafter, the government subsidy on maize-meal, the basic worker's staple, was removed to reduce the real wage. By 1984, inflation was increasingly creeping into the economy as foreign exchange shortages began to be felt in industry and agriculture.

The above example concerning Zimbabwe illustrates the dilemma facing the African neo-colonial state. Monetary and fiscal policy came into sharp contradiction as soon as the latter was used to advance economic development objectives. The two seemed to operate together in a colonial situation. With independence, development efforts are seen to contradict 'monetary stability'. The Zimbabwe case also reveals the close relationship that soon emerges between banks and other financial institutions with the state through neo-colonial state debt.

Adjustment and Stabilisation Processes

It is, therefore, understandable that in their supervisory role the International Monetary Fund, and to some extent the World Bank, have concentrated on exchange rate adjustments and accompanying structural adjustment measures to this end. This also explains why the IMF's original objectives of automatic balance of payments adjustments, which would have penalised surplus countries and

required them to adjust their internal economies to remove their own disequilibria, did not work. To have done so would have meant that Third World countries could have had access to the surpluses of these countries to adjust their economies over the longer-term to take care of their development needs. In the end, the various policies adopted from time to time by the multilateral institutions in general and the IMF in particular came to centre on one essential item: requiring Third World *deficit* countries to adjust instead to the adverse changes emanating from developed, capital-surplus economies. The single most potent instrument to achieve this demand for adjustment also came to revolve around the exchange rates of Third World countries through the drive to reduce *public expenditures* and increase the intermediary role of commercial banks.

While the approaches of the two multilateral institutions differ in that whereas the IMF's stabilisation policies emphasise 'demand management' in order to bring about a balance of payments equilibrium, the World Bank's structural adjustment policies emphasise the 'supply side' of the problem by stressing institutional and policy reforms to bring about 'growth' in production (especially for export), both policies in fact complement each other. This indeed was stressed by the World Bank itself in its 1982 annual report when it stated that its programmes were 'complementary and mutually reinforcing' of those of the IMF, since the World Bank facility could only be extended after the country concerned had agreed to a 'standby agreement' with the IMF. Both have the common objective of achieving an equilibrium in the affected countries' external sectors by shifting resources to desired points. These revolve around contracting domestic monetary growth and the demand for foreign balances by modifying exchange rates in order to encourage the supply of exports, as well as using saved foreign balances for import substitutes and capital goods at increasing relative prices and higher profitability. This, it can be noted, is in line with the actual tendencies in the economies of the developed capitalist states, already discussed in previous chapters.

To achieve these basic objectives, the following policy instruments have been adopted: First, to modify the exchange rate, as we have already noted, and to this end the devaluation of the currency of the affected country. This has the immediate effect of raising the domestic price of the external currencies so that these currencies

have a higher purchasing power over local resources. But since the most important local resource in these countries is the *labour-power* of the peasantry, who constitute over 80% of the population and who produce the export goods required, together with the workers in the plantations, mines, factories and transportation systems, the devaluation means that foreign capital can now buy their labour-power more cheaply through the devalued local currencies.

This is what is behind the argument that devaluation increases exports by making them cheaper. But by the same token, the domestic prices of imported goods – particularly capital goods – are *increased*. This enables the importing monopolies to make higher profits on the sale of their goods, both consumer and capital. Since the real objective of this capital is to exploit labour, this capital still stands poised to make a double profit when it is applied to production, and this is another reason why it is necessary to reduce wages through devaluation. The other demand on the exchange rate is the insistence by the IMF on increasing interest rates on domestic credit, which is assumed to increase the desire to save. In fact its main impact is to give the new devalued money in the hands of the money capitalists a higher value within the banking system, which is intended to strengthen the privatisation of the economy by discouraging the state from borrowing from the central bank. In short, the manoeuvre is intended in the short-term to encourage savings and deposits, although in that short-term it undermines domestic productive investment and therefore encourages imports. This demand is, in fact, intended to undermine the fiscal policy of the state and the strengthening of the monetary arm, the basic strength of which is in the external sector.

The second important demand of the IMF that the country should liberalise its trade with external firms also goes a long way in assisting foreigners with increasing their imports and access to cheap exports. This has the effect of removing all subsidies and tariffs, which are used to protect domestic markets against the imports of strong monopoly competitors from outside through raising the prices of their products. While this does not in fact entirely exclude the external monopoly power, it is not favoured by international finance-capital, particularly under the present, critical conditions. The high tariffs used advantageously by the monopolies when the import-substitution policy was first implemented are now

considered outdated by both them and new competitors. It is now argued that these should be removed to allow capital goods, inter-mediate goods and other production inputs to be brought down to a lower cost. In the same breath, all price controls are dismantled, to the clear disadvantage of both urban and rural populations, as well as to local industry.

The effect of the above stabilisation and structural adjustment measures in reality often have the opposite effect, except those relating to the cheapening of labour-power. The devaluation leads to higher inflation in the next period, since the higher prices of imports are added to the prices of inputs in domestic production as the import element in domestic production is usually very high. We have seen this in relation to import-substitution enterprises. Even in agriculture, the import cost of oil, insecticides and fertilisers and sometimes seed increases the cost of production of agricultural prod-ucts for export, which in turn makes it necessary to further reduce wages and prices paid to the workers in plantations and peasant producers in the subsequent period. This is achieved through the mechanisms of constant price 'increases' to the peasant producers with constant inflationary spirals. The increase in producer prices is always one step behind the increase in basic consumer prices, otherwise the devaluation would not have the desired effect. As an economist with the African Development Bank has observed:

> A third consequence of an exchange rate adjustment relates to price increases. But this effect would depend very much on supporting wage policies. The main purpose of devaluation is to reduce real demand for resources and to divert the saved resources to the external markets. If permissive policies could let real domestic demand remain unchanged or increased, the exchange rate adjustment would become counter-productive. Thus, a partially compensatory increase in wages would be possible.[16]

This is because although the economist does not say it directly, any increase in producer prices and wages that results in unchanged or increased consumer demand would undermine the devaluation. In order to reduce domestic demand, the producer price and wage increases must decline.

Thus it is not surprising that stringent IMF doses of stabilisation

and World Bank adjustments have led to an increase in urban and rural poverty and increasing rural–urban migration, turning both rural (mainly female and young) and urban labour into mere slave labourers on their own lands, plantations and factories. In cases like Zambia, Nigeria and Sudan, they have led to riots in which several hundreds have been killed by the armed forces, leading to the reversal of the policies or their modification. In other countries, such as Ghana, surprising innovations have been adopted to deal with unmanageable situations. Here, the first phase of stabilisation for the years 1983–86 were brought into action with two standby agreements worth $3 billion. The objective was to reverse the decline in the productive sectors, stabilise fiscal and monetary discipline, and 'rehabilitate' the economic and social infrastructure. This phase saw to the devaluation of the cedi from 2.75 to the US dollar in 1983 to cedi 181 in 1988. Although exports were said by the IMF to have increased in 1987 and 1988, the cost to the economy as a whole was quite devastating. Ghana's external debt built up to an unprecedented $2.4 billion, with 75% of the 1988 export earnings going to the servicing of the debt. To achieve this miserable 'upturn' in the economy, 81,000 employees were sacked from the public sector and millions impoverished in the urban and rural areas.

By 1987, Ghana was faced with the devastating side-effects of the stabilisation programme and in order to ameliorate the suffering of the population, the Ghanaian government was forced to work out a 'counter-IMF' action programme called the Programme of Action to Mitigate the Social Costs of Adjustment (PAMSCAD), which was also funded by new 'donors'. The objectives of the PAMSCAD was to *re-create* 40,000 public sector jobs and to support employment-generating projects in rural and urban areas, including public works such as rural housing and food production. These were said to be aimed at 'drawing people away' from the urban centres back to the villages and at dissuading the rural population from migrating to the urban areas. Furthermore, 'food-for-work' projects were being put in place based on 'food-aid' from external 'donors'! The action programme had attracted $85 million from a donor's conference in Geneva, which recognised 'the widespread poverty and economic hardships which, for some groups, have been exacerbated by the economic recovery programme and [which] may in turn make the programme itself unsustainable.'[17]

This, if anything, proved the bankruptcy of IMF stabilisation and World Bank structural adjustment programmes. They had turned Africa into an impoverished continent with nothing to show for the 500 years of capitalist 'civilisation' save the skyscrapers and fly-overs of Johannesburg, Nairobi, Abidjan and Lagos. International finance-capital had impoverished the majority while enriching the capitalist minority and their local comprador class. The crash of international finance-capital, therefore, represents from a Third World perspective the destruction of the countryside and the deaths of millions out of a poverty generated by the capitalist accumulation of wealth on a global scale.

The Impact of the Financial Crash on the Third World

The October financial crash has had a tremendous impact on this weak economic structure in Third World countries. The initial elements of this impact were a direct consequence of the financial adjustments of Third World countries, which we have examined above. These adjustments were intended to bring these countries in line with the financial deregulation taking place on the New York, London and Tokyo stock exchanges. Indeed, the stabilisation and adjustment measures just described, together with the debt-repayment manoeuvres, were part and parcel of this impact. Bankers who had 'overlent' found themselves caught up with large 'sovereign' debtors who were finding it difficult to repay their debts. Now the financiers, together with the international financial institutions, were working day and night to restructure the debts in order to maintain the debt structure. This is what IMF 'stabilisation' meant.

This became evident as the bankers in unison worked out schemes to mortgage Third World countries' resources even further to the international financiers. A 'plan' worked out by a New York brokerage of Drexel Burnham Lambert, the creator of the junk-bonds, envisages the creation of another kind of bond – a resource-backed bond – which Third World debtor countries could use to sell and then buy back their debt from the same or other bankers at a discount. The new bonds would be backed by the natural resources of the Third World countries concerned, such as oil, mines and forests. The debt could then be 'converted' into these resource-backed

securities at as much as an 85% discount, bought on the secondary market and then traded on stock exchanges.

Since 1980, many Third World countries have converted some $6 billion into these kind of bonds by entering into arrangements with transnational banks and corporations, enabling these monopolies to swap assets among themselves at speculative prices. This activity is what has added to the 'securitisation' of Third World resources, which was expected by 1987 to have expanded into a huge market of $10 billion on the strength of the privatisation taking place in a number of Third World countries. Such countries as Argentina, Brazil, Chile, Costa Rica, Ecuador, Mexico, the Philippines and Venezuela had accepted some kind of conversion scheme, while even smaller countries such as Colombia, the Dominican Republic, Jamaica and Uruguay were all being pulled in to accept the schemes.

On the African continent, the African Development Bank had also bought the idea of the 'securitisation' of debt, which was being advocated with the full backing of the President of Senegal. The bank advocated the reduction and conversion of the existing debt into long-term bonds. This would amount to the marketing of the debt into further debt, the redemption of which would be paid into a redemption fund by African states for the account of the creditors.

A process of de-parastatalisation has thus been under way on the African continent at the urging of international financiers to strengthen small-businesspeople in African economies, who would then be linked to the international financial markets in a new 'partnership' with the international banks.

Ivory Coast, at one time considered the most 'private' capitalist economy on the continent, was found to be highly dependent on state-sponsored enterprises. As part of the $93 million World Bank Structural Adjustment Programme Loan, 10 parastatal organisations were put up for sale, and another seven were earmarked for privatisation. Indeed, a Commission for State Disengagement was set up to see to this enforced privatisation of the Ivorian economy.

This anti-state drive of the World Bank had also been strengthened by the 'socialist' countries, who in their own 'reforms' were doing virtually the same thing. But this attack on public expenditure was in fact only one side of the equation in the drive to strengthen the monetary sector at the expense of the real sector.

The second side of the equation, which was seen as undermining private bank intermediation in African credit-creation and management, was the financing of cash crops. This sector has always been seen as contributing to the expansion of the 'money supply', and has therefore been accused of contributing to increasing 'inflation' and thus undermining the value of money assets. The reluctance of commercial banks to lend to this sector, and in particular to traditional agriculture, is essentially rooted in this understanding. African states had tried to intervene in the process by requiring banks to lend to this sector on its guarantee through crop-marketing boards or cooperative unions, but the World Bank and IMF insisted that these arrangements be dismantled in Uganda under a standby arrangement. International financiers argued that the financing of coffee through these means was placing a liquidity burden on banks. The IMF insisted that this 'burden' be removed in order to enable the private commercial banks to 'resume' their initiative in savings-deposit intermediation. Indeed, in order to lay the ground for this development, the World Bank, through its sister organisation, the International Finance Corporation (IFC), had put forward initial capital of $50 million from the IFC and private capital to set up an Emergent Markets Growth Fund to be quoted on major exchanges, which would set the ground for a securities market for Third World debt. The new fund was also supposed to take up minority shares in Third World private enterprise in order to encourage the 'privatisation' drive of the IMF. This fund has in fact already been floated and is currently being sold on the major exchanges.

This was seen as giving strength to the Baker III plan announced by the US administration in October 1985, under which a number of indebted Third World countries would have access to a new layer of loans on the condition that they carried out the IMF and World Bank structural adjustment programmes. Under the plan, the policy of 'privatisation' was to be central. The financiers were clearly intent on using the debt as a leverage to deepen the enslavement of Third World peoples. Through 'privatisation' the financiers wished to compel Third World states to sell public-owned property to individual capitalists – both domestic and foreign – who would then 'securitise' these assets for speculation on financial markets. One US economist has remarked:

> Privatisation – the enhancement of [the] private sector through [the] management, leasing, or ownership of current state-owned assets or through greater private sector/public sector competition – represents one of the most promising approaches for overcoming the economic and political risks of debt conversions and the constraints on the demand side of the secondary market.[18]

Such a strategy would enable both local and foreign private interests to wholly take over the national economies of Third World countries in order to integrate them further into the world economy on an even more exploitative basis. Such an approach has been seen as part of a 'comprehensive package' which would entail the further 'liberalisation' of Third World economies, a process which would *directly* link peasant producers and small-scale capitalists to the global securities markets.

This is why the World Bank wanted these global loans to the marketing boards to be discontinued, because it was an inefficient way of lending as it tied large amounts of money at points where they might lie un- or mis-used. There was also no incentive to utilise the loans effectively and this tended to raise interest rates while other sectors of the economy were being starved of credit. The answer, according to the World Bank, lay in 'privatising' crop financing and this would mean that direct links would have to be established between primary cooperatives societies and the banks without the intermediation of marketing boards. Credit would be on an *overdraft rather than a loan* basis so that the cooperative societies would open a line of credit with the banks secured by the collateral of the crop itself and, where necessary, the peasants own lands directly, instead of a government guarantee. Such an arrangement would enable the banks themselves to monitor the needs, the utilisation and the repayment of the advances on a regular basis.[19]

It can be seen, therefore, that international finance-capital was on a sustained offensive to take over direct control of production relations in the countryside, turning peasants into their direct labourers without the pretence that they 'owned' their lands and linking these privatised, rural units to financial markets. These financial devices and techniques were being evolved on the international financial markets, as we have seen, to market and securitise these rural assets directly on the stock exchange. The IFC Emergent

Marketing Growth Fund was one such attempt to create the institutions and structures to achieve this purpose. Indeed, the World Bank was also arguing that commercial banks and development banks should strengthen the generation of local funds as a means of 'utilising external funds'. This, it advised, could be best achieved by the banks if they strengthened their deposit base through the creation of 'new instruments and devices' with different maturities and with varying credit risks 'to allow savers to keep their wealth without fear of them being eaten up by inflation'.[20] Here it can be seen that the whole stabilisation and structural policy of the IMF and World Bank is to strengthen the monetary sector at the expense of the productive sectors, with every attempt to increase production undermined by monetary pressures through exchange rate and international payments imbalances.

We should not be lulled into believing that the 'debt relief' announced by the Group of Seven at their Toronto summit in June 1988 will help Africa to strengthen itself. This package, intended for the 'poorest of the poor', is itself an admission of failure which will be used to tighten the noose around the necks of African countries. Although the total debt relief is expected to amount to $85 billion – a sizeable amount in relation to African total debt – it is not an outright cancellation. It involves a variety of detailed negotiations around interest rate reductions, debt reduction, re-scheduling and an increase in concessionary aid. These measures were intended to 'send a very strong signal' to the Paris Club overseeing into these detailed manoeuvres. The US government has announced that its participation in this 'deal' will be *conditional* on African countries carrying out the Baker Plan structural adjustments.

Thus it must be concluded that the crisis that international finance-capital increasingly pushed onto the shoulders of the oppressed and exploited majority in Third World countries will intensify, even if it appeared to be ameliorating in the short-term by these manoeuvres. Such short-term 'shot-in-the-arm' solutions will in fact add to the ever engulfing crisis which, in the end, must undermine the very existence of international finance-capital itself. The 'crash', while it must not be seen as a 'doomsday' scenario, is in my view evidence of an ongoing phenomenon which will worsen as the system of production becomes incapable of responding.

Notes

1. The discussion on this issue was exhausted in Chapter Three of my main book, *The Rise and Fall of Money Capital*.

2. Marx, K. *Capital*, vol. 2, Progress Publishers, Moscow, 1956, p.113.

3. This discussion arose out of the Dar es Salaam debate. See Tandon, Y.T. *The University of Dar es Salaam Debate on Class, State and Imperialism*, Tanzania Publishing House, Dar es Salaam, 1982.

4. See International Monetary Fund (IMF) *Surveys of African Economies*, vols. 1–6, Washington, DC, 1984.

5. Kamarck, A.M. *The Economics of African Development*, Praeger, London, 1965.

6. Frank, A.G. 'Capitalism and Underdevelopment in Latin America', *Monthly Review*, New York, 1967, pp.70–2.

7. Quoted in extensio in *ibid.*, pp.172-3.

8. Little, A.D. *Tanganyika Industrial Development*, Dar es Salaam, Government Printers, 1961.

9. Kuuya, M. 'Import Substitution as an Industrial Strategy: The Case of Tanzania', in Rweyemamu, J.F. (ed) *Industrialisation and Income Distribution in African Countries*, CODESRIA, 1982.

10. *The Herald, Zimbabwe.*

11. Goreaux, L.M. 'Compensatory Financing Facility', *IMF pamphlet series no. 34*, IMF, Washington, DC, 1986.

12. Cole, T.K.E. 'Monetary Management in Africa: The Role of the Treasury or Government in African countries', mimeo, 1981.

13. Reserve Bank of Zimbabwe, 'The Role of Government in Monetary Management', mimeo, 1981.

14. *Ibid.* See also Moyo, T. *Zimbabwe Journal of Economics*, vol. 1, no. 4, Harare, Zimbabwe.

15. *Ibid.*

16. Bhattia, A. 'The Exchange Rate Policy in African Countries', *Monetary Management in Africa*, May 1985, p.238.

17. *Daily Nation*, Nairobi, Kenya, 2 May 1988, p.11.

18. *Economic Impact*, no. 6, 1987/4, p.14.

19. International Bank for Reconstruction and Development (IBRD) 'Uganda: Agricultural Sector Memorandum', Washington, DC, July 1984, p.18.

20. IBRD 'Uganda: Towards Recovery and Prospects for Development', Washington, DC, 1985, p.19.

Conclusion

The objective of this book was to demonstrate the relevance of the Marxist theory of money and credit to the analysis of the crisis of international finance-capital and the crash that increasingly threatens its financial markets. The analysis started from Marx's basic proposition that money evolves as an aspect of commodity production in general and that it retains its essential characteristics and functions under capitalism, although in this evolution under capitalism in particular, credit money develops to its utmost limits in the aspect of money as a means of payment. The increased accumulation of capitalist wealth is expanding beyond anything known before, while money-commodities place a definite limit in that although credit brings this form of production to the highest possible level, the demand to accumulate such wealth in gold in periods of crisis – when faith and confidence in paper money is shaken – makes money-commodities a central and essential element in capitalist development. This means that although money-credit enables capitalism to expand, it does not do away with money-commodities entirely, in contrast to the one-sided expectations of David Ricardo, and this element comes to the fore with each and every crisis and impending crash of financial markets.

This has been clear in the analysis. All that needs to be said here in conclusion is that the problems that build up to threaten international finance-capital are, as we saw earlier, to be found within the contradictions of the capitalist system of production itself. The basic contradiction is that which exists between labour and capital as social forces on a global scale. When capitalism in its early stages of development faces its first crises, it extends the contradiction to the fields of the peasant and proletarian masses in the colonies. This attempt, while strengthening capital out of these early crises, creates new oppositional forces on the side of labour. Although new

bourgeois forces are added, the mass of an exploited peasantry that joins the world market as direct producers for capital soon counterbalance these new exploiting forces – many of them recruited from the old feudal or semi-feudal forces.

The colonial enclaves of production and the colonial state therefore become sub-centres of the reproduction of capitalist relations and struggles. As these exploitative relations are exposed to the bulk of the population, a national contradiction emerges which creates the first battle line between these forces and finance-capital. Although a national state is created out of these battles and although the native bourgeoisie emerges and tries to consolidate bourgeois relations in collaboration with international finance-capital, this new alliance of bourgeois forces is once more opposed by the exploited and oppressed worker–peasant masses. This forms the second battle line against international finance-capital, or imperialism.

As these battles intensify and as the working-class in the capitalist states intensify their own struggle at home, finance-capital increasingly finds it difficult to reproduce itself at a 'reasonable' rate of profit and, as this happens, it closes down production points to try to diversify and concentrate on the most profitable outlets. But here too the going is not made any easier and open revolts of exploited masses in the form of 'IMF riots' or strikes take place. With mass starvations in the former colonies, capital finds it cannot reproduce the labouring classes that it needs to perpetuate its rule. Thus both in capitalist and Third World states, a point is reached when no further 'reform' or restructuring is possible, and as the urge to make money without the intervention of production increases, so does finance-capital take on a more and more speculative, parasitic composition. But since capital cannot reproduce itself by making money out of fictitious capital without the intervention of production, it must collapse out of these struggles of the exploited and oppressed classes. These struggles must ultimately result in the political overthrow of the bourgeoisie as a ruling class and the eventual elimination and abolition of class rule.

Thus the crisis of the international finance system cannot be reformed to remove these fundamental contradictions of capitalism. Plans to create a new international currency after the dollar cannot work, just as appeals for the creation of a new gold-based

monetary system to bring about fixed exchange rates have all proved abortive in the past few years. Capitalism will come to an end with the abolition of the nation-state system, and only this can provide the basis for a truly international economy. Capitalism arises with the modern nation-state and it is behind this nation-state structure that the bourgeoisie are able to maintain their class rule over labour. Capitalism also has the tendency to create super nation-states in the form of imperialist states to maintain an international hegemony. But this is also undermined by the very contradictions of imperialist finance-capital. This hegemony is in fact the very evil being fought by the people of the world.

Indeed, the struggle to eliminate imperialism and its servant international finance-capital is the struggle to eliminate national exploitation and oppression, and within the same struggle are contained the roots of the elimination of the nation-state itself. The elimination of the nation-state is the elimination of capitalism and with it the elimination of money-capital as a system of productive relations which, as we have shown, is increasingly happening within the activities of capitalism itself. Socialism must emerge as capitalism's opposite but only momentarily, for the march of society to a free world – a world under communism – can no longer be stopped. This will be a *one-world* without class exploitation and oppression.

Part Two (2009)

The 2007–08 Meltdown

Postscript: the 2007–08 Meltdown

Background

The global economic crisis that struck the world in 2007–08 had long been predicted. Writing at the peak of the Asian financial crisis of 1997–98, George Soros, one of those financial 'wizards' who participated in that crisis, wrote a book, *The Crisis of Global Capitalism: Open Society Endangered*, in which he analysed the problems behind that crisis and its implications for global capitalism and called for the regulation of economic globalisation. Soros observed that unless there was such control, the global economy was bound to 'break down'.[1] In early 2008 before the September financial meltdown, he wrote another book entitled *The New Paradigm for Financial Markets: The Credit Crisis of 2008 and What it Means* in which he attempted to advance his views about the need for 'reflexivity' in understanding of the operations of financial markets, which mainstream economic theories did not accommodate.[2] Earlier in 1989 in the original edition of this book, I made similar warnings. We observed:

> There can be no doubt in anyone's mind, least of all in the minds of the financial oligarchy that manages and exploits the world's resources, that the international capitalist system is in utter crisis. The crisis of the system has, since the 1929–31 crash and depression, apparently been 'pushed off' from time to time by various adjustment innovations. However, each crisis management innovation has added the ills of the previous solutions to the new ones and complicated possibilities for future innovations. Furthermore, the crisis loops have become shorter and shorter for most of the countries of the world with the result that in a

majority of these countries the loops have become merged into one gigantic continuous and ongoing *mega-crisis*.[3]

What was said then has come to pass, with the leading capitalist countries becoming caught up in a crisis that had been building up all these years but whose signs were simply ignored. Indeed, it can be said that the Asian financial crisis of 1997–98 was a warning of the impending collapse. But this crisis was used purely as another opportunity to adjust, for world capitalism had by then developed a new sense of triumphalism – especially after the collapse of the Soviet Union – based on never-ending success. Now we are faced with a mega-crisis, which few of the world's leading capitalist countries know how to overcome. How did this come about? We try to analyse the current crisis and in a concluding chapter we indicate The Way Forward.

What is the Root Cause of the Crisis?

In examining the origins of the credit crisis of 2008, Soros traced it to the activities of financial institutions from 6 August 2007 and the subsequent events that led to the near insolvency of the British-owned Northern Rock on 13 September 2007 – the largest British mortgage banker – a crisis that had triggered off an 'old-fashioned bank run for the first time in Britain in a hundred years'.[4] Even after tracing these immediate events which led to the 'credit crunch' in the UK and the US from August 2007, Soros still found it necessary to state: 'The crisis was slow in coming, but it could have been anticipated several years in advance. It had its origins in the bursting of the internet bubble in late 2000.'[5] But that was a misstatement and underestimation of the deep origins of the crisis.

Indeed, as the analysis in this book's original edition sought to demonstrate, the Black Monday crash of 9 October 1987 was traceable even further back to the events of the 1970s with the de-industrialisation of the capitalist economy, especially within Britain. Chapter Five of this book referred to the serious contraction in British industrial production between 1970 and 1980 (the British Minister of Industry, Anthony Wedgwood Benn, had dated this contraction to several years before, going as far back as 1965), and this contraction had reflected a serious struggle between capital and labour, a

struggle that ultimately resulted in the election of Margaret Thatcher. But even then, those problems leading to the contraction of industry had their origins in Britain's earlier economic activities. Having campaigned to fight the powers of the trade unions – whom she blamed for all Britain's economic problems – Thatcher adopted policies to advance the interests of the country's financial oligarchy by deregulating the state's capacity to intervene to protect labour against capital. This was aimed at setting in motion a new period of capitalist accumulation that relied less on industrial production and more on the 'financial industry' and 'financial services'.

The crash of 1987 was therefore very much in keeping with previous developments in the capitalist economy that had led to the fall of the rate of profit in industry, which Karl Marx had only tentatively referred to as a 'tendency' in the evolution of industrial profits. Marx had argued that the capitalists would increasingly exhaust the possibilities of extracting surplus-value from living labour, trying as they did to replace living labour with machinery. Since machinery was dead labour unable to produce surplus-value, there would be a 'tendency' for the rate of profit to fall *pari passu*. As the oldest industrial economy in the world, it was not surprising that this historical tendency in capitalist production should have first taken root in Britain, leading to the de-industrialisation of production and the emergence of the era of production of money-out-of-money without substantial material production from industry.

It is this tracing of material capitalist production that must inform the emergence of 'globalisation' as a phenomenon increasingly reliant on 'financial services' as its dynamic driving force in earning 'profits'. This is also the context in which the events of 2000 onwards have to be analysed and understood. It is therefore not enough to simply focus on the years 2000–01 as the beginning of the current financial crisis, as George Soros has done. While it can be stated that the crisis 'originated' in the bursting of the internet bubble in late 2000 that led the Federal Reserve to cut interest rates from 6.5% to 3.5% within the space of just a few months, a development followed by the 9/11 terrorist attack in 2001 (which forced the US government to counteract the effects of the attack on the economy by cutting the interest rate even further down to 1% in July 2003), such 'cut-off' points can be misleading because they obscure

the more long-term and creeping problems faced by the capitalist economies in general.

The internet bubble itself has to be explained, as well as the 9/11 terrorist attacks. If this is done, it will be found that the internet bubble arose from dot-com investment in information technology that pushed the relationship between capital and labour to the maximum level that could have been permitted by 'the market'. It is also true that the 'cheap money' which became possible after these two events led to the beginnings of the housing bubble that followed in 2007, but this bubble had deep roots in the 'real economy' that was increasingly weakening against the financial markets. Indeed, the internet bubble was just part of the manifestation of the sharpening of this contradiction between capital and labour. It reflected the sharp struggle between labour and attempts by the capitalists to find new ways of utilising dead labour in the form of technology to reduce the cost of living labour (variable capital) in order to increase profits. Ultimately, living labour turned out to be too expensive to sustain a long-term exploitation of this option.

In his remarks before the New York Association for Business Economics on 6 June 2001, the Governor of the Federal Reserve Board of New York State argued that the acceleration in productivity made possible by the 'New Economy' had set off complex dynamics. The Governor stated that these had been the encouraging of an investment boom to take advantage of the new profit opportunities provided by technological advances and a consumption boom in response both to expectations around quicker growth in labour-income and a surge in equity values reflecting optimism about higher earnings growth. As a result, the unemployment rate became progressively lower, while at the same time the higher rate of productivity growth meant a lower cost of production for a given level of wages. That, he noted, had initially boosted profits, only to be quickly followed by a 'dis-inflationary virtuous cycle' that allowed the economy to accommodate a progressively tighter labour market, resulting in a reduction in employed labour.

This raised the question of whether the economic performance of that period, especially between 1996 and mid-2000, was sustainable. In other words, did new-economy forces eliminate the risks of overheating and higher inflation that were so much a part of

the 'old' neo-Keynesian economy of full employment? This was doubtful and therefore, given the uncertainties around a sustainable configuration of unemployment, output growth and inflation, there was a lack of a precise roadmap of where the 'New Economy' needed to go. This is what prompted the tightening of monetary policy from mid-1999 onwards. Therefore, it can be said that 1999–2000 was a new watershed in the adjustment of the relationships between capital and labour in manufacturing that led to new policy drive to upstage the financial services as an engine of growth.

This was also because economic growth in the pre-1999 period fell more sharply than had been anticipated. Employment had slowed down, in part because monetary policy was committed to such an outcome. But late in the year, the economy decelerated even more sharply. This sharper slowdown reflected, partly, the contribution of several additional shocks that reinforced the effect of monetary policy tightening. The result was increased interest rates for low-rated borrowers and tighter underwriting standards at banks. The decline in equity valuations for high-tech firms, the virtual closing of opportunities for initial public offerings, and the higher quality spreads for low-rated borrowers naturally hit start-up and new technology firms especially hard. Equity prices fell sharply, particularly technology stocks, with the NASDAQ (National Association of Securities Dealers Automated Quotations) declining nearly 60% and internet stocks about 70% from their peaks.

This was, according to the Governor, a perfect example of an unwinding of a pre-existing imbalance in the unsustainable rise in equity values in the technology sector caused by the initial rise in profits of the New Economy. The correction of equity prices presumably reflected, at least in part, a re-evaluation of the profitability of owning and producing high-tech capital and software, a deterioration in the expected earnings of telecommunications firms, and a reappraisal of the earnings prospects of dot-com firms. These reassessments of the value of these firms had in fact much to do with earlier developments in the decline in industry and little to do with monetary policy or the overall slowdown in growth. The frenzy of investments arising from advances in technology resulted in some investments that were successful and others that were not. This was

a second example, and one that was perhaps less noticed earlier, of the unwinding of an unsustainable trend in this new sector. At any rate, a shake-up in the high-technology area and retrenchment of investment spending followed because of weakened demand, and the accumulation of inventories led to firms moving to cut down production to not just a level supported by the slowdown in demand, but one even lower to shed off the excess inventories. These were adjustments that were made to move away from the 'old' industrial model, as well as the new one.

So the dot-com bubble and the consequent slowdown in the economy were part of a much deeper malaise than that which was being advanced by many economists about the current 'financial crisis'. In fact the New Economy had suffered the same old Dutch disease, resulting in an almost fully fledged recession due to these developments. Just like today, the wealth that had been accumulated in the dot-com economy in a few years had quickly disappeared, almost as mysteriously. In much the same vein, many firms had gone bankrupt, especially riskier ventures in the technology sector. This is what led to the drastic cut in interest rates by the Federal Reserve from 6.5% in 2000 to 3.5% in order to prevent the full-scale recession that was feared. The fear was worsened by the 9/11 terrorist attacks, resulting in a further cut to rock-bottom interest rates of 1% in July 2003.

But instead of resulting in an overall economic recovery, these low interest rates instead resulted in a new strategy of recruiting new investors in the form of 'sub-prime' borrowers, leading to a growth in housing construction that was seized upon by speculators. The housing bubble was itself the result of leveraged buyouts and other financiering excesses characteristic of the late monopoly capitalism of speculators, a new form of speculation which involved large numbers of borrowers and buyers of houses. As pointed out, the market value of the housing market grew by 50% between 2000 and mid-2005, resulting in a frenzy of new construction. Estimates by Merrill Lynch indicated that about half of all American GDP (gross domestic product) growth in the first half of 2005 was housing-related as this was where 'easy money' could be made from the 'cheap money' engendered by the housing boom.

From 1997 through 2006, sub-prime consumers were able to draw more than $9 trillion in cash out of their home equities, which

were in turn financing personal consumption. These were the beginnings of sub-prime easy credit, which the new financial oligarchy was unleashing to create 'new wealth'. By the first quarter of 2006, home equity withdrawals accounted for over 10% of all personal disposable income. This led to double-digit price increases in house prices engendered by speculators, leading in turn to the construction of 'second homes' simply for the purpose of extracting 'free income' for speculators and giving rise to the securitisation mania, as we already observed. This is the background to the speculative frenzy that led to the 2008 credit crunch and the consequent financial crisis, both of which are deeply rooted in the crisis of the global capitalist economy, which is unfolding within a new, fully fledged recession already showing signs of deflation and depression.

The Credit Crunch and the 'Sub-Prime' Mortgage Crash

The attempt to detach the creation of credit in the name of 'money' from its material production base and to try to make money out of 'money' without production was foreseen by Marx as one of the weaknesses and limitations of the capitalist form of production. This problem has been exacerbated by the more recent power of investment banks to leverage and create credit instruments such as 'collateralised debt obligations' (CDOs) and 'derivative contracts' that were not backed by any form of material production of goods or wealth-creating services. This became possible because in the US and Britain the financial capitalists had managed to create new levels of capitalist 'wealth' in tiered credit and financial instruments and 'products' which were structured in great part around working-class earnings, pension funds and even the prospect of future employment as the basis for sub-prime mortgage lending.

This development had exposed the real limitations of capitalist production in that while technological development permitted the production of material goods and services to almost unlimited levels, the relations of production – expressed in the form of private profit and money as wealth, which were extracted from labour – had held back that production and limited it to the money-wealth needs of that class. On the other hand, there emerged a group of financial capitalists – whom Marx had called the 'financial

oligarchy' or 'financial bandits' – whose sole interest was to make money out of money without the backing of production. This they attempt by endeavouring to equate the 'values' of their credit instruments to 'real money' backed by some form of production such as houses, which were themselves a form of 'hedge' against possible threats to real wealth. Interestingly, this 'sub-prime' wealth was itself a consequence of drawing the working-class into new forms of exploitation represented by the new loans extended to them for purposes of securitisation and leveraging.

This fundamental reality was in fact behind the so-called 'sub-prime' mortgage crisis, which was in essence a last ditch attempt by the financial oligarchy to bring the gains made by labour in the form of wages and other wage acquisitions and entitlements into the web of money-making without production. Having exhausted all their 'capital' acquisitions in the dot-com New Economy, they now tried to tap the workers' earnings by 'capitalising' and 'financialising' them into speculative activities and new financial instruments. This was done in the name of making workers have a share in the new 'wealth' that was being created by speculators of the New Economy. Although it is said that most of the financiers who engaged in this new 'trade' were 'unregulated' companies, it should be noted that in fact the placing of workers' earnings into speculative hedge funds was conducted by 'responsible' bodies such as governments, municipalities, corporations and mutual funds, among others. In the US the Securities and Exchange Commission (SEC) reported that about 20% of corporate and public pension funds were among hedge funds in 2002, up from 15% in 2001. When other developed countries were included, it was estimated that pension funds overall constituted 30% of the investor hedge-fund base as these funds were 'attracted' by high returns and as a strategy for 'diversifying' their holdings.

All this sweet new vocabulary could not hide the fact that what was actually happening was that capital had exhausted its capacity to drain enough surplus value from productive labour. Likewise, having also exhausted their profits, deeply rooted in the collapsed dot-com New Economy, the new financiers now wanted to tap workers' wages from their safe havens into the more 'profitable' housing economy. The mortgages became known as 'sub-prime'

for that reason, because those who were being wooed into the new speculative activity were not simply workers but also the retired and the unemployed, who did not have a secure income. It did not matter anymore whether you were employed, retired or unemployed so long as you could be lent 'free money' with which to buy a house, because the new loan so created through sub-prime lending could be securitised and leveraged several times to create more wealth for the financial oligarchy.

Collateralised Debt Obligations

This drive by the financial oligarchy to earn 'free money' is what led to the creation of these baseless credit instruments, instruments that soon became blown out of all proportion to their material base and began to infect the 'real economy' of which they were a product. According to George Soros, the real problem began with the 'bursting of the internet bubble' of 2000 and the 9/11 terrorist attack, which resulted in the US Federal Reserve lowering interest rates to around 1% by July 2003, as already observed. For Soros, it was this 'cheap credit' which 'engendered the housing bubble' as the 'explosion of leveraged buyouts and other excesses' begun to take place.[6] Soros equates this low rate of interest to the availability of 'free money' and argues that, 'when money is free, the rational lender will keep lending until there is no one else to lend to.'[7] At this level, mortgage lenders 'relaxed their standards and invented new ways to stimulate business and generate fees' in the form of 'free money' and 'free income' for themselves.[8]

This is what led investment banks such as Merrill Lynch, as well as privatised former state institutions such as Freddie Mac and Fannie Mae, to expand mortgage lending by almost 50% between 2000 and mid-2005, which reflected itself in US GDP growth. This housing property boom was reflected directly in a frenzy of construction, including the valuing of new furniture, and indirectly in the spending of the cash generated from the refinancing of mortgages, estimated to have constituted more than half of US GDP in the first half of 2005. This wealth 'was created in' structured investment vehicles (SIVs) so that investment banks could keep it off their balance sheets in order to deceive investors that their credit position was safe.

This contrivance made it possible for the banks to create yet more credit instruments in the shape of 'collateralised debt obligations' (CDOs), which they were able to hold in large amounts and through them sell off their most risky mortgages to other banks by 'repackaging them into securities' and thereby keeping them off their balance sheets. It is the SIVs that were used to finance their positions by issuing asset-backed commercial paper, and when these dried up the banks were forced to bail out their own SIVs, at least for a time. The CDOs frenzy took on an autonomous momentum. They were used to channel the cash flows from thousands of mortgages into a tier-structured tranche credit system, more like a pyramid. This tier-structured credit mechanism was 'tranched' into bonds with varying risks 'tuned to different investor tastes' and involving a class of asset-backed securities through 'special purpose vehicles' (SPVs) comprising assets rearranged into different tranches with different credit ratings, interest rates and priority payments. The top tier, which held about 80% of the bonds, had the first call on all underlying cash flows (very much preferential shares in the equity market) with an AAA rating given by rating agencies that give value to the assets. The lower tiers were made to absorb first dollar risks but they carried higher yields and were rated lower.

With this frenzy, houses were by 2005 built not so much for permanent residential purposes, but merely as 'investments' or 'second homes'. The most popular devices used to make houses appear affordable were the 'adjustable rate mortgages' (ARMs) with a 'teaser' consisting of below-market rates for an initial two-year period. This manipulation was based on the false assumption that these lower-rated mortgages would be re-financed from new, higher housing prices, which would generate new set of fees for the lenders, with the overall result being the creation of a vast pyramid scheme that seemed to be self-financing.

It was in these circumstances that standards based on 'rational' economic 'reasoning' collapsed, and this made it possible for the new group of 'financial bandits', as Marx called them, to create mortgages and construct houses for workers who had low credit ratings or who were without any meaningful income. These new mortgages were then rated 'Alt-A' or sub-prime mortgages. They were in reality 'liar loans' (as some economists called them) given

to unsuspecting working-class and unemployed customers. These loans were commonly available and came with no documentation, along with the 'ninja loans' given to people with no jobs, no income, and no assets but perhaps with some future hope of being employed. Indeed, this was done with the active connivance of the mortgage brokers and mortgage lenders. This is how the (securitised) collateralised debt obligations came into being, in part by speculating on the possible future employment of labour in some form.

Securitisation was meant to reduce risks through this risk-tiered and geographic diversification of assets, but instead this technique increased risks by transferring the ownership of mortgages from bankers who knew their customers to investors who did not, with securities sold 'off the counter'. This was achieved through a series of transactions whereby 'loans' based on mortgages were 'sourced' to brokers who temporarily 'warehoused' them in thinly capitalised 'mortgage bankers'. The 'loans' were then sold *en bloc* to investment banks who had manufactured the CDOs to be resold to institutional investors. The institutions that handled the CDOs earned 'fees' on them, which were passed on to the next buyer. The logic was, 'The higher the volume, the bigger the bonus.'

Leveraging was the next step in this game. It was the stuff that made 'free money' for the financial oligarchies that were behind the credit-creation mania. In countries such as the United States, this new credit system increasingly became a kind of inverted Ponzi pyramid, with the 'real' money in the form of deposits and time deposits constituting only 10% of the system – called M1, M2 and M3 by the Federal Reserve – at the base of the inverted pyramid. The next tier of the pyramid was the securitised debt accounting for 20% in the middle. The remaining 70% was constituted by the new wealth of derivative financial instruments and other forms of future options that had little or no link to the base. This financial structure when compared to global GDP became a real burden to the productive capacity of the people of the world, which stood at slightly under $50 trillion in 2006. The leveraging had got out of hand. According to estimates, the average Wall Street bank was leveraged 30 times in 2006 compared to 12 times in 2004, while the leverage in ordinary commercial banks (those without investment bank activities) amounted to 10 times in 2006. If 'off-balance-sheet'

items such as SPVs are included, the leverage became much higher, perhaps as much as 20 times the 'real' assets held by the banks in the real economy.

It is with this frenzied activity that securitisation took on a momentum of its own, beginning around 2005. In this frenzy, 'synthetic' securities that were tailored to mimic the risks of real securities without the expense of buying and assembling actual loans became commonplace. Risky paper could be created and multiplied several times beyond the actual supply in the marketplace. Creative investment bankers were able to 'slice' up CDOs and repackage them into CDOs of CDOs or CDO 1-2-3, as well as new financial 'products' called 'synthetic collateralised debt obligations' (SCDOs).

Towards the end of 2007, these synthetic products accounted for more than half the trading volumes of all securities, which were not restricted to mortgages. Securitisation and leveraging were spread to other forms of credit with the consequence that by far the largest synthetic market was constituted by 'credit default swaps' (CDS), which Soros has called an 'arcane synthetic financial instrument' invented in Europe in the 1990s.[9] Prior to the invention of the CDS, a bank wishing to diversify its portfolio would buy or sell pieces of loans, which was a complicated process because it required the permission of the borrower. For this reason, this new form of diversification became very popular with the customers. It also enabled terms for taking loans to be standardised so that by 2000 the notional value of these contracts in the US amounted to about $1 trillion.

The picture changed when hedge funds entered the market in the early 2000s, when specialised credit hedge funds effectively acted as unlicensed insurance companies, collecting premiums on the CDOs and other securities that they insured. Estimated to be around $42.6 trillion by 2008, the value of this market grew exponentially until it overwhelmed all other markets in nominal terms and was believed to equal 'almost the entire household wealth of the United States'.[10] The estimated capitalisation of the US stock market was $18.5 trillion, and the US Treasury bills and bonds market was only $4.5 trillion in comparison.

It was this securitisation mania which led to another 'innovation' in the form of 'financiering' called the 'debt leverage'. This became a mechanism by which 'margins' were created between

different kinds of assets, allowing hedge funds to show good profits by exploiting risk differentials on a leveraged basis, which assisted with 'driving down' risk premiums and became a new form of credit-creation. This is what created the environment in which new forms of credit-creation and credit-manipulation emerged called the 'Derivative Contract'. It was also this form of financial manipulation that created environments in which individual hedge fund firms such as that of Bernard Madoff were able to set up Ponzi pyramid-like schemes through which they could defraud rich families and foundations of their investments by paying off the old investors with monies received from new investors, thereby earning themselves 'free money' in the form of 'fees'.

But Soros is here also inverting reality because it is not the 'cheap credit' that 'engendered the housing bubble' and which then began to affect the real economy. Rather it was the unproductive 'real economy' caused by the falling profitability of labour in industry that had led to the dot-com New Economy in the first place. The large numbers of unemployed that followed became a problem but also an opportunity for the new financial oligarchy, because in the new financial economy, employed labour as was good as unemployed labour so long as both could be brought into the speculative economy to create 'cheap credit' and 'free money'. In short, 'cheap credit' was created for sub-prime borrowers so that a new pyramid of loans could be constructed for labourers – whether employed, retired or unemployed – to borrow from, and it is this manoeuvre that widened the base for the creation of 'free money' based on speculation for the oligarchy.

The Derivative Contract

A hedge fund created by an investment bank, the derivative contract is a credit default swap arrangement through which the contracting party is promised to be paid the full amount of the contract in case of loss. The hedge fund would be created from 'real money' and the fund would be used to 'insure' different kinds of debts that have been created out of assets such as mortgages. Thus there are different kinds of derivatives used for different purposes. Interest-rate swaps are used against changes in interest rates, which might adversely affect the contract. They are said to be more

reliable because such changes will only cause a crisis in the event of 'highly unlikely spikes in interest or inflation'.[11] These derivatives accounted for a nominal value of $393 trillion at the end of October 2007.

The more 'dangerous' sector of the derivative market was said to be credit swaps, which according to *Newsweek* in October 2007 were the more likely to 'implode'. The notional value of these 'assets' was estimated by *Newsweek* to be 'worth' $55 trillion. They are considered particularly risky because 'they work like hurricane insurance', with a likely large payout in case of loss. This occurred when Lehman Brothers, one of the 'respectable' investment bankers, suddenly failed, thereby putting a huge strain on CDS holders. Indeed, in a newsletter to investors reported on the BBC World Service in March 2003, a financial expert by the name of Warren Buffet had already described derivatives and CDS credit instruments as 'financial weapons of mass destruction' owing to their vulnerability to crisis. Buffet added that they constituted a 'catastrophic risk' to the economy because of their exposure to risk themselves.

Derivatives were at first regarded as 'insurance products' intended to spread risk where one pays a premium and gets 'protection'. But according to Buffet, they soon developed to become a means of investment in their own right. It has been estimated that the 'notional value' of all derivative instruments in their different forms was somewhere between $668 trillion and $700 trillion by 2007. This is not 'real money', illustrated by the fact that the total world market value – most of which is also 'fictitious' in Marxian terms – is only estimated to be in the region of $15 trillion. This means the rest of the 'value' of the derivative contract arrangement, estimated to be 'larger than the US economy' and counting before the collapse, is worthless. Derivates were said by *Newsweek* to be 'doubling in size every two or three years for the last decade' and likely to continue due to the fact that there is 'no real alternative' to the arrangements so long as capitalism is in place. Indeed, there was a likelihood, according to *Newsweek*, that the derivatives market 'could become a quadrillion-dollar market'. At this rate and given the current crisis in the system, the capitalist system has become 'over-ripe', as Lenin once said, and ready for fundamental transformation at its core.

According to the same publication, there are several reasons for the growth of the derivatives behind the leveraging mania. The first is the invention of sophisticated computer programming that has made it easier 'to create price complicated derivatives'. Another reason, it added, 'is the continuing rise of "quants"', by which *Newsweek* meant maths geniuses who were recruited by Wall Street in the mid-1980s precisely to invent exotic new financial products. As top universities smelt 'the new money', they also intensified their own 'production' of graduates engaged in 'financial engineering' for deployment in the new market.

It was therefore not surprising that in their initial recommendations, the G20 summit of the heads of state who met in Washington, DC, on 15 November 2008 'tasked' their Ministers and experts in their summit declaration to 'strengthen the resilience and transparency of the credit derivatives markets and reduce their systematic risks, including the improvement of the infrastructure of over-counter markets.[12] This proves that this form of speculation is endemic to the capitalist system and no matter what the experts do, the risk of the over-extension of credit is bound to 'implode' even with the creation of a global clearinghouse for 'managing' and 'controlling' these kinds of transactions.

Yet with the rapid expansion of capitalist production and credit-creation, the problem still remained around the functions of money, especially as the system got 'reformed'. The classical political economy myth remains that money's main function is its role as a medium of exchange of commodities and not as an end in itself. This myth is still held despite that fact that the functions of money – as expressed in all modern textbooks – recognise money as having three functions: as a unit of account; as a medium of exchange and as a store of value. For this reason, George Soros – like Karl Marx – believes that the third function of money as store of value or 'intrinsic value' is 'not well understood' and therefore needs more consideration in the current crisis.

But this view of Soros is also partial because although the classical view still prevails in popular consciousness regarding the third function of money, this is a 'false consciousness'. Ultimately, when money in the form of over-extended credit cannot function properly as an exchange-value because of the loss of its 'value', the demand

for money in its third function still remains. This means that the $700 trillion 'wealth' created in the CDO and derivative markets also has a claim to the store of 'real money' or 'cash' whose base is increasingly diminishing.

This is so despite the fact that money as an exchange-value has become an end in itself in the sense that it is related to political power in which the state and elites are deeply interested. Therefore to maintain money as an exchange-value in some form becomes a reality in which the state (itself a debtor) is deeply interested. That is why the state must always 'bail out' the banks and the financial oligarchy in order to enable them to maintain some form of production to keep the political order in place and the existing 'values' maintained. This Soros acknowledges when he states, 'The ones who keep going end up wielding the most power and influence in the capitalist system.'[13] But this cannot go on forever. It merely proves what Marx long ago said of the capitalist state's being at the service of capital against labour.

At some point, money in its function as an end in the production and circulation of commodities must itself come to an end. According to Soros, this must come when those who hold wealth procured from the system – the financial oligarchy – decide that they prefer to accumulate their 'real' wealth in some form of reliable money-commodity in view of the threat posed by 'toxic assets' with no value. Currently most people insist on 'hard cash' instead of parting with it in excessive shopping. In that case money will become the 'ultimate goal' sought after by all wealth holders. This is because when everyone is struggling for more money, the competition becomes so intense 'that even the most successful are reduced to the position of having to fight for survival'.

In that case the past autonomy and discretion enjoyed by the capitalist state and the financial oligarchy to create credit will have been lost. At this stage, even the demand for gold as real money will not be met for most of the wealth holders since there will not be enough of it to go round. Therefore, those most favoured by the state and who are at the centre of its political power will have access placed in the state to 'mint and coin' money. The rest will fall by the wayside to join the large army of the unemployed labour force, which will have been discarded by capital. For that reason, gold

will provide no safe haven for the majority of the financial oligarchy and will therefore come to an end.

Speculation and the Food Crisis

It has transpired that one of the factors behind the sudden rise and fall in the prices of commodity products, especially food products, has been the speculation that entered this sector of the economy. According to a study carried out by the Institute for Agriculture and Trade Policy (IATP) based in Minneapolis, Minnesota, titled 'Commodities Market Speculation: The Risk to Food Security and Agriculture' released in September 2008, $317 billion had by July 2008 been invested in speculative commodity index funds, led by major traders such as Goldman Sachs and the American Insurance Group (AIG). These index funds create constant upward pressure on commodity prices and 'bundle' futures contracts of up to 24 agricultural and non-agricultural commodities, including oil, energy and base precious metals. This 'bundling', according to the report, means that the price movements of these commodities can trigger the sale of a fund contract, regardless of the supply and demand situation in an agricultural commodity.[14]

The result is increased volatility and uncontrollable price movements. Although commercial speculation is not new, having been used even in the 19th century to enable commodity traders and processors to protect themselves against short-term price volatility, the current speculation, according to the report, has become too 'excessive' relative to the value of the commodity as determined by supply and demand and the other fundamental factors.[15] The report gives data from the United Nations Food and Agriculture Organisation (FAO) in which it is indicated that as of April 2008, corn volatility was 30% and soybean volatility 40% beyond what could be accounted for by market fundamentals. It added that price volatility had become so extreme that by July 2008, some commercial or 'traditional' speculators could no longer afford to use the market to hedge risks effectively. This meant that in addition to undermining industrial production, capitalist greed had undermined the oldest of the industries, agriculture.

Indeed, during the first three months of 2008, international nominal prices of all major food commodities had reached their highest

levels for 50 years. The FAO reported that food-price indexes had risen by 8% on average in 2006 compared with the previous year. In 2007, the food index rose by 24% compared with 2006 and in the first three months of 2008, it rose by 53% compared with 2007. This sudden surge was led by increases in the price of vegetable oil, which on the average increased by 97%, followed by grains with an increase of 87%, dairy products with 58% and rice with 46%.

An article that appeared in Toronto's *The Globe and Mail* on 31 May 2008 argued that it was the deregulation of financial markets and the systematic exploitation of US regulatory loopholes that had led to the upsurge of speculative investments in food commodity markets, much of it by institutional investors such as the managers of pension funds. 'These funds', wrote the authors, 'have ploughed tens of billions of dollars into agricultural commodities as a way of diversifying their assets and improv[ing] returns for their investors.'[16] But it is clear that the malaise was much deeper and it is this malaise in the real economy that led to the relaxing of regulatory controls.

According to the authors, the amount of fund money invested in commodity indexes had climbed from just $13 billion in 2003 to a staggering $260 billion in March 2008, according to calculations based on regulatory filings. There were warnings that this amount could easily quadruple to $1 trillion if pension fund managers allocated a greater portion of their portfolio to commodities, as some consultants suggested they were poised to do. Thus it was the progressive loosening of regulatory requirements which made possible the enormous influx of money, much of it fleeing the meltdown in the market for mortgage-backed securities and the wider fallout, including big leveraged buyouts in banks.

Because agricultural markets are small – relative to stock markets – the amount of cash pouring into these markets gives these funds substantial clout. The authors observed that these big institutional investors controlled enough wheat in futures instruments to supply the needs of American consumers for the next two years. They blamed the 'demand shock' from these recent entrants to the commodities markets as the primary factor behind the sudden soaring of food prices. They noted that if no immediate action was taken, food and energy prices were bound to rise still further,

leading to catastrophic economic effects on millions of already stressed US consumers and the possible starvation of millions of the world's poor.

The Response by States to the Financial Crisis

At first the US leaders thought the crisis was just a 'credit crunch' arising from the sub-prime mortgage crisis. But the crisis soon spread to the whole financial system and eventually to the entire 'real' economy. The shock took a definite dimension when it dawned on the Bush administration that the collapse of one of the leading investment banks – Bear Stearns – was imminent, but by then it was too late because soon after Lehman Brothers and Merrill Lynch went the same way. These 'standalone' investment banks were taken over by universal banks, leaving only Morgan Stanley and Goldman Sachs, both of which had also given up their status as leading investment banks to become bank-holding companies in order to have access to the 'bailout' that they were pressing the US government to make available to them through the Federal Reserve Fund.

This situation was compounded by the response to the crisis by individual countries, when in fact the crisis was a global one. The process of 'bailing out' the failing financial institutions begun with President George W. Bush rushing through Congress a plan of a colossal $700 billion under the name of the Troubled Assets Relief Program (TARP) to 'buy out toxic assets' that were threatening the collapse of these institutions. Congress passed the law on 3 October 2008, and the idea of buying 'toxic assets' was intended also to stabilise these banks and create an atmosphere of confidence for them to begin lending to each other and to industry and individuals once again. This turned out to be a misunderstanding of the crisis and so the first $250 billion pumped into the banks at this time ended up coming back to the Federal Reserve Bank as deposits by the very banks that were supposed to be 'saved' from collapse. This was because the banks calculated that their real problem was not extending credit but enhancing their credibility, which was perceived to lie in their increasing their liquidity reserve assets with the Central Bank – the Federal Reserve.

The 'toxic assets' that were being 'bought out' were the collateralised debt obligations and the credit default swaps, as well as the mortgage-backed securities that had clogged these institutions. But the problem was that the magnitude of the liquidity reserve assets of these banks was not known. Therefore, what the US Federal Reserve Fund was doing was pouring water over a vast fire in the hope that this would help to extinguish the troublesome flames on the credit market while installing confidence in the whole banking system. This however did not happen since the problem was not properly understood. It began to spread to Europe, where British Prime Minister Gordon Brown was the first to take note of what was happening. He too rushed through Parliament his own 'rescue' plan, but with a different approach. He proposed a £50 billion plan, which unlike the US 'bailout' programme was to buy shares in three commercial banks perceived to be near collapse, including Northern Rock. This was soon revised and raised to an £87 billion plan when it became clear that the problem was much bigger than had at first been thought.

The consequence was that the British government had become an investor in those banks. This response sent a different message to the British banks, which unlike the American banks began to slowly 'unfreeze' credit by lending to each other cautiously. But this was because in addition to buying shares, the British government had also required the banks to engage in inter-bank lending without the risk of losing their money. Even then, inter-bank lending and lending to small businesses were restrained, as confidence had not fully returned to the financial institutions. This put the US government on the spot, who with a lot of trepidation adopted the British approach by pumping $250 billion to re-capitalise nine banks with the purchase of shares in those banks, such 'unthinkable' 'socialist' measures helping capitalism to survive. But this time these banks had to give away part of their cake to the US government, which it was to use to manage the operations of those banks to return to 'normalcy', even though no one had any idea as to when the crisis would end.

In the meantime the crisis was spreading to the rest of Europe. Kaupthing, the leading bank in Iceland, collapsed, jeopardising the country's solvency. With the collapse, Iceland suspended all

trading in its finance sector. It began to negotiate a large loan with its Scandinavian neighbours, but it was Russia, with its large reserves, that was willing to listen. Other countries such as Ireland and Greece decided to guarantee individual savings bank accounts to the extent of 100%, which created problems for other countries, especially Britain, as individual depositors in Britain began to move their savings to Irish banks. As stocks continued to fall throughout the world, Switzerland also decided to come to the defence of its prized UBS bank with a $60 billion package. UBS was one of biggest losers from the US mortgage sub-prime crisis.

In these circumstances, an emergency summit of the European Union's (EU) member states was called in Paris over the weekend of 4–5 October 2008 to consider a number of proposals, and prominent among these was Gordon Brown's six-point plan for global financial reform. For their part, the EU leaders failed to adopt a single response to the crisis. Some countries such as France demanded greater oversight over financial institutions in Europe after they were forced to commit more than €1.8 trillion ($2.45 trillion) to their banks and the money markets. Other European countries wanted to set up a financial crisis cell to act as an early warning system. Britain demanded reviving plans to beef up Europe-wide supervision of cross-border finance groups.

Then Germany, fearing a run on its banks after the failure of the country's largest real estate company, the Hypo Real Estate, on 5 October 2008 announced a government plan involving $70 billion to guarantee banks' private deposits. This caused a shock in other European countries, who decried the go-it-alone policy and the lamentable absence of a common approach. In all, in this haphazard manner Europe (apart from Britain) came to the rescue of six banks. With no coordinated regional response, the European countries ended up only with a 'commitment' to 'cooperate', but with no concrete common plan.

The real problem for the Europeans was the fear of each country that there would be a run on particular banks in their countries if they did not respond individually, or that there might be a general run on their banks by depositors fearing that not only particular banks but also the financial system in the country would face collapse. Depositors had become jittery as they feared that their

savings were no longer safe and had concerns around whether the governments would guarantee their savings (or to what extent) in the event of banks' failure.

Brown's six-point plan went beyond just creating a global early warning system, which in the case of Britain would identify future risks to global economic and financial stability, calling for the reform of international financial management institutions such as the International Monetary Fund (IMF). His plan also recommended that national financial regulators coordinate their supervision amongst themselves, while calling for banks to disclose more of their trading positions. He wanted all this to be accomplished by the end of 2008 so that by that time each of the world's top 30 banks would be under the supervision of a panel of regulators from the countries where the IMF was most active.

But the German Finance Minister, Peter Steinbrueck, pointed out that Brown's plan had come 'two years too late'. It turned out that the German Chancellor Angela Merkel had, during her presidency of the Group of Eight (G8) in 2007, advanced similar measures. These proposals were rejected by the US and the UK when Gordon Brown was Chancellor of the Exchequer under Prime Minister Tony Blair.

In fact, the calls for the coordination of financial systems had been in place for a number of years. Many of the institutions mentioned by Brown in his plan such as the IMF, the European Central Bank and the Financial Stability Forum had all written earnest reports warning the world of the risks posed by the securitisation of credit, falling capital ratios, unregulated hedge funds as well as other financial market problems which had been building up in the global economy. But these calls had fallen on the deaf ears of these same politicians now calling for tougher measures.

It appeared that the real issue was that governments, including the British Government, were at the time reaping considerable benefits from the credit boom in the form of taxes to think too seriously about the problems. At the time, they were happy rewarding the banks with low interest rates, which encouraged them to dole out more and more credit to borrowers to purchase houses and hedging. Although Gordon Brown's plan for the formal reporting of risks by the banks might therefore help in the short run, it is highly unlikely to address the global imbalances which have fuelled this crisis over time.

Therefore what the EU and the US are planning to do is not enough without bringing together other countries throughout the world to look at the entire post-war economic architecture. The free movement of capital throughout the world based on securitised credit-creation is what has contributed to this global economic crisis. But this phenomenon is a very recent one due to the economic globalisation that began in the 1980s, before which time economies were more national in character.

The Persistence of the Crisis

These piecemeal responses did not avert the crisis. On the contrary, the worries continued when it began to dawn on the leaders that the crisis was not just a 'credit crunch' affecting financial institutions alone, but that the 'real economy' was weakening and adding to the momentum of the meltdown. 'Effective demand' began to decline as unemployment rates also began to increase in the US and European countries. What had added to the feeling of panic was the crisis in the money markets in which banks lend to one another when the so-called 'shadow banking system' made up of 'structured investment vehicles' (SIVs) came to a total collapse. The shadow banking system operates outside the rules of the normal banks. On 1 October 2008, one of these large 'shadow banks' called Sigma Finance closed down, sending panic throughout the system. This was because the SIVs were funding themselves with short-term credit carrying low interest rates and got their 'cut' by depositing the same funds in long-term investment instruments with high profits.

Such lending was therefore vulnerable to the freezing of credit in short-term funding and could not access central bank rescue funds as they were operating outside the official system. The banks had made use of these 'vehicles' as their credit could be placed outside of their balance sheets. Therefore, as the inter-bank lending begun to freeze up, the SIVs were the hardest hit. Inter-bank lending was normally for three-, six- or twelve-month periods and since they were not available at all, banks were forced to rely on 'overnight money' while keeping on 'hunting' for funds on a daily basis.

This meant that the banks could not fully run the 'money market funds' which provided short-term loans in the form of

commercial paper to companies in the 'real economy'. There was therefore a virtual freeze in that market, and this is what began to create tremors around the world as global corporations began to feel the pinch and the smell of a recession. Even top corporations such as General Electric in the US and AT&T were unable to tap into this market. During September alone, $200 billion was taken out of the commercial paper market and in the week beginning 29 September alone the amount lent to companies fell by $95 billion. The turning point in the freezing of the market had happened when one such large 'shadow bank' called Reserve Primary Fund lost the money it had lent to Lehman Brothers, which was frozen when the bank went bankrupt. These funds had been regarded as 'super safe' and therefore the failure of Lehman Brothers and the fall of the Reserve Primary Fund made investors and funds nervous about extending more loans, even to well-known companies.

More problems were making the system worse, especially in the $54 trillion credit derivative market in the US, when in October the effects of the collapse of credit companies such as Fannie Mae, Freddie Mac and Lehman Brothers, which went under because of their failure to settle their debts from these derivative contracts, began to be felt. This had added to the crisis of the insurance business, which resulted in these companies losing billions of dollars as well as those of the banks that had offered credit insurance. This meant that the insurance investors that had given protection and insured Lehman Brothers against defaulting on its debts were made to pay 80 to 85 cents to the dollar as Lehman's bonds on the financial markets plummeted to a mere 15 to 10 cents to the dollar – a problem that was bound to have wide repercussions across the entire system.

Then it transpired that there was the added problem of the expected shake-up of the hedge funds. It turned out that there were over 10,000 hedge funds in the US with assets of $2 trillion. Some investors in these funds were already demanding their money back as the near-Ponzi system begun to roll back, which forced some of these funds to be liquidated with the *Sunday Times* of London predicting that 'the firestorm' would be 'quick and violent'. In fact this violent firestorm resulted in the freezing of billions of dollars in hedge funds after the collapse of Lehman. It also resulted in a ban

on 'short-selling' stocks by governments in the US and Europe, creating an extremely volatile situation in financial markets and the 'evaporation' of credit as a result of the 'deadly climate' that had been created.

This 'clogging' of the financial system meant that credit could be available for 'real economy' investment, and this began to become an additional worry for governments in the US and Europe where the problem had begun to be felt by October. The problem was immediately felt with the sudden collapse of oil prices from $170 per barrel in June down to $90–5 by September. By December, prices had gone below $37 dollars per barrel in the global market. While this relieved consumers in the short run, the oil price collapse had more fundamental ramifications because the oil market seemed to be the victim of speculators fearing that the economy was running into a recession. This indeed led to a fall in the demand for oil, thus creating the very scenario that speculators had feared. This began to herald the end of the commodities boom as the S&P GSCI (Standard & Poors Goldman Sachs Commodity Index) fell by 28.6% in the third quarter of 2008, which was 5% below the 1 January level.

The fall in oil prices was followed by a fall in metal prices, followed by a fall in agricultural products, the decline of which continued as many poor commodity-exporting countries begun to feel the crisis in a sharp manner, with hundreds of workers in countries such as the Democratic Republic of Congo (DRC) and Zambia going without work. The lowering of oil prices also led to the overall cutting of prices in other sectors, which threatened a deflationary spiral even in the developed world as the fear now began to focus on both deflation and recession. This led to a new panic in which governments scrambled to cut interest rates in order to ignite borrowing on the part of consumers and producers, but this did not happen given the fact that these 'solutions' did not go to the real fundamental problem of the economy – namely the historical fall in the rate of profit in manufacturing.

The Bank of England announced several cuts in interest rates, but with no significant response in the economy. The US Federal Reserve in December 2008 joined the scramble by cutting its key short-term interest rate to a record 0.25%, citing 'falling prices' as the reason behind the cut. It was also described by *USA Today* on

17 December 2008 as an effort to fight 'the worst financial crisis since 1930s'. The key short-term interest rate was the federal funds rate, which banks charge each other for overnight loans. This low rate, which is a benchmark for business and consumer loans, was intended to stimulate consumer and business activity, but with this cut the Federal Reserve expressed its determination, according to *USA Today* of the same date, 'to use less conventional methods to pump money into the economy and spur business activity'. Indeed, President-elect Barack Obama, speaking around the same time, agonised that the government had used almost all the equipment in its arsenal to quench the slide but to no avail, while indicating that even more 'unconventional methods' would have to be called upon.

But this also indicated an excessive focus on the crisis in the developed countries of the US, Europe and Japan. Little was being done to deal with the crisis in the 'emerging markets' and less developed areas of the world, where the situation was also getting out of hand, as indicated in the falling agricultural and commodity prices affecting these countries' export earnings. This had led the UN Secretary-General, Ban Ki-moon, to cry out in reference to the large 'bailouts' that there was something 'fundamentally wrong... when money seems to be abundant, but funds for investment in people seems so short in supply.'[17] Ban called for $72 billion per year additional external financing to achieve the Millennium Development Goals (MDGs) by 2015. Even then he predicted that the meltdown in the major developed economies would be a major setback to the MDG drive, from which it had been expected that there would be a 50% reduction in 'extreme' poverty and hunger. An Asian delegate to the UN General Assembly exclaimed that even the $72 billion demanded by the Secretary-General was 'peanuts' compared to the US $700 billion bailout package for the banks.

The Stimulus Packages

The response to the general global crisis was not even seen as being crucial to the recovery of the global economy by the leaders of the developed economies. Indeed, when the G20 summit issued their declaration, the issue of stimulating the global economy was not even discussed. The matter was left to each country to deal with

according to their means and devices. It is therefore not surprising that the responses of the US and the EU were piecemeal in dealing with those demands, which were regarded by the leaders as significant politically in the individual countries. In fact the first country to take the issue of stimulating the economy seriously was China, which on 9 November 2008 advanced emergency measures to protect jobs and stabilise the Chinese economy in the wake of the factory closures and mass layoffs that had swept the country over the previous few months. The Chinese Minister of Human Resources and Social Security, Yin Weimin, said that: 'The global economic crisis is picking up speed and spreading from developed to developing countries and the effects are becoming more and more pronounced here. Our economy is facing a serious challenge.'

Thus with its focus on keeping its own economy on track, China announced a 4 trillion yuan ($586 billion) stimulus package, the largest in the country's history. China's State Council unveiled it on 9 November, with a two-year time span. The stimulus is aimed at injecting funds into 10 sectors, including healthcare, education, low-income housing and environmental protection, along with schemes to promote technological innovation, transport and other infrastructure projects. The plan was also to be directed into reconstruction efforts in areas that had been struck by natural disasters, such as Sichuan Province, which was devastated by a massive earthquake in May 2008. The measures also included a loosening of credit policies and tax cuts. They also called for reforms in the country's value-added tax regime that would save industry 120 billion yuan. Credit ceilings for commercial banks were to be abolished in the hope that this would result in channelling more capital to small enterprises, rural areas and unspecified 'priority projects'.

The EU for its part found great difficulty agreeing on a single stimulus plan for the region as a whole. The EU Commission in Brussels tried to put together such a plan, but this was at first resisted by Germany. Later the German Chancellor stated that Germany would support the European Commission's initiative, which limits member states' contribution to only 1.5% of their gross domestic product. With the spectre of recession looming large, the European Commission requested heads of state and government to sign up to its proposed stimulus plan, amounting to only €200 billion ($260 billion) for the European economy.

The plan, which was based on a series of national measures, was expected to enhance public investment across Europe and allow for some tax cuts. Germany, Europe's biggest economic power, had been under pressure in the run-up to the summit to contribute as much as possible to the European package. However, the German Finance Minister was reluctant to spend any more than was necessary to get the German economy moving again. Instead, the Minister launched an unusual attack on Britain's economic stimulus package, saying that it would not fend off recession and would leave the next generation saddled with debt. In an interview with *Newsweek*, the Minister argued that the British Government's switch from financial prudence to heavy borrowing was 'breathtaking' and equated it to 'crass Keynesianism'. This indicated the level of disagreement among world leaders, a situation certainly not conducive to any possible concerted efforts at combating the global crisis.

The US government was caught out in an unenviable situation of having two presidents – one in the White House in Washington, DC, and the other in a waiting house in Chicago – from whom conflicting solutions were being proposed. Bush at his lowest level of popularity was seen as a non-performer and a generator of the crisis. Moreover, Republicans in Congress were opposing many of his 'bailout' plans. This left him with only his $700 billion bailout, and even that he was having difficulties implementing. It was during this period that the automobile industry experienced a pressing crisis requiring some form of solution, which Bush aimed at when in mid-December he was able to work out 'stop-gap loans' for two of the three biggest automobile companies – Chrysler and General Motors – to 'stop their collapse'.

At this stage, President Bush acknowledged the impact of the 'credit crunch' on the entire US economy and its global implications. He argued that failing to 'bail out' the automobile industries and to permit their collapse would create 'a ripple effect' that would 'lay waste to business far beyond the auto-industry', but made it clear that the 'bailout' was just a 'stop-gap' measure to enable these companies to put their houses in order. Otherwise, they would have to be prepared for bankruptcy proceedings under Chapter 11 of the US Bankruptcy Code. President-elect Obama had, in his own attempt to face the challenges of assuming office, also argued

for support for industry, something of particular importance if his aim of creating two and half million jobs in two years was to be realisable.

But unlike Bush, Obama had to face the task of reviving the US economy, which continued to deteriorate before his own eyes even before his inauguration. In a December 2008 press conference, President-elect Obama declared that the US economy was 'very sick' and was getting worse with each passing day. He warned that unless something drastic was done quickly, the recession, which was under way, could go on for the next four years and in such a scenario, the situation could become 'irreversible'. Faced with this situation, it was not clear what the new President, and indeed the whole leadership of the world, would do to deal with a potentially irreversible situation, short of having to face the chaos that comes with civilisations' 'end of history'.

But in order to avoid the situation from becoming 'irreversible', Obama hurriedly put in place a stimulation package for the US economy. On 3 January 2009, the President-elect unveiled his plan, which was to become the top priority for his incoming administration come 20 January 2009. The broad proposal's main objective was to boost job growth and revamp the troubled American economy. Obama pointed out in his weekly radio address that economists 'from across the political spectrum' had warned that if the country did not act swiftly and boldly, 'we could see a much deeper economic downturn that could lead to double digit unemployment and the American Dream slipping further and further out of reach.' He added that: 'That's why we need an American Recovery and Reinvestment Plan that not only creates jobs in the short term but spurs economic growth and competitiveness in the long term.'

Top of the agenda in this Recovery and Reinvestment Plan was to create three million jobs, revised from the earlier two and a half million jobs in the short run, with 80% of them in the private sector. Obama also called for 'long-term investments' in areas such as infrastructure, along with the updating of the American healthcare system and the building of '21st century' learning institutions. This was in addition to the direct tax relief which was to be granted to 95% of American workers. According to President-elect Obama: 'This plan must be designed in a new way; we can't just fall into the

old Washington habit of throwing money at the problem.' Instead Obama called for 'strategic investments', 'vigorous oversight and strict accountability' and 'fiscal responsibility' on the part of financial and business institutions.

But the problem facing this plan was the magnitude of its financial implications. The Democratic Speaker of the House of Representatives Nancy Pelosi had already been working on an earlier economic stimulus package in the range of some $600 billion, which included key elements of Obama's stimulus ideas for a greener and more energy-efficient economy. But the plan was experiencing difficulties due to its financial magnitude, leading the Speaker to be unsure that such a package would be ready for Obama's signature by the time of his swearing-in on 20 January 2009. The plan included many measures which the Bush administration and the Republican Congress had earlier opposed. They included key components of the Obama stimulus package such as more money for food stamps and emergency assistance to states, tax breaks for middle-income households, and money for public works investments ranging from energy-saving technology in public buildings and schools to the modernisation of university research facilities.

This meant that the real hurdle in Congress was to be over how much the stimulus package would cost. By mid-January 2009, this question was becoming important as new figures about the US economy coming out of the Congressional Budget Office revealed that the US Federal Government would be in deficit to the tune of some $1.2 trillion for the fiscal year ending 30 September 2008, said to be the largest on record. Even then, this figure did not include the projected $850 billion required for Obama's stimulus plan. Furthermore, the plan was expanding to such an extent that it was being suggested in some quarters that it would in fact ultimately need close to $1.4 trillion to get off the ground. In such event or situation, the budget deficit would have doubled for the 2009 fiscal period, increasing national debt in the process, itself already over the $10 trillion mark by the end of 2008. In the end, after hard bargaining with the Republicans, Congress passed a $787 billion package that Obama insisted was the bare minimum to 'save' the economy from collapse. But as one economist commented on CNN (Cable News Network), 'you cannot cure an alcoholic by giving him/her more alcohol!'

Indeed, the only 'solution' that was being debated by Obama's team of economic experts, even before assuming office, was that the US government should carry out a nationalisation of the banks and failing enterprises. This it would achieve not by saying so, but by 'aggregating' and buying all 'toxic assets' in the hands of the banks and corporations in order to 'unclog' their liquidity so that they could begin to lend and borrow 'afresh' to begin to activate the economy. The idea was floated of creating a 'bad bank' to take over 'toxic assets' and deal with them so that they would not inhibit the operations of commercial and investments banks in their 'normal' lending activities. This was supposed to be done in the hope that the government would later cleanse these assets of their 'toxicity' and resell them at some future time at the rate at which they were bought or with a profit 'to the taxpayers', who had nothing to do with the matter.

It was not clear whether at that point the government would then resell these 'cleaned' assets to the banks and corporations or set up new institutions to 'own' them. Such a solution would still smack of the US state 'socialising' the losses of the financial oligarchy, making the poor contribute to the private profiteering that had led to the crisis in the first place and failing to require the oligarchy to compensate for their greed. Although President Obama went as far as fixing the fringe benefits of the Chief Executive Officers of the corporations that were being financed by the state, there was no indication that the state would control the way the corporations made their profits, for which the CEOs were being rewarded. In short, whether the word 'nationalising' or 'socialising' was used or not, the US state would always have used backhand methods of bailing out the rich at the expense of the poor.

The G20 and the 'Reform' of the Bretton Woods System

As expected, the G20 met in Washington, DC, on 15 November 2008 under the Chairmanship of President Bush to review the global financial system and find solutions to the global financial meltdown. The group laid out detailed proposals for restructuring the global financial system, but fell short of offering a concrete or coordinated fiscal action plan aimed at pulling the world economy out

of its present crisis. Given their failure to recognise that the respective crises underway within their own countries, and indeed the global capitalist crisis as a whole, this was perhaps to be expected. British Prime Minister Gordon Brown had consistently reiterated this point, but with little action even on his own part. Brown, as we have already noted, had fuelled mortgages' credit-creation under the illusion that he was defining an economic paradigm that he called a 'bust-free boom'.

The Declaration

Meeting with the leaders of the major powers at the summit for the first time were leaders of the strong emerging economies such as China, Brazil, India and South Africa. Although the leaders collectively laid out an outline of the 'common principles' behind financial market reforms, they left the implementation of fiscal measures to stimulate domestic demand up to individual countries, which proved that these leaders did not fully comprehend the scale of the crisis and its global reach. At the end of the summit, they issued a 16-point declaration together with an action plan, which they expected their cabinet Ministers to begin to implement and achieve results from by 31 March 2009 before a new summit could be held to consider longer-term solutions.

The declaration began by stating that what the leaders had done was no more than taking steps to hold 'an initial meeting amid serious challenges to the world economy and financial markets'. They expressed their determination to enhance their cooperation in order to 'work together to restore global growth and achieve needed reforms in the world's financial systems'. They acknowledged that over the past few months different countries had taken urgent and exceptional measures to support the global economy and stabilise financial markets. These efforts must continue, they declared. At the same time, the declaration stated that the summit wanted to lay 'the foundation for reform' to help to 'ensure that a global crisis, such as this one, does not happen again'. They reiterated that the work they had embarked on would be 'guided by a shared belief that market principles, open trade and investment regimes, and effectively regulated financial markets foster the dynamism, innovation, and entrepreneurship that are essential for economic growth, employment, and poverty reduction.'[18]

Root Causes

Regarding the root causes of the current crisis, the summit argued that during a period of strong global growth, growing capital flows and prolonged stability earlier in the first decade of the 21st century, market participants wanted higher yields 'without an adequate appreciation of the risks and [having] failed to exercise proper due diligence'. At the same time, they added, weak underwriting standards, unsound risk management practices and 'increasingly complex and opaque financial products and consequent excessive leverage' had 'combined to create vulnerabilities in the system'. These they added were vulnerabilities which policymakers, regulators and supervisors in some advanced countries had not adequately appreciated and which did not address the risks building up in financial markets, keep pace with financial innovation or take into account the systemic ramifications of domestic regulatory actions. With inconsistent and insufficiently coordinated macro-economic policies and inadequate structural reforms, it is these 'major underlying factors' to the current situation which, among others, had led to 'unsustainable global macro-economic outcomes', including 'excesses' that had 'ultimately resulted in severe market disruption'.

But these analyses fell short of facing up to the realities of the crisis. As we have seen, European leaders had blamed the crisis on the American 'free market' style capitalism that had encouraged greed and 'unethical' capitalist practices. These practices had been 'guided' by the same principles that the leaders expressed their commitment to at the summit, namely 'a shared belief that market principles, open trade, and investment regimes and effectively regulated financial markets foster the dynamism, innovation, and entrepreneurship that are essential for economic growth, employment, and poverty reduction'.[19] This implied that these leaders were still operating at the level of reiterating age-old principles of capitalist management, principles which had not stopped the system from descending to the point where the very existence of societies themselves was under threat. These clear incoherencies in the understanding of what was afoot in the crisis were reflected in the kind of proposals the leaders made to address the problem.

Immediate Steps

Based on these premises, the leaders declared that action must be taken to overcome the crisis in the short run. These actions were a repetition of the 'significant' steps they had so far undertaken to 'stimulate' economies and 'provide liquidity', as well as 'strengthening the capital of the financial institutions and protecting savings and deposits', in addition to 'addressing regulatory deficiencies', 'unfreezing credit markets' and working to ensure that international financial systems 'can provide critical support for the global economy.' The leaders, however, acknowledged that 'more needs to be done to stabilise financial markets and support economic growth'. They recognised the fact that economic momentum was slowing substantially in major economies and that the global outlook had weakened, adding: 'Many emerging market economies, which helped sustain the world economy this decade, are still experiencing good growth but increasingly are being adversely impacted by the worldwide slowdown.' This was correct because even those relatively successful local alternative approaches, especially in east and south-east Asia, were now being undermined by the crisis sweeping the whole world from the United States.

It is against this real background of 'deteriorating economic conditions worldwide' that these leaders agreed that 'a broader policy response' was needed based on closer macro-economic cooperation to restore growth, avoid negative spill-overs and support emerging market economies and developing countries during the decline. For this reason, they suggested 'immediate steps' to achieve these objectives, as well as for addressing longer-term challenges. But these steps fell well short of addressing the fundamental problems causing havoc in the global economy.

The 'immediate steps' the leaders suggested included vigorous efforts to stabilise the financial system, monetary support policy and the use of fiscal measures to stimulate domestic demand 'to rapid effect' (while maintaining a policy framework conducive to fiscal sustainability). These steps also included help for emerging and developing economies to gain access to finance (including liquidity facilities by the IMF and programme support), along with encouraging the World Bank and other multilateral development banks to use their full capacity in support of their development

agenda (such as through the recent introduction of new facilities by the Bank in the areas of infrastructure and trade finance). Finally, the steps proposed ensuring that the IMF, World Bank and other multilateral banks have sufficient resources to continue playing their role in overcoming the crisis. But despite their intended reach, in granting such a prominent role to banks and the Bretton Woods institutions – institutions that had consistently overseen policies that undermined rather than supported development – these measures pandered to the very players who had clogged up in the system in the first place.

Common Principles for Reform

That is why the summit itself recognised that these 'immediate' responses were not sufficient on their own to overcome the crisis and hence the need to embark on developing some common principles for the 'reform' of the financial markets and regulatory regimes in the medium and long term. These 'common principles' included a restatement by the leaders that regulation was first and foremost the responsibility of national regulators, who constituted 'the first line of defence' against market instability, when in fact such a line of defence is non-existent against the forces of economic globalisation that have historically blown across national borders. The leaders soon realised this fact and added that the financial markets were 'global in scope', leading them to call for 'intensified international cooperation among regulators and [the] strengthening of international standards and their consistent implementation' as part of efforts to protect against adverse cross-border, regional and global developments affecting international financial stability.

But this was also a cry in the wilderness since the leaders again reverted, in a kind of vicious circle, to their national borders by calling on the new 'cross-border' regulators they were proposing, while carrying out this new duty, to 'avoid potentially adverse impacts on other countries', including regulatory arbitrage. Instead they advised that the 'cross-border' regulators should 'support competition, dynamism and innovation in the marketplace'. The new regulators, they insisted, 'must ensure that their actions support market discipline' and see to it that the financial institutions that had contributed to the crisis 'also bear their responsibility for

the turmoil'. They advised that these institutions 'should do their part' to overcome the crisis by recognising losses, improving disclosure and strengthening their governance and risk management practices. But these principles, it can be seen, were such that the regulators could not enforce their cross-border function since all the powers of enforcement, if any, lay with national governments. The 'principles' were such that they could not be implemented and became confusing to the new 'College of Supervisors' even before they were created. This was so even though the leaders committed themselves to implementing policies consistent with the common principles for reform, which they merely spelt out. These principles also included the following:

- Strengthening transparency and accountability in financial markets
- Enhancing sound regulation by exercising strong oversight over credit-rating agencies, consistent with the agreed and strengthened international code of conduct, while also ensuring that regulation is efficient and does not 'stifle innovation' and encouraging 'expanded trade in financial products and services'
- Promoting integrity in financial markets by bolstering investor and consumer protection, while avoiding conflicts of interest, preventing illegal market manipulation, fraudulent activities and abuse, as well as protecting against illicit finance risks arising from non-cooperative jurisdictions
- Reinforcing international cooperation by calling upon national and regional regulators to formulate their regulations and other measures in a consistent manner. Regulators were called upon to enhance their coordination and cooperation across all segments of financial markets, including cross-border capital flows. Regulators and other relevant authorities as a matter of priority were argued to strengthen cooperation on crisis prevention, management, and resolution.
- Reforming international financial institutions such as Bretton Woods so that they can more adequately reflect changing economic power in the world economy in order to increase their legitimacy and effectiveness. In this respect, the G7 recognised the role of the emerging and developing economies, including the poorest countries, to 'have a greater voice and representation'

in financial institutions, including through the urgent expansion of the Financial Stability Forum (FSF) to a broader membership of emerging economies, while other major standard setting bodies were also asked to 'promptly review their membership'. This was called for in view of the fact that 'emerging economies' such as China and Brazil were active participants in regional markets. China was a key player in the financing of the US deficit budget by buying US Treasury bills. In these circumstances, it could not be seen how decisions regarding the global economy could be made without including these countries.

Even though the guidelines the leaders had given to the regulators were far from clear due to the urgency of the crisis, they went even further to 'task' their ministers and experts from the G20 countries to take 'rapid action to implement these principles'. The Finance Ministers, coordinated by Brazil, the UK and the Republic of Korea were to initiate processes and set timelines towards their implementation. This was the agenda that the Ministers had to perform between the end of the summit and the end of March 2009, when the summit was to be recalled. To assist the Ministers to comprehend their task, the summit spelt out an action plan, which they were to carry out.

Action Plan

An initial list of specific measures, including high priority actions to be completed prior to 31 March 2009, was stipulated in the summit's Action Plan. The Plan detailed a number of actions, among them: 'mitigating against pro-cyclicality in regulatory policy'; reviewing and aligning global accounting standards, particularly for complex securities in times of stress; strengthening the resilience and transparency of credit derivatives markets and reducing their systemic risks, including the improvement of the infrastructure of over-the-counter markets; reviewing compensation practices as they related to incentives for risk taking and innovation; reviewing the mandates, governance, and resource requirements of the international financial institutions; and defining the scope of systemically important institutions and determining their appropriate regulation or oversight.

The Plan set forth a comprehensive work plan to implement the five agreed principles for reform, which the Ministers, together with the relevant international bodies such as the IMF, an expanded FSF and standard setting bodies, were to undertake. These measures included the immediate actions to be undertaken sum-marised above and in particular the strengthening of transparency and accountability. In the medium-term the actions included the creation of a single quality global standard for accounting bodies, cooperation between regulators, supervisors and accounting stand-ard setters, and financial institutions' greater disclosure of all losses on an ongoing basis, 'consistent with international best practice, as appropriate'. The regulators were also required to ensure that a financial institution's financial statements include 'a complete, accurate, and timely picture of the firm's activities (including off-balance-sheet activities) to be reported on a consistent and regular basis'. But to carry out these tasks the regulators and the Ministers would need the backing of legislation – at which level it was not clear – before they could be expected to produce the results by the required deadlines.

This is because each country or region was required to pledge to review and report on the structure and principles of its regulatory system to 'ensure it was compatible with a modern and increasingly globalised financial system'. To this end, all G20 members com-mitted themselves to undertaking a Financial Sector Assessment Program (FSAP) report and to support the transparent assessments of countries' national regulatory systems, including a review of the differentiated nature of regulation in the banking, securities and insurance sectors, and to provide a report outlining the issue and making recommendations on needed improvements. A review of the scope of financial regulation was to be undertaken, with spe-cial emphasis on instruments and markets that were currently unregulated, along with ensuring that all systemically important institutions were appropriately regulated. National and regional authorities were also tasked to review resolution regimes and bankruptcy laws in light of recent experience to ensure that they permitted an orderly winding-down of large complex cross-border financial institutions in addition to providing 'definitions of capi-tal', which should be 'harmonized in order to achieve consistent

measures of capital and capital adequacy'. But this was a tall agenda for cross-border complexity under conditions where there was little regulation in place.

Among important actions to be undertaken by regulators regarding 'prudential oversight' was the need to ensure that credit-rating agencies meet the highest standards of the international organisation of securities regulators and that they avoid conflicts of interest, provide greater disclosure to investors and to issuers and differentiate ratings for complex products. This was supposed to help ensure that credit-rating agencies have the right incentives and appropriate oversight to enable them to perform their important role in providing unbiased information and assessments to markets. They were also required to ensure that financial institutions maintained adequate capital in amounts necessary to sustain confidence by setting out strengthened capital requirements for banks' structured credit and securitisation activities.

In addition to building on the imminent launch of central counter-party services for credit default swaps (CDS) in some countries and speed efforts to reduce the systemic risks of CDS and over-the-counter (OTC) derivatives transactions, the regulators were insisting that market participants support exchange-traded or electronic-trading platforms for CDS contracts, expand OTC derivatives market transparency and ensure that the infrastructure for OTC derivatives can support growing volumes. But this was under conditions where very little regulation existed, as the Washington Consensus had ensured in its neo-liberal ideology that no such institution existed in any state.

Ministers were also required to promote integrity in financial markets by working together to enhance regulatory cooperation between jurisdictions on a regional and international level in areas where 'integrity' was never insisted on before. They were to promote information sharing about domestic and cross-border threats to market stability and ensure that national (or regional, where applicable) legal provisions were adequate to address these threats. How this was to be done in such a short space of time was not clear. The regulators were also to review business conduct rules to protect markets and investors, especially against market manipulation and fraud and to strengthen their cross-border cooperation to

protect the international financial system from illicit actors. In cases of misconduct, there would be an appropriate sanctions regime.

The leaders committed themselves to reinforcing international cooperation by establishing supervisory colleges for all major cross-border financial institutions, as part of efforts to strengthen the surveillance of cross-border firms. Major global banks were required to meet regularly with their supervisory college for comprehensive discussions of the firm's activities and assessment of the risks facing it. They were also to take all steps necessary to strengthen cross-border crisis management arrangements, cooperating and communicating with each other and with appropriate authorities to develop comprehensive contact lists and conduct simulation exercises, as appropriate.

Regarding the reforming of international financial institutions, the summit directed that the FSF should expand to a broader membership of emerging economies. The IMF, with its focus on surveillance, and the expanded FSF, with its focus on standards setting, were called upon to strengthen their collaboration, enhancing efforts to better integrate regulatory and supervisory responses into the macro-prudential policy framework and conduct early warning exercises. The IMF, given its universal membership and core macro-financial expertise, was required, in close coordination with the FSF and others, to take a leading role in drawing lessons from the current crisis, consistent with its mandate.

The summit undertook to review the adequacy of the resources of the IMF, the World Bank Group and other multilateral development banks and to stand ready to advocate for their increase where necessary. The international financial institutions were also asked to continue to review and adapt their lending instruments to adequately meet their members' needs and revise their lending role in light of the ongoing financial crisis. The big powers committed themselves to 'explore ways to restore emerging and developing countries'' access to credit and to resume private capital flows, which were said to be critical for sustainable growth and development, including ongoing infrastructure investment.

Finally, the summit 'underscored' the point that the Bretton Woods institutions must be 'comprehensively reformed so that they can more adequately reflect changing economic weights in the world economy and be more responsive to future challenges'.

They added that emerging and developing economies should have a greater voice and representation in these institutions. The IMF was required in the process to conduct vigorous and even-handed surveillance reviews of all countries, as well as to give greater attention to these countries' financial sectors and to better integrate these reviews with the joint IMF–World Bank financial sector assessment programmes. The advanced economies, the IMF and other international organisations were required to provide capacity-building programmes for emerging market economies and developing countries on the formulation and the implementation of new major regulations, consistent with international standards.

These measures are complex and require a political framework negotiated by all the countries involved. Many of the activities 'tasked' to the Ministers and experts cannot even be undertaken without such a framework, nor can the responsibilities given to the cross-border regulators even be imagined. Reforming the existing international financial system, including the IMF, cannot be undertaken unless the problems of these institutions that have built up over the years are analysed to the satisfaction of all countries. These problems can then be discussed at a global conference where solutions can be discussed and agreed by all. Before this is done, there is very little likelihood that even the G20 countries will be in a position to promote anything acceptable to other countries.

The London G20 Summit

The second summit met in London as scheduled at the beginning of April 2009 under the chairmanship of British Prime Minister Gordon Brown. Leading up to the summit, the global economic situation had continued to deteriorate. The only thing to have changed was the new leadership of a major player – the US – with the election of President Barack Obama. President Obama sought to inspire a change in his country's approach by trying to keep a low profile and creating a new image of the US as a country that wanted to work side-by-side with others to try to find solutions to a common problem. But it was clear that behind the scenes the US was working closely with Prime Minister Brown to lay down the main approach that would be presented to the rest of the summit.

Concretely, the G20 summit came out with a programme that fell

short of addressing the underlying causes of the global crisis. The summit's leaders declared a five-point plan of action that included pledges to:

• Restore confidence, growth, and jobs
• Repair the financial system to restore lending
• Strengthen financial regulation to rebuild trust
• Fund and reform international financial institutions to overcome the crisis and prevent future ones
• Promote global trade and investment and reject protectionism to underpin prosperity
• Build an inclusive, green and sustainable recovery.

They recognised that by acting together to fulfil these pledges the group will bring the world economy out of recession and prevent a crisis like this from recurring in the future. But these decisions were being made in the same old way with the same kind of institutions still in place, which the leaders at the G20 merely promised to 'regulate'. The first stumbling block they encountered was how to deal with the IMF, whom the major economic powers had relied on to run the global economy in their favour by pushing policies causing the contraction of the economies of poor countries. Now the G20 decided, seemingly without looking at the IMF's record and legitimacy, to treble the resources available to the Fund to $750 billion to support new special drawing rights (SDRs) allocations of $250 billion, which were to supplement at least $100 billion of additional lending to ensure $250 billion of support for trade finance. The new SDRs were also to be used as the additional resources from agreed IMF gold sales for concessional finance for the poorest countries. This package was supposed to constitute an additional $1.1 trillion programme of support to restore credit, growth and jobs in the world economy, and to constitute 'a global plan for recovery on an unprecedented scale', in addition to the measures that were being undertaken by each country nationally.

But, as in the past, these developments have simply marginalised the economies of poor countries, appearing to be helping them when the advantages have all been weighed in favour of the rich countries. For instance, although the G20 summit appeared to

imply that the $250 billion of SDRs to be created by the IMF were to supplement the $100 billion of additional lending and gold sales to support trade for the poorest countries, the reality was that the new SDRs were to be allocated to the 186 IMF members according to their shares of voting rights. As a result, 44% of the new SDRs will be allocated to the seven rich countries, while only $80 billion will be available for middle-income and poor developing countries, who constitute the bulk of the 186 IMF members. The balance was to be allocated to the other countries not falling under any of the above categories. This allocation to the poor is by no means generous because the IMF is to implement these allocations on the basis of its old *modus operandi*, with policies that are pro-cyclical and likely to drive these countries into even deeper crisis, as happened during the Asian financial crisis of 1997–98.

Even then the 'success' of the summit cannot therefore be assessed in view of these decisions, which affect poor countries adversely. These measures were very much short of what was needed to deal with the immediate consequences of the crisis. In an article in the *Financial Times* of London on 3 April 2009, Chris Giles challenged the figures given by the summit of their contributions to the IMF. He observed that rather than the $1,100 billion that had been announced, only less that $100 billion was in fact available and that 'most of those were in train without the G20 summit.' In this, Giles added, the IMF had been the biggest 'winner' by being promised an additional $500 billion (less the $250 billion SDR allocations). Giles also pointed out that of this 'commitment' Japan and the European Union had already offered $100 billion each even before the summit. To make matters worse, the summit did not announce where the other $300 billion – to take the total up to $500 billion – would come from, although there were unconfirmed reports that indicated the US would contribute $100 billion and China $40 billion. These would then be recycled to the poor countries as new loans running out of foreign reserves.

According to Yilmaz Akyüz, a former United Nations Conference on Trade and Development (UNCTAD) Chief Economist, the IMF should not have been enabled to provide loans out of official funds.[20] Instead the IMF should have been required to obtain its additional funding from the financial markets or through the issuing of new SDRs in order for it to fulfil its surveillance function of disciplining

the policies of countries providing loans. But if this G20 commitment was supposed to act as a 'stimulus package', it was definitely not a 'bailout' similar to those being dished out in the G8 countries and some emerging market countries such as China. What was instead happening was that the IMF was being used to implement its age-old strategies of forcing emerging and developing country economies to adopt pro-cyclical policies to deal with the crisis, policies which would actually accentuate the economic downturn by preventing countries from increasing government expenditure as a means of counter-cyclical policy aimed at strengthening their economies. This, of course, was the very opposite of what was happening with the 'stimulus packages' and 'bailouts' of the G8 countries.

In their so-called support for poor countries, the G8, with the silent support of the 'emerging economies', were therefore using the IMF to continue policies that were bound to keep poor countries' economies in recession, all the while claiming that by attending to their own economies rich countries would enable poor countries to themselves gain in a trickle-down manner from new 'growth' by continuing with their exports to G8 markets. But even if this was possible, all that would be achieved would be a return to business as usual for multilateral institutions such as the IMF and the World Bank, who would have their legitimacy 'restored' through the back door. This would be in spite of the 'commitment' by the G20 to build on the current reviews of these institutions and to consult widely with the Ministers of Finance being required to 'report back to the next meeting with proposals for further reforms to improve the responsiveness and adaptability of the International Financial Institutions'. In addition, the G20 summit further committed rich countries to implement the World Bank reforms agreed in October 2008 and to 'look forward' to further recommendations at the next meetings on voice and representation reforms on an accelerated timescale, to be agreed by the 2010 spring meetings.

In the meantime, in order to solicit the support of the emerging economies attending the summit, the G20 agreed that the heads and senior leadership of the international financial institutions should be appointed through 'an open, transparent, and merit-based selection process'. The G20 also issued a declaration for strengthening the financial system by agreeing in particular to:

- Establish a new Financial Stability Board (FSB) with a strength-ened mandate, as a successor to the Financial Stability Forum (FSF), including all G20 countries, FSF members, Spain and the European Commission
- Ensure that the FSB would collaborate with the IMF to provide early warning of macro-economic and financial risks and the actions needed to address them
- Reshape regulatory systems in each country so that the authori-ties are able to identify and take account of macro-prudential risks
- Extend regulation and oversight to all systemically important financial institutions.

Realising that the new situation within which they were work-ing had radically changed, those at the G20 summit, in addition to agreeing to reform the international financial institutions for the new challenges of globalisation, also recognised 'the desirability of a new global consensus on the key values and principles that will promote sustainable economic activity'. They did not go as far as spelling out these new 'principles' but merely expressed 'sup-port for a discussion on such a charter for sustainable economic activity' with a view to 'further discussion at [the] next meeting.' The declaration stated: 'We take note of the work started in other fora in this regard and look forward to further discussion of this charter for sustainable economic activity at the next meeting.'[21] Despite several 'commitments' requiring a concrete response with the involvement of all countries part of the global community at large, this is the most that they could promise. All they could agree to as a final statement was: 'We agreed to meet again before the end of this year to review progress on our commitments.'

The 'End of History' for Global Capitalism

The failure of the political leaders of the developed industrial coun-tries to understand the dynamics of the current global economic crisis is a reflection of their loss of vision of the system that has been in place in their countries for over three hundred years. As I have already remarked, the present crisis has not arisen out of the blue. This crisis is part of various crises that have been building up

all along. The deep crisis that is now under way lies in the destruction of industrial production in all the countries of the capitalist world since the 1960s. In the original version of this book reflecting on 1987's Black Monday crash (see Chapters 5 and 6), I discussed this development and noted how de-industrialisation had affected the composition of capital in favour of fictitious capital and had led to the decline of equity (that is, capital invested in industrial production). This had led to the emergence of the service sector and the dumping of industrial labour.

It was not therefore surprising that one of the immediate policies pursued by Margaret Thatcher and Ronald Reagan in the period 1979–80 was a struggle against 'big labour' and 'big government'. As the working-class was 'de-classed' with the collapse of the trade unions and the introduction of 'flexible' employment without the protection of labour laws, there emerged a new 'class of workers' called young MBAs (Master's of Business Administration). The difference was that this 'class' of workers worked on computer desktops 'trading' in financial markets to produce 'new money' without any meaningful intelligent or physical productive labour. The 'de-classing' of labour was not just in its displacement from the production process. Working-class pension funds were used by the new 'downsized' corporations for the purpose of financing the 'take-overs' and 'mergers' that characterised new capitalism in the 1980s. The capitalists still wanted to make money out of the 'de-classed' workers by inducing them to sell off their housing investments – in a process Margaret Thatcher called 'de-mutualisation' in the UK, which we shall discuss below – and then turning the properties over for financial speculation.

In the United States, they tried to do the opposite but with the same result by creating a 'new economy' based on workers owning houses rather then selling them. The houses, which the workers, the middle-class and even the unemployed bought, were then used for leveraging different kinds of 'financial instruments' to create an image of the economy as 'growing', which the US state encouraged for the purposes of deficit budget financing. During the 1970s and 1980s, this 'dramatic shift' in the financing of the budget resulted from the fact that governments were faced with large deficits caused by sustained stagnation in their economies due to the loss of

profitability of productive enterprises, especially in manufacturing. This is what brought neo-Keynesianism to a halt, never to reappear. In the 1990s, governments in the developed capitalist countries tried to overcome this stagnation by adopting neo-liberal strategies of 'balancing the budget', which ultimately backfired. This was because the 'balancing' only produced a 'jobless' recovery in the US due to lack of profitability arising out of de-industrialisation.

This is what led the US government to resort to risky forms of 'stimulating' its economy to counter the tendency towards stagnation, which it attempted by replacing traditional Keynesian public deficit financing with a form of private deficit financing, or what Robert Brenner has called 'asset price Keynesianism' or 'bubble-nomics'.[22] This resulted in the 1995–2000 New Economy and the historic equity price bubble that drew directly from the massive paper wealth that was being 'produced' through the new financial instruments. It is this massive paper wealth emerging out of the dot-com New Economy that enabled the record-breaking increase in borrowing, borrowing that sustained a powerful expansion of investment and consumption from which the US state was able to raise its 'revenue' in the form of deficit financing.

But the 'growth' that arose from this expanded investment and consumption was driven by the rise in equity prices that were not solidly based in industrial production. These equity prices rose, according to Brenner, 'in defiance of the falling profit rates', exacerbating industrial over-capacity and soon resulting in the 2000–01 stock market crash and recession, and depressing even further profitability in the non-financial (i.e. industrial) sector. This was what constituted the 'shift' in financing, as industry became an 'old industry' giving way to the 'new' dot-com economy. There were no longer restraints on the determination of 'value' since with a declining labour force and a declining surplus value, 'value' could only be determined through the financial markets and not in the 'fundamental' or 'real' economy.

This was why Alan Greenspan of the US Federal Reserve tried to counter the new cyclical downturn of 2000–01 with another round of 'asset price Keynesianism' by inflating equity prices, resulting in new financial speculation that included the boom in the housing sector. To achieve this, the Federal Reserve reduced interest rates, as

we have noted, at near-zero levels, something that George Soros has attributed to the fallout from the 9/11 terrorist attack on the World Trade Centre. In fact the real purpose of the reduction in interest rates over the three preceding years was for President Bill Clinton's administration to catalyse a historically unprecedented explosion of household borrowing, which contributed to and fed into the rocketing house prices and household 'wealth' and the bubble that accompanied them. This explains why in this period 90–100% of the growth of US GDP was attributable to personal consumption and housing construction. The housing sector alone accounted for 50% of GDP growth in this period.

But all this happened because the housing explosion was being used not so much to house the middle-class (which it also did), but primarily to give the corporations time to work off the excess 'capital' that they had 'earned' out of the dot-com New Economy. This breathing space enabled the corporations and banks to resume investing in order to expropriate higher levels of surplus value from the workers in the non-financial (industrial) sector and thereby raise the rate of exploitation of labour. This is why in this period of the 'New Economy' there were high levels of growth in the financial sector or 'paper economy' and a very slow rate in industrial production in all the advanced industrial capitalist countries. This is also what explained the rise in housing prices with which the workers and the middle-class were drawn into the housing bubble economy in the name of the 'sub-priming' of the housing mortgage economy. The concept of 'sub-primers' emerged precisely in this period as a direct extension of the housing bubble, the bubble having been pushed to the maximum level through lending to people without a stable income.

Sub-priming was the means by which the financial oligarchy in charge of the economy was able to induce the workers and the middle-class to borrow without limits, borrowing to buy a house, for housing-related expenditure or even for an extra house. This had two related consequences. On the one hand, it ate into the workers' and middle-class households' disposable incomes and home equity withdrawals and added to their consumer credit borrowing and capital gains payments. On the other hand, this financial manipulation left most households with zero balances in real dis-

posable incomes and as the credit crunch begun to emerge, the sub-primers found themselves without viable collateral on which they could maintain their earlier borrowing to pay for the houses. This is what led to the 'sub-prime mortgage crisis'. With the 'de-leveraging' of the credit mountain of $15 trillion that had been created out of their earnings and expectations, the sub-primers found they could not hold the houses they had been induced to buy. The collapse of prices in real estate markets led to further defaults and foreclosures so that the earlier house owners could no longer keep them. Soon even those who had been employed found themselves out of work, with the recession that followed leading to unemployment rates of up to 500,000 per month by the beginning of 2009, according to the monthly announcements of the federal authorities.

With this development large numbers of sub-primers found themselves without houses. This, indeed, was essentially the same situation that Margaret Thatcher had overseen in the UK in the 1980s, dispossessing British workers of their houses through using different financial mechanisms of de-mutualisation, through which she took over the workers' organised cooperative property owner-ship scheme (which had previously enabled workers to own houses by paying for them in instalments). Thatcher hatched an economic programme under her 'Big Bang' financial 'revolution' in 1986, through which financial services were 'deregulated'. This turned friendly and building societies, previously owned by working-class members and run on a cooperative basis, into commercial banks through a process of 'de-mutualisation'. De-mutualisation, the jargon used at the time to carry out this public theft and the destruc-tion of workers' cooperative initiatives, was achieved through inducing the workers to sell their shares in building societies with hefty 'offers' of cash. Most workers accepted to sell, with only a handful of cooperatives refusing.

Although this process made the working-class part and par-cel of the new money-making machine, in the end it proved unproductive as the system later came down crumbling, start-ing with the very institutions that had been promoted by the de-mutualisation of the workers' property. The most prominent example of these institutions was the most successful bank in de-mutualisng workers' building societies, Northern Rock, a

bank that had built its success on the workers' wealth. Although Northern Rock had been formed in 1965 by the earlier merger of two building societies based in the north-east of England – where de-industrialisation had hit the shipbuilding, coal mining and steel industries to the core – it was not until Thatcher's financial revolution that the bank got a real lift-off. It built a 'business model' greatly admired by the high-street banks in London's 'financial centre' of the world. But it caught the same British disease of industry's loss of profitability that had plagued the UK economy in the early 1960s, a disease which ultimately brought it down only for it to survive through nationalisation by the British state (itself in an increasingly weak position in its capacity to 'coin money').

This is why the history of the rise and fall of Northern Rock can be said to be the story of the rise and fall of the capitalist system. It rose from the ashes of the collapsed feudal system that capitalism fought so hard to replace only to represent the decline of British capitalism in 2007. Jeremy Seabrook has given us a short history of this evolution, transformation and collapse, arguing that capitalism has never changed: while the prices of its products can always go up, they can also always go down.[23] This is just as the Kiganda proverb of the Baganda people of Uganda reminds us: 'Ekibukiira wagulu okitegeera wansi' (in essence, 'Whatever flies high must always come down'). With Northern Rock on its wings, the British capitalist economy flew high, but has now come down.

Housing workers' savings and collective property under the friendly and building societies came out of the workers' spirit of 'mutuality' and 'solidarity', a spirit which formed the foundations of the mid-19th century building societies. The societies were a response to the Poor Laws that were passed by the British Parliament to ensure that the condition of a poor person who took refuge in workhouses – to which the poor ran in desperation – should 'always be', according to Jeremy Seabrook, 'in a worse condition than the poorest labourer who remained outside'. It is this 'iron law' of capitalism that led the poor workers and the unemployed to form 'friendly societies' to 'bear ye one another's burden'.[24] With the general increase in the size of the working-class during the industrial revolution, these societies increased in membership on the basis of workers making regular contributions towards their shares, and

when sufficient funds were accumulated, a ballot would be held and the winning member would have the advance of the other members' shares to purchase a house. The societies were called 'terminating societies' because once all their members were housed, they ceased to exist. By the end of the 19th century, these societies had increased to over 1,700 and many now referred to themselves as 'permanent building societies'.

These societies were the beginnings of the Northern Rock bank, which was the result of a merger of the Northern Counties Building Society (formed in 1860) and the Rock Building Society (formed in 1865). A century later in 1965, this merger of two mutual friendly societies to form a capitalist enterprise spelt the beginnings of their demise. The apparent success with which the bank operated turned it into a 'model' to be imitated by other financial institutions, with the principle of its 'successful' operation no longer based on the shares provided by its members and its mutuality and solidarity but rather on the sheer weight of its capacity to accumulate 'profits' from 'securitising' and 'repackaging' mortgages for re-sale to other banks. According to Jeremy Seabrook, 'These were parcelled up into numerous "instruments", all with varying levels of risk, and were bought by hedge funds, which borrowed against them or used them to gamble against future rates of default.'[25]

On the basis of this 'business model', Northern Rock had by 1994 become the 10th biggest mortgage lender in Britain and by 1997 it was fourth in the ladder of success. It was a 'virtuous circle' and a high level of efficiency in creating high-yield 'savings' that were put into 'products' buyers wanted and which attracted 'volumes' that reduced the unit costs of their 'production', which went back into the pricing of the 'products'. So far so good, as Northern Rock's success won accolade after accolade, but within what Seabrook has called 'a twinkling of an eye', Northern Rock came crumbling down. In September 2007, it was revealed that the bank was on the verge of collapse due to the 'credit crunch' that had started in relation to US sub-prime mortgages, mortgages of the same class of people used as cannon fodder to the 'crumbling wall of money'. According to Jeremy Seabrook:

> The fate of friendly and building societies, owned in the first place by their members, is a potent illustration of the capacity of

capitalism to absorb even those institutions which are set up in opposition. The assumption is that everything – and everyone – has a price, and it is inconceivable that anyone invited into the wealth creating machine would choose to remain outside. This is, after all, how the wider working-class movement became part of the system: organised labour, which in its early days formulated a desire only for a secure sufficiency, was instead overwhelmed by a consumerism which so far exceeded the modest demands it originally made that it was disarmed against what it had regarded as hostile to its interests.[26]

Seabrook's analysis should be pushed beyond the level of the personalities involved in the different manipulations, such as the role of Gordon Brown, who supported the activities of Northern Rock when he was the Chancellor of the Exchequer. This only proves the different levels of contradiction in the capitalist system represented by its leaders' actions, as well as revealing its strengths, weaknesses and limitations. Only by locating the specific contradictions of the system as a whole can we gain a glimpse of the way forward out of the capitalist malaise. It is this analysis that can enable us to see that this system cannot go on forever, and this realisation should motivate us to think and act both locally and globally to save the planet and the future of humankind. Northern Rock has given us a glimpse into the nature of the capitalist system, a system whose survival is only possible when the labour of the working people gives the capitalists the power to rule. That power is now on the wane and this can be seen materially in the fact that capitalism can no longer function in the way Northern Rock was privileged to operate. If it can no longer generate savings or put in place a new credible capitalist system without greed, nor can the path that capitalism has traversed be reversed to let it pick up from where it went wrong and chart a new path, such as Brown and French President Nicolas Sarkozy have been praying for through a new 'moral' capitalism. In short, it can no longer 'save' in order to 'invest' to exploit labour, because the exploitation of labour and its savings can no longer support the system.

We already had a glimpse of this malaise when we saw that capitalism had already begun to negate the very basis of its production by turning savings into negative balances in banks and other

financial institutions. This phenomenon had emerged long before Thatcher ordered the de-mutualisation of workers' property leading to profit-earning financial enterprises like Northern Rock. The problem that Thatcher tried to circumvent was the power and strength of the labour force, a force that had created property of its own. At that stage capital could not profitably employ labour in industrial production, and in order to reduce its power it was decided that its trade union organisations should be weakened, and by weakening them proceed further to buying up labour's properties in order to turn them into profitable capitalist financial enterprises.

As we have seen above, this backfired not only in Britain but also in the US with the sub-prime mortgage scandal. This experience demonstrated that capitalism could not reproduce itself from the surplus value produced by the labourers, and this failure was reflected in capital's inability to maintain an ethic of savings and turn those savings into profitable industrial production. In short, savings from whatever source could not capitalise themselves. Capitalism had even exhausted the power to turn workers' savings into a battle against labour. In a revealing issue entitled, 'Where have all your savings gone?', an editorial in *The Economist* of 6 December 2008 characterised the previous decade as one lost for American and European savers because after two booms and two busts, stock markets had earned them 'nothing or less' than they had originally saved.[27] This was the very decade in which the Northern Rocks of this world were simply minting money out of money, with no form of substantive profitable production through industry, which is where real profit is made. The editorial also added that low interest rates had made bonds and bank deposits 'unrewarding' and that had it not been for a tax relief, contributors to pension funds, 'would have been better off keeping their money under the mattresses' than saving it with the banks.

The financial figures for 2008 demonstrated that those investors who had saved their money in mutual fund assets had lost out, with these assets declining by $2.4 trillion.[28] This represented a fifth of their value since the beginning of 2008 in the USA, while in Britain there had been a drop of almost $195 billion in the savings over the quarter. In the same period, the value of global stock markets had shrunk by approximately $30 trillion, 'or roughly half'. These losses were in fact in equities, which according to *The Economist* had

placed the losses on credit-related securities 'into the shade' where the ongoing crisis had begun. This had also demonstrated that the previous belief that putting money in 'alternative assets' to prevent investors losing money in the bear market 'had proved false'. This 'alternative investment' included investing in the housing sector, where Northern Rock had developed a 'successful business model'. Thus both the prices of corporate bonds and those of commercial property all plunged, indicating that there was no longer a safe haven for investments of any form of capital and that savings could no longer carry any 'value', which can only be derived from living labour.

What was even more revealing was that figures around American pension funds given by the US Congressional Budget Office (CBO) calculated in October 2008 revealed that these funds, which formed a significant proportion of the country's savings, had dropped in value by $2 trillion over the previous 18 months and that these losses were just a portion of the global total. By way of comparison, the Bank of England had estimated that $2.8 trillion of pension funds had been lost in the credit-related instruments into which these funds had been invested through banks such as the Northern Rock. These declines in stock markets had, according to *The Economist*, 'erased all the gains made in the rally from 2003 to 2007'.[29]

These losses had dire consequences for both the capitalist financial oligarchy and especially for the workers, many of whom lost their savings and housing properties. Estimates by a US financial publication, the *Morning Star*, concluded that an American worker who had put $100 a month into an average equity fund for the past 10 years would have accumulated just $10,932. This, it added, would have resulted in a loss of $1,068 on the investment. European workers who had likewise invested a flat amount of money every month for the past decade would have lost 25% of their savings, *The Economist* reported. The consequence, according to the magazine, was that many workers in these countries were therefore contemplating 'opting out of the system altogether'. As an indication to this end, the American Association of Retired People estimated that 37% of workers were already without pension funds, perhaps preferring to put their money in mattresses!

The consequence of these developments has been the emergence of a 'dilemma' for capitalism. On the one hand, working- and

middle-class savers are not prepared to spend the money they hold in savings by buying commodities so long as the recession lasts since they can no longer trust that their investments will be safe. Instead of investing in order to have a return on their 'savings', they therefore now prefer to have a return *of* their 'savings', most of which are held in 'toxic assets' by speculators and the financial oligarchy. On the other hand, faced with a recession, governments have been arguing that savers need to purchase goods and services in order to create effective demand in the economy, which will, they hope, create employment and conditions for real wage incomes. The workers, however, many of whom are unemployed, would rather stick to their savings as consumers of the last resort under a failing capitalism. They will only spend their savings in order to feed their families and buy basic necessities, rather than saving in stocks or equities for the revival of a capitalist economy that has run them to the brink.

In short, the workers have 'opted out' of capitalism by withholding their savings, leaving the financial oligarchy to be 'bailed out' by the state from the mess they created for the workers and the entire global capitalist economy, as capital pulls back and as 'toxic assets' are de-leveraged to a proper size with the support of the state. This may spell not the 'end of history' that was supposed to occur with the collapse of the USSR (Union of Soviet Socialist Republics) but rather the 'end of capitalism', notwithstanding the hope that the state will 'bail out' the financial oligarchy by nationalising or partially nationalising the banks and the corporations through creating 'bad banks' to buy off 'bad toxic' assets. Should that come to pass, the financial oligarchy will be reluctant to invest their ill-gotten gains into nationalised state banks or corporations and will simply live opulent lives similar to those of the age-old merchant class of the feudal era, lives which the nascent bourgeois class had castigated as being extravagant in the heyday of young capitalism. The then 'revolutionary' bourgeoisie too, it appears, have become a reactionary, backward-looking class, one which deserves to be left in the graveyard of history and with it, the end of the capitalist era. We next look at The Way Forward out of this capitalist meltdown.

Dani Wadada Nabudere
Mbale, Uganda, 15 May 2009

Notes

1. Soros, G. *The Crisis of Global Capitalism: Open Society Endangered,* Public Affairs, New York, 1998, p.xix and p.xxix.
2. Soros, G. *The New Paradigm for Financial Markets: The Credit Crisis of 2008 and What it Means*, Public Affairs, New York, 2008.
3. Nabudere, D.W. *The Crash of International Finance-Capital and its Implications for the Third World*, SAPES Trust, Harare, 1989.
4. Soros, G. *The New Paradigm for Financial Markets*, p.xiv.
5. *Ibid.*
6. Soros, *The New Paradigm for Financial Markets*, p.84.
7. *Ibid.*, p.xv.
8. *Ibid.*, p.xv and p.84.
9. *Ibid.*, p.xvii
10. *Ibid.*, p.xix.
11. *Newsweek*, 27 October 2008.
12. Declaration of the G20 Summit, White House website, 16 November 2008.
13. Soros, *The Crisis of Global Capitalism*, p.113.
14. Institute for Agriculture and Trade Policy (IATP), 'Commodities Market Speculation: The Risk to Food Security and Agriculture', Minneapolis, Minnesota, September 2008.
15. *Ibid.*
16. *The Globe and Mail*, Toronto, 31 May 2008.
17. *Third World Resurgence*, Issue No. 216, 2008.
18. Declaration of the G20 Summit, White House website, 16 November 2008.
19. *Ibid.*
20. Akyüz, Y. 'South Centre Bulletin', 36, Geneva, 24 April 2009, p.7.
21. Declaration of the London G20 summit, conference website.
22. Brenner, R. 'From budget-cutting to "Bubblenomics"', *Third World Resurgence*, issue no. 217–18, Third World Network, Penang, Malaysia, 2008, p.42.
23. Seabrook, J. 'From Northern Rock to Northern Wreck', *Third World Resurgence*, issue no. 217–18, Third World Network, Penang, Malaysia, 2008, p.39.
24. *Ibid.*, p.39.
25. *Ibid.*
26. *Ibid.*, p.40.
27. *The Economist* 'Where have all your savings gone?', London, 6 December 2008.
28. *Ibid.*
29. *Ibid.*

The Way Forward

It is clear that this crisis goes to the very foundations of the modern capitalist economy, a system which is coming to an end. The measures proposed by the 2009 London G20 summit to deal with the crisis cannot restore the capitalist system to operate on its old or indeed any 'new' basis, as British Prime Minister Gordon Brown and French President Nicholas Sarkozy would have us believe with their dream of a 'new capitalism'. What is required is that those social forces that have been most affected by the crisis take the responsibility for a new order into their hands and try to work out a completely new system to replace the existing capitalist one. The elements of this new system already exist in the contemporary alternative models of economic and social organisation, including alternative credit systems, informal 'survival' activities and even the old and new forms of cooperative production, marketing and management. What is being raised here is a political-power issue, meaning that the workers and the unemployed middle-classes in the developed capitalist countries, who are increasingly falling by the wayside, must together with the marginalised masses in the south organise themselves politically and put forward their own 'packages' for taking over collapsing industries from the hands of the financial oligarchies who have laid to waste the economies on which they the workers and the people of the world have been dependent.

They should not sit silently while they allow the financial oligarchies to 're-organise' and put forward 'plans' for 'bailouts' from their governments, who are using workers' savings and pension funds to cushion themselves from the pains of a collapsing system. Instead they should work out their own plans for taking over industries and managing them on a new, cooperative basis, while also assuming the responsibility of taking over the states whose

power structures are based on the exploitation of labour, a reality which can no longer be accepted. In so doing, they should attempt to link up with poor communities in the south and establish a new 'glocal' civil society – a global society rooted in local nationalities and global citizenship – on the basis of which a new federated system of states can emerge and a new glocal economy and glocal market can be created.

The ultimate objective of this political strategy is the emergence of new forms of political organisation based on local power centres with the simultaneous capacity to exist globally, hence the use of a new concept – glocal – a combination of the global and the local. These new forms of political power are already emerging and will continue to emerge at the local level as states weaken, unless new warlords try to occupy the political space. But these bandit forces will only emerge where populations have left them the space to do so. Our understanding is based on an emerging political consciousness among the poor, whose interests are taking root in diverse 'survival' activities. But for this new political force to be effective, it will have to take measures to structure itself at local power levels with inter-linkages on a wider cooperative basis under the model of 'confederal' or federal–regional states.

There is no doubt that the character of the African post-colonial state, market and society–state relationships were crafted to reflect the interests of the ruling classes in the imperialist countries under European imperial state systems. Indeed, these state forms are reflected in the current post-colonial states' failure due to their lack of legitimacy. In these circumstances to try to imagine the reform of these states or to reinvent them in their present form is to try to imagine the impossible. What is instead required is a completely new state power structure that has legitimacy among the people, for whom it will promote new forms of social, economic and political organisation. Such a new state system has to respond both to favourable global conditions as well as favourable local conditions that are part of our real world. They will not come about in a single 'Big Bang' but through the concerted, smaller struggles of ordinary people to form new states from below.

Moreover, the globalisation of the economy under existing capitalist systems – systems that have created mal-development –

has created a situation that is noticeably different from conditions in the developed economies in a state of collapse. Since the imposition of structural adjustment programmes in Africa from the mid-1980s, the African post-colonial state has weakened further and the economic activities currently referred to as the 'informal' sector have actually become part of the survival economy of the poor, which in many countries represents up to 80% of all economic activity, activity regarded by most states as 'illegal'. Africa has become one of the fastest urbanising continents with the result that vast numbers of the 'rural' population are moving into mega-cities where the only economic activity is to join the 'reserve army' in the informal economy. This is a new power that can be galvanised into a political force for radical change.

In addition, there is a 'social capital' out there which can likewise be galvanised to enable the people still living in 'traditional' societies to survive the crisis and embark on new ways of organising their lives. In its 1989 report, 'From Crisis to Sustainable Growth', the World Bank recognised that far from impeding future development strategy, 'many indigenous African values and institutions can support it'. It argued that while the 'modern sector' had been in recession in many African countries, 'the informal sector', that was strongly rooted in the community, had been 'vibrant'. In particular, according to the World Bank, this sector had shown a capacity 'to respond flexibly to changing circumstances'.[1] These changing circumstances that the Bank referred to included the growing relationship between the global economy and the 'informal sector' based in local communities, which were basically survival strategies.

It is well recognised that 40–50% of African savings find their way out of Africa to be invested in other, mainly developed economies. In addition, there is the large-scale plunder of revenue resources, some of which is given as 'aid' for African development. Those in authority, including the presidents signing the New Partnership for Africa's Development (NEPAD) framework, carry out this plunder. It is because they recognise the corruption in their countries that these leaders have 'committed' themselves to 'good governance' as a basis for a 'new partnership' with the 'donor' countries. It is doubtful whether the Peer Review Mechanism that NEPAD has been promoting will be able to deal with this disease however, one which undermines African transformation at its very root. The

disease is within the leadership and not in African culture, as some academics and scholars have argued. However, it is the duty of civil society to focus on this in order to get to the truth of the matter. To do this we need to carry out research into the causes leading to $350 billion in African savings having left the continent over the last ten years. Some of the indicators which can help us carry out such research include:

- Researching the hostility of African regimes to indigenous capital development under the fear that such a capitalist class would become politically 'dangerous'
- The denial of investment inducements to African capitalists to invest in their own countries. Attractive inducements are instead given to foreign capital, which in turn discourages local capital from playing its part in the transformation of its own continent. The lack of domestic investment, as it were, also tends to act as a disincentive to foreign capital
- The harassment of political opposition within African countries and the lack of a democratic culture promoting tolerance. Capitalists belonging to opposing groups are marginalised and denied access to state contracts, with the result being that they are forced into corrupt practices themselves.

Conflicts within African countries frighten not only foreign capital but also national capital, which instead runs out of the continent to find 'green pastures' elsewhere. However, in the new changed conditions, it is our view that for these global linkages to be made more fruitful and positive for the local actors they must reconstitute a 'flexible' state supportive of these local political and market opportunities instead of looking at them as appendages of the global economy, itself in a state of collapse. The Bank also argued that the modern sector 'should support the traditional sector, instead of seeking to replace it'. The Bank therefore called for changes that are 'rooted in the country's social context', although it did not think of this as a strategic development.

Be that as it may, there are strong signs which demonstrate the fact that there is already slowly emerging within the womb of the collapsing capitalist system a new economic activity based on the synergetic cooperative linkages that can now be found within much

of the 'informal sector'. In this economy, money, which already exists as credit, will become the dominant form of relationships based on trust. This is a system in which individuals will manage their 'disposable time' in the way they want and not on the basis of a competitive chase for money-wealth for its own sake. This is a world in which the 'societal individual' will become a responsible, moral and ethical actor for the sake of society and not for the sake of self.[2]

Evidence is also emerging on a daily basis of how ordinary people are trying to find alternative ways of investing their money as well as engaging in new forms of self-reliant production. It was reported on the BBC in mid-May 2009 that many people were resorting to home grown food production in their small gardens around their houses to grow potatoes, tomatoes and consumable crops of that kind. In France, it was also reported that instead of putting their money in savings accounts in banks or buying shares or stocks in companies ordinary people were buying cows and other forms of investments, which were of a new kind. This was happening in the economies of developed countries and suggested that new thinking was beginning to emerge about finding alternative economic systems, which need to be explored and encouraged on a global basis.

At a political level, therefore, we shall increasingly see the emergence of a global civil society alongside a new global market based on these emergent social forces, that is, a glocal society. The current concept of 'civil society' in Africa applies only to a small group of urban-based elite organisations which are basically westernised and serve donor interests. The concept does not include the majority of the rural communities who are still attached to their cultures and traditions.

While recognising the role of traditional society, this is why the World Bank in its 'From Crisis to Sustainable Growth' report regarded it as simply not part of 'civil society'. In order to 'modernise' these rural communities, the Bank therefore emphasised the role of 'intermediary classes', by which it meant urban-based 'civil society' organisations to deal with the rural communities in the 'delivery' of certain services in the adjustment programmes in Africa. The idea was to use these intermediary classes to co-opt groups engaged in rural and 'informal' activities so as to bring them within the existing, disempowering mainstream economic activities

that had failed to 'develop' with the assistance of the state. In the World Bank's view, this was 'empowering' intermediation through these intermediary classes. But this was not sustainable however as it underestimated the capacities and capabilities of the 'rural' communities and these 'informal economy' actors as well as the role of their social and intellectual capital.

Hence, this new kind of glocal civil society must be inclusive of the 'urban' poor and the 'rural' poor who have survived through informal activities. It also includes all the members of society who struggle for the creation of a new glocal society at local and global levels. It promotes networks of people engaged in similar activities both locally and globally. In this is an attempt to build a truly global citizenship based on interlinked networks of local and global activity in which the sum total of the local is what constitutes the global or the glocal. Indeed, this confirms what is actually happening already on the ground. It is estimated that 72% of the African continent's population now lives in peri-urban slums as large numbers migrate from the countryside to mega-cities to join the 'informal economy'. So what is needed is the recognition of this new glocal civil society, a civil society that survives on the margins of the mainstream economy linked to the now collapsing global economy.

Thus, it is these glocal civil society organisations that will eventually organise themselves into new local state forms of regional federation. These federal–regional states will eventually lead to the emergence of a federated or confederated global state, to be developed by the local powers. These developments indicate that with the collapse of the existing systems of governance at both national and global levels the new social forces will have a future that is better coordinated and better organised. No, we shall not with the collapse of the existing order return to the caves – we shall only move forward to a new world. Yes, a new world is possible, and it can now be stated with certainty that it is inevitable.

Dani Wadada Nabudere
Mbale, Uganda, 15 May 2009

Notes

1. World Bank 'From Crisis to Sustainable Growth', Washington, DC, 1989.
2. Nabudere, D.W. *The Rise and Fall of Money Capital,* Africa in Transition, London, 1989, p.354.

Bibliography

Akyüz, Y. 'South Centre Bulletin', 36, Geneva, 24 April 2009.

Bacon, R.W. and W.A. Eltis 'Too Few Producers', *Sunday Times*, 14 November 1976.

Bain, A.P. *The Control of Money Supply*, Penguin, 1980.

Baker, R. *Capitalism's Achilles Heel: Dirty Money and How to Renew the Free Market System*, John Wiley & Sons, Hoboken, New Jersey, 2005.

Bhattia, A. 'The Exchange Rate Policy in African Countries', *Monetary Management in Africa*, May 1985.

Bork, R.H. *The Antitrust Paradox*, Free Press, New York, 1979.

Brenner, R. 'From budget-cutting to "Bubblenomics"', *Third World Resurgence*, issue no. 217–18, Third World Network, Penang, Malaysia, 2008.

Brittan, S. 'De-Industrialisation Revised', *Financial Times*, London, 26 January 1977.

Cole, T.K.E. 'Monetary Management in Africa: The Role of the Treasury or Government in African Countries', mimeo, 1981.

The Economist 'Where have all your savings gone?', London, 6 December 2008.

Einzig, P. *The History of Foreign Exchange*, London, 1970.

Eiteman D.K., A.I. Stonehill and M.H. Moffett *Multinational Business Finance*, Addison Wesley, New York, 1979.

Ellsworth, P.T. *The International Economy*, Collier Macmillan, New York, 1964.

Fand, D.I. 'The Post-1965 Inflation in the US', September 1969.

Fisher, I. *The Theory of Interest*, Kelly, New York, 1930.

Frank, A.G. 'Capitalism and Underdevelopment in Latin America', *Monthly Review*, New York, 1967.

Friedman, I.S. *Inflation: A World-Wide Disaster*, Hamish Hamilton, London, 1979.

Friedman, M. *Free to Choose*, Penguin, London, 1980.

—— and A.J. Schwartz *The Monetary History of The United States, 1867–1960*, Princeton, 1963.

Galbraith, J.K. *The Great Crash 1929*, Penguin, London, 1980.

—— *The New Industrial State*, Hamish Hamilton, New York, 1979.

Gardner, R.N. *Dollar–Sterling Diplomacy*, McGraw Hill, New York, 1969.

Goreaux, L.M. 'Compensatory Financing Facility', *IMF pamphlet series no. 34*, IMF, Washington, DC, 1986.

Goschen, G. *The Theory of the Foreign Exchanges*, London, 1932.

Hansen, A.H. *Business Cycles and National Income*, Norton & Co., New York, 1951.

Harrod, R.F. *Money*, Macmillan, London, 1969.

Heller, W.W. *New Dimensions of Political Economy*, Harvard, 1960.

Hendrickson, R.A. *The Future of Money,* MacGibbon Still, New York, 1979.

Hicks, J.R. *Critical Essays in Monetary Theory*, Clarendon Press, Oxford, 1967.

Hilferding, R. *Finance Capital*, Routledge & K. Paul, London, 1981.

Hirsch, F. *Money International*, Penguin, London, 1969.

Institute for Agriculture and Trade Policy (IATP), 'Commodities Market Speculation: The Risk to Food Security and Agriculture', Minneapolis, Minnesota, September 2008.

International Bank for Reconstruction and Development (IBRD) 'Uganda: Agricultural Sector Memorandum', Washington, DC, July 1984.

—— 'Uganda: Towards Recovery and Prospects for Development', Washington, DC, 1985.

International Monetary Fund (IMF) *Surveys of African Economies,* vols. 1–6, Washington, DC, 1984.

—— 'What Happens During Recessions', *working paper (WP/08/274)*, IMF, Washington, DC, 2008.

Jenkins, A. *The Stock Exchange Story*, Heinemann, London, 1973.

Jenks, L.H. *Migration of British Capital to 1875*, Nelson, London, 1971.

Johnson, H.G. *Essays on Monetary Economics*, Harvard, 1967.

Kamarck, A.M. *The Economics of African Development*, Praeger, London, 1965.

Kaufman, H. *Interest Rates, the Markets and the New Financial World*, Taurus, New York, 1986.

Keynes, J.M. *A Tract on Monetary Reform*, London, 1923.

—— *How to Pay for the War*, London, 1940.

—— *Treatise on Money*, vols. 1 and 2, Macmillan, 1953.

—— *The General Theory of Employment, Interest and Money*, London, 1963.

—— *Collected Writings*, vol. XXV, Macmillan, London, 1980.

De Leeuw, F. and E. Gramlich 'The Channels of Monetary Policy', *Federal Reserve Bulletin*, June 1969.

Lenin, V.I. *Imperialism: The Highest Stage of Capitalism*, Progress Publishers, Moscow, 1965.

Lerner, A.P. 'On Generalising the General Theory', *American Economic Review*, March 1960.

Little, A.D. *Tanganyika Industrial Development*, Government Printers, Dar es Salaam, 1961.

Lundberg, F. *The Rich and the Super-Rich*, Bantam Books, New York, 1968.

Marx, K. *Capital*, vols. 1, 2 and 3, Progress Publishers, Moscow, 1977.

—— *Contribution to the Critique of Political Economy*, Moscow, 1967.

—— *Eighteenth Brumaire of Louis Bonaparte in Revolutions of 1848*, 1965, Moscow.

Mattick, P. *Economic Crisis and Crisis Theory*, Merlin Press, London, 1981.

Monetary Management in Africa, African Centre for Monetary Studies, May 1985.

Monthly Review, New York, vol. 18, December 1966.

Moyo, T. *Zimbabwe Journal of Economics*, vol. 1, no. 4, Harare, Zimbabwe.

Nabudere, D.W. *The Political Economy of Imperialism*, Zed Press, London, 1977.

—— *The Rise and Fall of Money Capital*, Africa in Transition, London, 1989.

Nove, A. *Soviet Economy*, George Allen Ellwin, London, 1986.

O'Connor, J. *The Fiscal Crisis of the State*, St. Martins Press, New York, 1973.

Osadchaya, I. *Keynesianism Today*, Progress Publishers, Moscow, 1983.

Powel, E.T. *The Evolution of the Money Market 1385–1915*, Frank Cass, London, 1966.

Reserve Bank of Zimbabwe, 'The Role of Government in Monetary Management', mimeo, 1981.

Rist, C. *History of Monetary and Credit Theory from John Law to the Present Day*, New York, 1940.

Rweyemamu, J.F. (ed) *Industrialisation and Income Distribution in Africa*, CODESRIA, 1982.

Samuelson, P.S. and R.M. Solow 'Analytical Aspects of Anti-inflation Policy', *American Economic Review*, May 1960.

Schumpeter, J.A. *History of Economic Analysis*, Oxford University Press, 1954.

Seabrook, J. 'From Northern Rock to Northern Wreck', *Third World Resurgence*, issue no. 217–18, Third World Network, Penang, Malaysia, 2008.

Smith, J.F. *The Coming Currency Crisis*.

Soros, G. *The Crisis of Global Capitalism: Open Society Endangered*, Public Affairs, New York, 1998.

—— *The New Paradigm for Financial Markets: The Credit Crisis of 2008 and What it Means*, Public Affairs, New York, 2008.

South Centre, 'South Bulletin: Reflections and Foresights', Geneva, 16 November 2008.

Strange, S. *International Economic Relations of the Western World 1959*, Vol. 2: International Monetary Relations, RIIA, 1976.

Sweezy, P. and P. Baran 'Monopoly Capital', *Monthly Review*, New York, 1960.

Tandon, V. 'Americanisation of Security Industry and Pension Funds', mimeo, London, 1986.

Tandon, Y.T. *The University of Dar es Salaam Debate on Class, State and Imperialism*, Tanzania Publishing House, Dar es Salaam, 1982.

Thurow, L.C. (ed) *American Fiscal Policy for Prosperity*, Princeton Hall, 1967.

Timberlake, L. *The Crisis in Africa*, Earthscan, London, 1985.

UK Treasury *Proposals for an International Clearing Union*, section v., paragraph 20, 1943.

US Government *Economic Report of the President*, Washington, DC, 1963.

Walter, H.C. *Foreign Exchange and Foreign Debts*, Methuen, London, 1978.

Wichard, O.G. *Survey of Current Business*, February 1981.

Welzk, S. *Boom Without Jobs*, Bonn, 1987.

World Bank 'From Crisis to Sustainable Growth', Washington, DC, 1989.

Index

More books from Pambazuka Press

Available at www.pambazukapress.org

Ending Aid Dependence
Yash Tandon

Developing countries reliant on aid want to escape this dependence, yet appear unable to do so. This book shows how they may liberate themselves from the aid that pretends to be developmental but is not. It cautions countries of the South against falling into the aid trap and endorsing the collective colonialism of the OECD – the club of rich donor countries. An exit strategy from aid dependence requires a radical shift in both the mindset and the development strategy of countries dependent on aid, and the direct involvement of people in their own development. It also requires a radical restructuring of the global institutional aid architecture.

ISBN: 978-1-906387-31-0

September 2008 £9.95 157pp

Food Rebellions!
Crisis and the Hunger for Justice
Eric Holt-Giménez and Raj Patel

Food Rebellions! takes a deep look at the world food crisis and its impact on the global South and underserved communities in the industrial North. While most governments and multilateral organisations offer short-term solutions based on proximate causes, authors Eric Holt-Giménez and Raj Patel unpack the planet's environmentally and economically vulnerable food systems to reveal the root causes of the crisis. By tracking the political and economic evolution of the industrial agri-foods complex, *Food Rebellions!* shows us how the steady erosion of local and national control over their food systems has made African nations dependent on a volatile global market and subject to the short-term interests of a handful of transnational agri-food monopolies.

ISBN: 978-1-906387-30-3

July 2009 £12.95 273pp

Aid to Africa: Redeemer or Coloniser?
Hakima Abbas and Yves Niyiragira (eds)

As the global economic crisis raises alarm – not least for its likely effects on overseas development assistance – this book offers a critical analysis of aid to Africa from the diverse perspectives of African academics and activists, including Samir Amin, Patrick Bond, Demba Moussa Dembélé and Charles Mutasa.

The authors explore the very nature and premise of aid, juxtaposing the system with colonisation and reparation, while providing alternative frameworks for Africa to meet its development goals. *Aid to Africa* examines the framework of aid from 'traditional' Western donors while also investigating how the emergence of new donors to Africa has changed the international aid discourse.

The uniquely African perspectives in this book provide both a framework for 'reforming' aid and an alternative development paradigm rooted in Africa's self-determination.

ISBN: 978-1-906387-38-9

July 2009 £12.95 203pp

Where is Uhuru?

Reflections on the Struggle for Democracy in Africa
Issa G. Shivji
Edited by Godwin R. Murunga

The neoliberal project promised to engender development and prosperity and expand democratic space in Africa. However, several decades on its reforms have delivered on few of its promises. Whether one is examining the rewards of multiparty politics, the dividends from a new constitutional dispensation, the processes of land reform, women's rights to property or the pan-Africanist project for emancipation, Issa G. Shivji, Mwalimu Nyerere Professor of African Studies at the University of Dar es Salaam, illustrates how these have all suffered severe body blows. Where, indeed, is Uhuru?

ISBN: 978-1-906387-46-4

April 2009 £16.95 257pp

0 1341 1273852 8

LaVergne, TN USA
30 March 2010

177579LV00004B/12/P

9 781906 387433